Deceptive Vows

Khardine Gray

Faith Summers

USA TODAY BESTSELLING AUTHOR
KHARDINE GRAY
writing as
FAITH SUMMERS

A Dark Mafia Arranged Marriage Romance

Author Note

Please note Faith Summers is the Dark romance pen name of USA Today Bestselling Author Khardine Gray

Dark Romance Note

Dear reader friend ,

Thank you so much for picking my book to read. I hope you enjoy it.
    I just have to warn you that this book is a dark romance.
    It contains scenes that may be triggering to some readers .
    Best of wishes xx

Also By Faith Summers

Series

Dark Syndicate

Ruthless Prince

Dark Captor

Wicked Liar

Merciless Hunter

Heartless Lover

Ruthless King

Dark Odyssey

Tease Me

Taunt Me

Thrill Me

Tempt Me

Take Me

Original Sins

Dark Odyssey Fantasies

Entice

Tease

Play

Tempt

Duet

Blurb

What kind of happily-ever-after do you get when you're forced to marry a monster?

A monstrous Bratva leader who binds your wrists and promises to break you.

Mikhail Dmitriyev is a beautiful devil with a villainous heart and a thirst for revenge.

The choices he gave me when he stole me away from my home with an army of men were very clear—*marry me or die.*

I chose to marry him and live.

But there's one small problem with his grand plan to rain Armageddon on the Mexican Cartel.

I'm not the woman he thinks I am.

I'm not the cartel princess he thinks he took to make his enemies bow to him.

When my captor finds out my secret and realizes he married the wrong woman, love won't be enough to save me.

And neither will his obsession.

Playlist

Ode to my Family – The Cranberries
Hollow- Four Star Mary
Wash it Away – Black Lab
Mine Again- Black Lab
The Obscurous- James Newton Howard
Torn- Natalia Imbruglia
Dilate- Four Star Mary
Señorita- Shawn Mendes and Camilla Cabello
And then I kissed Him- Hans Zimmer
Wildest Dreams- Taylor Swift
A Close Friend- James Newton Howard
Lucky Ones- Bif Naked
Jar of Hearts- Christina Perri

You can find the complete Deceptive Vows playlist on
Spotify xx

What kind of happily-ever-after
do you get when you're forced to
marry a monster?

Quotes of the Heart

"Damaged people are strong because they know how to survive." – Unknown

Prologue

Mikhail

New York

I drag in a staggered breath as I enter the church I've been attending since I was born.

I adjust my jacket, so the outline of my gun won't be as visible.

The priest doesn't need to be afraid of me, although I know he is.

Everything is ready now.

All that I need to carry out today's plan.

I just have this one last thing left to do before I leave.

My confession.

It may seem pointless because of who and what I am, but I'm still doing this anyway.

I'm the youngest son of Sergei Dmitriyev, the Pakhan of the Baranov Bratva. I am his Obshchak, part of the elite in the brotherhood, and my hands have been crimson with blood more times than I can count in this lifetime. Men like me have no hope, especially when we have no plans of changing and going back on the straight and narrow path that should lead to a blessed eternal life in heaven.

There's only one place for a man like me. I know my dark soul is already damned, but since I escaped my latest encounter with death and the gates of hell refused to let me in, part of me thinks I might not be as damned as I thought.

Or maybe it's just that the devil spat me out of his lair to do one last bidding.

I don't care how I made it back; my mother and sister should not be on the other side, and I should not be in the world of the living.

The plan I seek to enact will bring about vengeance for those who should still be living.

My gaze falls on the glass painting of Christ on my far left, and the nun arranging the flowers by the altar gives me the same welcoming nod she greets me with every time she sees me.

I nod back, despite knowing deep down she's probably wondering why I bother. I appreciate the non-judgmental look she gives me. I appreciate even more the sympathy I witness in the depths of her eyes for what happened to me and my family.

As much as she knows what kind of man I am, she'll know, too, that monsters aren't born; they're made.

They're created.

People made them that way.

Something happened to them to push them to the dark side, and the only way to battle your demons is to become a monster yourself.

I take the corner to Father Gabriel's office. He's expecting me. We stopped using the confessional years ago.

I prefer to look someone in the eyes and confess my sins rather than hide behind a wall.

His door is already open. When I enter the room, he lifts his graying head and acknowledges me in that fatherly way most priests do.

For me, his greeting is always more meaningful. When he looks at me, I know he sees everything I've lived through, from the boy to the man I am before him.

"Good day, Father," I say, giving him the polite greeting I don't feel.

"Hello, Mikhail. Take a seat and start when you're ready."

I sit in the leatherback chair in front of him and rest my hands on the edge of his desk.

Just like last time, I look straight into his dark gray eyes and gear myself up.

This confession is going to be different from any other because it's a declaration of war.

"Bless me, Father, for I have sinned, and I'm about to do it again..."

Chapter One

Natalia

La Paz, Mexico

My head throbs like a thousand knives are slicing through my skull at once.

I know even before I open my eyes that the cold pressing against my cheek is the floor.

I've slept on the floor enough times to know what it feels like.

What I don't know is what I'm doing on the floor.

I try to wake myself up, but the fog surrounding my mind fences in my thoughts like it's protecting me from the truth. As I move my head from side to side, the pain intensifies, and I screw my eyes shut tighter.

What the hell happened to me? I'm hurt.

The pain is coming from one side of my face, which feels numb and swollen, and is spreading all over my head.

It feels like ... like someone hurt me.

Like someone hit me.

The instant that thought hits, a dark feeling of doom settles in my heart and beckons to me to wake up.

It tells me to get the hell up. because something isn't right.

Something more than what's *already* wrong with my life.

When I open my eyes, I'm met with the hazy gray surroundings of where I am.

There's a dark ceiling above me, barely visible in the dimly lit room.

Room?

No, I've been here before. This isn't a mere room.

I'd know the ceiling of the dungeon below the estate anywhere. Asleep *or* awake.

Counting the grooves on the ceiling was how I passed the time when Raul locked me in here last time. And that weird smell of death and decay filling my nostrils was my only companion.

To me, it always smelled like the end.

Clinging to the edge of that scathing scent is blood. When I move my right hand and feel something sticky between my fingers and the cold concrete surface of the floor, I know what I'm touching is blood.

Blood.

Where did it come from?

What the hell happened?

Why am I back here?

I make the mistake of rolling onto my side. That's when I'm met with the grotesque sight of the headless body of a man lying next to me.

A scream tears from my throat, and another follows when I lift my hands and spot the pool of dark red blood filling the space between us.

I bolt upright, my screams turning louder when I scan my surroundings and see the dead, bloodied bodies of Raul's guards lining the floor.

Within the flash of a second, I remember what happened.

I remember *everything* that happened.

Looking down at the blood-soaked wedding dress molded to my body confirms the horrific images before me and those flowing through my mind like a movie stuck on fast forward.

I also know from the clothes the man beside me is wearing that this is Felipe Naveed. He's dressed in the sleek Armani suit he was supposed to wear to the wedding.

As I think of the monster he was to me and all he took from me, I conjure up the image of the man who killed him.

Felipe was shot first before... *this*.

It was while he was being shot that I ran away and tried to escape.

A hand grips around my leg, making me jump and scream even more. In the murkiness of the room, I make out José's face. He's been beaten—badly. One eye is swollen, and his face is covered in bruises and dried blood.

"Shhhh," he stutters, tapping the edge of my leg with one hand and placing a finger to his lips with the other. "Please stop screaming."

Seeing his legs are chained to the wall, I crawl over to him.

"What's happening? Who were those men?"

"Russian mafioso. Bratva men."

My blood freezes in my veins, and I start shaking.

"What do they want? What are they going to do to us? What—"

He silences me by catching my face between his trembling hands. "My dear girl, we haven't got much time. I need you to listen to me and do exactly what I tell you to do. You hear me?"

"Yes," I answer quickly. The weakness in my body reminds me of how much I rely on him.

As his dark brown eyes rivet to mine and I take in the fear brimming within the depths, the terror flooding my soul turns into something I can't describe. José Diaz is a man akin to my father, who never feared anything. Not even death.

He was Papa's best friend. José always took care of me, long before Papa was killed. He just took care of me even more after. He's giving me that look again that tells me what he's about to say is serious, and if I don't listen, it means death.

"They think you're Adriana," he explains in a low voice, barely above a whisper.

I suck in a breath. "What? *Me?*"

Although no one outside the estate knows Adriana's real identity, there's no way anyone would mistake a lowly peasant girl like me for the Cartel Princess.

"The wedding dress. They thought you were Adriana because of the dress," he explains, and my eyes snap wide as the realization truly dawns on me. "It's the only thing keeping you alive. You need to make them believe it's true."

"Where's Adriana?"

"Dead," he answers, and my brain freezes. I can't believe what he's saying to me.

My lips part as I try to process his words. "She's dead?"

"She was one of the first to die as the men stormed the grounds and opened fire. Her car never even made it through the gate. They killed everyone else and took Raul somewhere." He swallows hard and tightens his grip on my jaw. "Mija, you must do this. Everything is out of my hands now, and I don't know what these men will do next. When I realized their mistake could possibly save you, I confirmed you were her. They need Adriana for something, or you'd be dead, too. Outside these walls, anybody who has seen Adriana would never know she is Raul's daughter. That kept her safe, and it will keep you safe now, too. Promise me you will do this. Please promise me."

"I... promise," I stammer, choking back tears.

"Gracias, mi amor. I couldn't save your father or your mother. Please let me try to save you. You were not meant for this life."

When I glance at the chains binding him, the tears automatically stream down my cheeks. If he's chained up, it's for a reason, and he's not saying anything about himself. I can't lose him, too. Not him. Not the way I lost Papa. "What about you, José?"

"Do not worry about me. You have to think of yourself. They will keep me alive until they don't need to. That's why I'm here. You, on the other hand, might escape because of this dress."

He glances down at the still beautiful gown clinging to my body, now a bloodied mess and torn in several places. It's a one-of-a-kind original made specially for Adrianna, daughter of Raul Alvarez, the Cartel King of Mexico.

I look at the deceptive gown and recall how I came to be wearing it.

Splashed in diamonds and made of the finest silk, this dress would turn anyone into a princess. It wouldn't matter where I came from or who I was.

Nobody might have known Adriana's real identity, but everyone who was anyone important knew Adriana was going to be married to Felipe in a week's time.

It was supposed to be a grand event comparable to a royal wedding, and Raul planned to show off his daughter to his empire. The event was to be symbolic of the expansion of his reign and the continuity of his legacy through Felipe.

Now, Felipe and Adriana are both dead, and the Russian mobsters who locked us up down here think I'm her.

Footsteps sound on the other side of the door, and my nerves spike.

"Remember your promise, mi amor."

I nod, and he releases me just as the door bursts open. Two men with machine guns walk in first, and then I see *him*.

The man from before who shot Felipe.

Dressed in full black like the grim reaper himself, he strides in with that same cool, confident demeanor I witnessed mere moments before he shot Felipe.

I fix my gaze on the beautiful devil I encountered earlier. It could have been hours ago. I have no idea how long I was out. A day could have passed.

Regardless of how much time has gone by, the same shiver of fear wracks my body, and he has the same effect on me with his good looks, power, and dominance.

Those good looks could fool you. His has the eye-catching masculine beauty and ruggedness that makes you want to stare, but it's the power and dominance rippling off him in effulgent waves that highlight how dangerous he is.

He's not the man you swoon over. He's the man you run from the first chance you get.

Just looking at him is suffocating.

His dark, dominant presence robs me of my senses, and I feel like a hand is clamped around my lungs, squeezing tight from inside of my body, strangling me.

The corners of his lips turn into a wicked smile, and as he approaches, I feel like I might die from fright before he reaches me.

I'm paralyzed with terror as he bends down, grips me by my throat, and lifts my trembling body.

He grins wide at the obvious fear I'm showing.

"The princess is awake, boys," he states. And now I know the faint accent I picked up earlier is Russian. The deep baritone of his voice is cool and husky with a lingering effect that works its way into me. "And even with the blood of her bastard fiancé on her face, she's still as beautiful as she's rumored to be."

Those honey-colored eyes of his drink me in, and the darkness within makes my mouth dry and my heart gallop in the cavity of my chest.

There's only one thing that darkness can mean.

Death.

Darkness means death, and I don't want to die.

Right now, I don't know if being Adriana will kill me or keep me alive as José said. If the latter is true, for how long?

"Please don't kill me," I beg when he digs his fingers into my skin.

"Kill? Oh, I have much worse in store for you, Adriana Alvarez."

It feels so strange to hear him call me by that name. That insipid name that always fuels my blood with rage.

However, if he has worse than death in store for me, being called Adriana Alvarez is the least of my worries.

When he turns his smile up a notch, undiluted fear roils within my belly.

"What are you going to do to me?" I choke out, not knowing how I manage to form words.

"Let's start with you watching me kill your father."

He's talking about Raul, but he wouldn't know that Raul is my monster. He's the monster who took everything from me. Killing him would be like slaying my demon.

Redemption and justice spark in my soul but are quickly extinguished when I allow reality to school my emotions. No redemption or justice will be sought here when I'm sure this man is just another monster. One powerful enough to take down Raul.

And shit, if he takes me to Raul, that will give me away.

I shake when I think of my death.

He thinks I'm Adriana. When he discovers I'm not, I'm dead.

"Princess, you will watch me kill your father the way he killed my family," he states, giving me the crux of the problem, but my head is now spinning and bile is rising in my throat. "And then you'll watch your kingdom fall before your eyes. When I'm done, I plan to fuck you and own your virgin pussy."

My body stiffens as shock flies through me. Shock fueled

11

by rippling waves of trepidation that hits me over and over again.

While he looks at me like he can't wait to devour me, my heart pounds harder as I stare at him wordlessly.

What the hell am I going to do?

When he releases me, I fall like a dead weight back to the ground, shaking.

"Bring her out, and the old man, too. Burn the rest of the bodies. Let's show these people how the Bratva deal with traitors."

Chapter Two

Natalia

10 hours earlier...

Knots twist and tangle in my stomach as I look at my reflection in the floor-to-ceiling mirror in Adriana's dressing room and scan over the beautiful wedding dress I'm wearing.

I'm in this dress again.

Her wedding dress.

Adriana walks around me, scanning me from head to toe in deep scrutiny as she looks me over. I keep still and pretend I don't know what's wrong.

Even though we're virtually the same petite size, my hips are curvier and my breasts bigger. Since the fucking dress is supposed to be tailored to fit, it's more suited to my body than hers. That's why we're having problems, and there are going to be more problems that won't get fixed in time.

Her wedding is now a week away, yet she wants me to do

the fitting with the seamstress again so she can go on a date. Not with her fiancé. Oh no. This is with some new guy she met in a club last week.

The dress is beautiful and not just the most gorgeous dress I've ever seen in my life. It's the most beautiful *everything* I've ever seen. I'm sure any woman would love to be in my shoes. Just the chance to try it on would entice anybody.

Anybody who isn't me.

Every time Adriana makes me put it on, it feels like an anchor to my hell and the omen of the darkness and death that await me once she says 'I do.'

I think she knows how I feel about wearing her dress, and outside of the convenience of having me here, she does shit like this to taunt me.

Once she gets married, I'll be sold. Owned by someone else.

Her father plans to sell me as a sex slave in the virgin auction for what I know will make Raul a pretty penny. So, if I don't find a way out—and escaping is near impossible—in approximately one week's time, I'll become some rich bastard's pet. A sex slave. That's what I need to worry about. Not this.

The thought makes the backs of my eyes sting, but I hold back the tears. I refuse to cry in front of these people. I refuse to cry at all, because I know I won't come back if I break down.

She stops in front of me, tosses her long black hair over her shoulders, and strikes a pose worthy for the cover of *Vogue*.

"I need you to tell the seamstress to make the cleavage deeper and take in the waist so it shows off my hips." Her voice is heavy with her thick Spanish accent.

Speaking English is the one mercy I'm grateful for. My mother was from San Francisco. We spoke English most of the time at home, although my father was Mexican, and I was born and raised here.

I speak Spanish just fine, but when my fate was sealed to the Alvarez family, I pretended not to know the language as well as I do because I wanted them to speak to me in the language *I* was most comfortable understanding.

Speaking English reminds me of my mother and days of my childhood when my parents were still alive and I was free from this life in the cartel. It reminds me of hope, although with the threat looming over my head, every trace of anything that resembles hope fades with each passing day. For most of my nineteen years, all I've known is pain and suffering.

"Are you sure you shouldn't go to the fitting?" I offer, not because I care one way or the other. I'm only saying it because I know what she's like when things don't go as she wants them to. She ends up taking out her frustration on me or someone else.

"No." She waves me off with a flick of her wrist. "Obviously, I'll be away for the day."

Translation, she—*the supposed virgin bride*—is going to be out fucking this new guy senseless most likely until tomorrow morning. The last guy was one of her bodyguards. Raul killed him when he found out what was going on. He didn't want Felipe to know he wouldn't be getting a virgin on their wedding night. As if Felipe wouldn't discover that for himself or know what his wife-to-be is like.

That bastard knows and is just as disgusting as Adriana.

"I'll also need you to polish my shoes when you're done," she adds.

I frown. "I did them this morning."

She sets her hands on her hips. "Clearly, you haven't polished them properly if I'm telling you to do it again."

Bitch.

She's just fucking with me because she hates me. I'm a joke to her. We both know there are only so many times you can polish shoes and so much you can do to them to make them shine. This is just one of the host of games she's played with me since that ill-fated night when her father ordered the killing of mine and made me her slave.

She treats all the servants who work here on the estate like shit, and they do as they're told because they know the consequences.

Displease her, and you're dead. It's as simple as that. I've watched her order the deaths of many for petty things like dropping a bag or missing a spot of dust on furniture she'd ordered to be cleaned.

That's the kind of evil bitch Adriana Alvarez is.

She only plays with me like this because her father's plans for me mean she can't kill me.

Adriana slips the shoes onto her perfectly manicured feet, and even I have to admit they look good on her. I'd love to wear a pair of shoes like those instead of these tattered plimsolls I've been wearing for the last few years.

"Got it?" she asks cutting into my thoughts.

"Yes, Señorita Alvarez."

My voice sounds way too calm for the annoyance I feel. But I'll be the obedient servant if I can avoid being punished.

The last time I defied her, Raul starved me for a week and locked me in the dungeon for a month. That was terrible, but not as bad as when he whipped me for trying to escape after my father died.

Both instances were enough to keep me in line.

"Good girl. The seamstress should be here in about five minutes. Don't keep her waiting."

"Okay."

A knock sounds at the door just as she grabs her little Prada purse from the dressing table. She calls out to come inside in Spanish, and the door swings open.

When I see it's José, I feel some ounce of relief.

"Oh good, you're here," she says to him. "I need shelves done in the back."

"Sure," he replies, and we both watch her as she strides away like she's walking the runway.

He walks in, and as soon as the door clicks shut, I rush over to him, hoping he has some news for me.

He promised to help me escape, pursuing my father's dying wish. José has been my only hope for the last two years of my sentence here.

Nothing could explain the pain I feel for being the cause of my father's death.

After Raul raped and killed my mother right in front of us, Papa wanted to get me out of this hell. He was trying to do just that when our plan was discovered. José has been Raul's senior lieutenant for over twenty years, but there was nothing he could do to save my father as Raul ordered Felipe to kill him with my father's own gun.

When José takes both my hands into his and a solemn expression washes over his face, I know any news he has for me is not going to be the kind I want to hear.

With the shake of his graying head, he confirms I'm right.

"Lo siento, mi amor," he says, telling me he's sorry in Spanish. It's times like these when I appreciate how he always speaks to me in a mixture of Spanish and English. Just like my father did. It's as if he wants to keep his memory alive for me. "I'm still working on a plan. I promise you I am. It's just hard."

"I know," I reply. I do know. What we're discussing is no mere thing. It could mean death if anyone even heard us.

Raul would kill *him* because he'd lose too much if I died.

Sometimes, I wonder if death might be my only way out of this hell.

I pull in a deep breath and try to clear my head. I can't think like that. My parents would never want me to think like that, so I can't just give up. Not when they went through so much to keep me alive.

José, too.

He touches the edge of my cheek and gives me a warm smile.

"Be strong, mi amor." He lowers his voice. "I will die before I allow Raul to sell you."

"I don't want you to die."

"Do not worry about me, child." His pale brown eyes stare back at me with a fatherly warmth that worries me because I know he means what he said. He'll give his life for me. I don't want anyone else I love to die. "Go now. The seamstress is already here."

I nod, and he gives my shoulder a reassuring squeeze.

When I leave the room, I steel my spine and summon strength. The seamstress isn't going to like seeing me again.

When I get down to the hall where we do the fittings, her angry face is the first I see when I step through the grand oak wood doors. But I'm more concerned about the shit-eating grin spread across Felipe Naveed's face to worry about how angry the seamstress is or what she might say to me.

He's standing next to her dressed in his suit. It almost makes him look like a human being. *Almost.*

Felipe is Raul's second-in-command and just as evil.

I don't think I could be fooled into thinking this man was anything other than the bastard he is. Every time I see him, I remember how he placed that gun to my father's head and pulled the trigger.

He killed my father on Raul's orders, but he hated my father enough that he didn't need any orders to kill him.

"Wonderful. Leave us," he says to the seamstress with a taunting vibe laced through his voice.

I'm a joke to him, too, but he doesn't want to kill me. He wants me in other ways. He hasn't fucked me because he wants me sold in the auction as well, but that hasn't stopped him from playing with me.

The seamstress opens her mouth to protest, but she wouldn't dare say anything besides what she says now.

"Si, Señor Naveed."

As soon as she walks out the door, casting me a look of

disapproval as she passes by, that smile on Felipe's face widens.

"Come here to me, Natalia," he says, and I make myself move.

I will myself to move for the same reason I obey Adriana's orders.

It's his fault, though, why her dislike for me turned to hate. She hates that he wants me and only wants her because she's his path to the empire. As much as she screws around with any man who will have her, she wants Felipe to want her and only her. She likes his power and what it means for her future as the Cartel Queen when Raul hands over the kingdom to Felipe.

When I reach him, I make sure I stop a few paces away, but the bastard knows what I'm up to and steps forward, closing the space between us.

The closeness makes my skin crawl, but I root my feet to the ground and try to look like I'm stronger than I am.

"Adriana sent you again?" he asks.

"Yes."

"I'm sure she didn't say where she was going."

"No."

He smiles wider to reveal straight white teeth, reminding me of a well-dressed shark.

He cups my face and lowers his head to brush his lips over my forehead.

"I know she's spreading her legs for that cunt at the club," he whispers. "No matter. I get to play with you."

His large hand covers my right breast and squeezes. When I try to step away, he slips his arm around me and holds me in place.

"Let go of me," I cry, trying to break free of his grasp.

"Fucking stop fighting me." A harsh laugh rumbles in his chest, and he crushes his lips to mine.

As soon as he forces his disgusting tongue into my mouth,

the crash of the door makes us jump apart. Or rather, he releases me, and I move away from him at the sound.

We both look toward the door as a man walks through it.

A tall, tall man I'd place to be around six foot six with the kind of muscle you'd find on a military man. He's gorgeous. Breathtaking even, and despite the danger rippling off him, I'm captivated by his beauty.

His face with its sun-kissed skin and deep angles and planes looks like it was carved by the gods. And the thick locks of wild, unruly obsidian hair covering his head and a neatly trimmed beard give him a rugged edge. The gold hoop looping through his ear makes him look like one of the pirate captains of the old world who sailed the Caribbean.

What gets me even more is his eyes.

The color and the emotion.

They glow like a warm honey, but there's nothing warm about them. The emotion I detect is ice-cold hatred.

It makes the hair on the back of my neck stand to attention, and my soul cowers as he takes measured steps toward us.

"Impossible," Felipe gasps, looking like he's just seen a ghost.

I've never seen him look so scared. Even I know that when the monster who terrifies you gets scared, you should be worried about the thing that's scaring him. In this case, it's this man. This man I've never seen before.

"Y-you," Felipe stutters.

"Yes, me," the man answers, speaking with a hint of an accent I can't quite place over the drumming of my heart in my ears.

"You're supposed to be dead."

"Clearly, I'm not. But you will be." The man pulls two guns from his pockets, and before Felipe can do anything, the echo of bullets bounces off the walls as the man shoots him.

I scream and back away, knowing I have to get the fuck out of here.

The man doesn't look at me. Instead, he continues to shoot Felipe.

I run toward the doors at the other end of the hall, hoping he doesn't shoot me down as I run away. I just make it through the doors when I hear him coming.

"There, there, princess, run as fast and as far as you can. You won't escape me."

His voice carries down the passageway.

He's right, too. I don't get far, and I know I won't escape when another man—this one masked—jumps out from behind one of the columns and elbows me in my face so hard the impact knocks me out.

Chapter Three

Mikhail

Present time

I keep my gaze trained on the princess in her wedding dress as she walks ahead of me with two of my soldiers on either side of her.

The old man—Raul's senior lieutenant—is behind me.

I want Raul to see her first. I need him to recognize I was serious about his destruction and taking his only pride.

His beloved daughter, Adriana Alverez, will be the last thing he sees before he leaves this world.

Three weeks ago, when I awoke from the coma I'd been in for nearly three months, Felipe's face was the first image that came to my mind.

What followed next was the full memory of the ambush that motherfucker set up to kill my mother and sister right before my eyes. At that moment, the realization struck me that

Raul sent him because Felipe Naveed doesn't do anything outside Raul's orders.

It was a good assassination plot, except for the fact that I lived. I was the thing that went wrong.

I wasn't supposed to be alive to place Felipe at the scene of the crime, or to track anything back to Raul to bring on the massacre I rained down earlier today.

Dead men tell no tales, but I lived to sing them and avenge my mother and sister.

Raul will feel my wrath, and Adriana will witness it.

She's the reason he kept his silence as I tortured him. He thought he could save her by refusing to talk and tell me why he did what he did.

All his refusal did was confirm the suspicion already churning my gut, telling me he wasn't working alone.

His actions were already suspicious as fuck. Sure, Raul Alvarez is a powerful man with the type of thirst to conquer akin to most cartel kings. I wouldn't be exaggerating by saying he runs Mexico, but the Baranov Bratva is world-renowned for our infamy. You wouldn't be idiot enough to kill the wife and daughter of the Pakhan out of the blue and think you could get away with it.

But there's a hell of a lot more to this story than simply wanting to conquer a world-renowned giant. I will find out exactly what's going on.

The princess stumbles, and one of my men rights her by grabbing her arm.

That's when I notice the bruise on her cheek she would have gotten when that imbecile knocked her out.

I dealt with him after for doing so. He went against my orders and harmed her.

I meant what I said back in the dungeon. Even with blood, guts, and bruises on her, she is beautiful with the striking beauty to rival all the angels.

I'd be a liar and more of a sinner than I already am if I

didn't admit to finding her as insanely attractive as my men, who I catch stealing glances at her.

People everywhere have only heard whispers of how beautiful Raul Alvarez's daughter is. The fact Raul kept her a mystery only increased the allusion to her beauty.

The real-life version of her certainly beat what I conjured in my mind.

Those bright, large hazel eyes against her vibrant olive skin are breathtaking. As is her body.

She's petite at about five four but has that perfect shape with the right amount of curves to define her hips and fully rounded breasts I'm going to enjoy playing with.

That silky black hair flowing down her elegant back is an invitation to run my fingers through it. Or lace them through the silky fibers as I thrust my cock into her gorgeous mouth.

That was the first thing I wanted to do when I saw those lips of hers.

Such a pity our first meeting was of me killing her fiancé.

Then again, I can't imagine which other way I would have met her. That wedding of hers was only going to be between the cartel members that make up Raul's empire.

She's a woman any man would want to keep. People like me take note of beauty for different reasons. Even in my dirty, filthy mind, in the moment I first saw her, my reason was purity, but that makes no sense. From what I've heard, there is nothing innocent about Adriana Alvarez and she's as evil as her father. So, I'll make sure she gets what's coming to her.

Right now, she's a trophy I've come to collect. An emblem of my victory and the bond that will glue my takeover of leadership in the cartel. That is all she is to me, and something to fuck.

For now.

Once I give her the hard fuck my dick is aching to wield on her, I'll get any fascination over her beauty and her body out of my system.

The only reason she's not dead yet is because I need her.

There's something, though, that struck me as peculiar about her.

When I told her I was going to kill her father, she never begged for his life. She never said anything.

Not a damn thing. And she never even looked shaken for him or shed the tears I thought she might.

It's a mystery to me, one I won't worry about right now. We're just approaching the hall Raul uses to conduct his business meetings.

That's where I have him tied up.

I left Sebastian, my second-in-command, in charge. Inside the same room the heads of the families in Raul's alliance should also be gathered—waiting.

My men open the doors, and we walk into the Arthurian-style hall.

I've got Raul shirtless and bound to two metal poles. Blood stains his skin from the top of his head down to the waistband of his pants, and bruises mar his aged face. I messed him up before I went down to the dungeon.

I haven't been here many times before. But two of those times, he'd tortured some poor bastard to death for entertainment. That's why those poles are there. Raul is a sick fucker with a penchant for watching people die.

Tonight, I have a box on the table with something special inside for additional entertainment.

I get the desired effect I was hoping for when Raul's gaze lands on his daughter.

His eyes widen with shock and his lips move, but he can't talk because I sliced out his tongue. The only sounds he can make are the groaning noises pouring out of his mouth. Tears run down his cheeks when he realizes no one can understand whatever the fuck it is he's saying, and his precious daughter is at my mercy. That garble coming out of his mouth is nothing but shit to me. My mother and sister never even had the chance to beg for their lives or each other.

Besides, I already gave him his chance.

I tortured the motherfucker for eight hours before I sliced out his tongue.

Eight hours, yet the man kept his silence. The only reason I knew his silence was to protect his daughter is because I tortured that part out of him after noting his behavior.

His resilience seemed to come from the love of a father wanting to protect his daughter. Knowing I was keeping her alive fueled his obstinance, and I could see he didn't care if I killed him. It's her he was worried about. I would have gouged out his eyes, too, in true Bratva style, but I wanted him to witness this moment.

The moment his kingdom falls.

Opposite him are the twelve cartel heads in his alliance. Like fucking knights, they're seated around the circular table in the center of the hall. When they see me, they look like they're ready to shit themselves.

Their reaction is not due to knowing me, but because they thought I was dead, too. My family kept my survival quiet.

From the way Raul is behaving, the men switch their shocked gazes from me to Adriana. This will be their first introduction to her.

While Raul's shrieks get louder and the asshole starts crying, I acknowledge my guests with a bright smile, like I'm hosting the Academy Awards ceremony.

"Evening, gentlemen." I speak in English so they will all understand me. I understand Spanish and speak it on a minimal basis, but I won't do it here. Right now, they need to understand what's happening and what's going to happen from here onwards. "As you can see, there have been some changes."

"What is happening?" the man closest to me asks cautiously. His name is Antonio. He deals primarily in gun trafficking, but like the others, dabbles heavily in the flesh trade. We met once at a fundraiser in New York my father hosted.

"You'll see." I reach for Adriana, pulling her right next to me. I then cup the back of her neck and grip her silky-smooth skin. Her neck is so tiny it would be easy to snap it. But I don't want to do that—not yet. "I wish to introduce you to Raul's daughter, Adriana Alvarez. Now that everyone knows each other, we can get down to business."

I walk Adriana closer to Raul, and he thrashes against the restraints in protests. Nothing he does will help him now. Or her.

Terror reigns in his eyes. As its wielder, I savor the surge of power intoxicating my blood.

I stop a few inches away, and she squirms against my grasp. Her fear, however, checks her and restrains her from doing more.

"Gentlemen," I announce, pulling my knife from the sheath on my side. "This is the traitor who killed my mother and my sister. Isabella and Talia Dmitriyev. This is the day I take his life for theirs. His blood will spill for theirs. This is also the day I will take his empire and everything inside it."

I look into Raul's eyes, and he starts shaking.

"Apart from you, these are the only two people I left alive," I tell him. "See you in hell, Raul Alvarez."

In one swift move I slash his throat, and blood sprays his princess and me. She screams a piercing sound, and still I note she never begged for her father's life.

Because I promised on my mother's life I'd kill Raul the same way he killed her, I drop the knife and pull out my gun as Raul sputters.

I cock the hammer and pull the trigger, giving him the final blow.

As his blood splashes on me once more, I don't even bother to note it.

Still holding Adriana by her neck, I straighten and hoist her up. There's very little white left on the front of her wedding dress. Most of it is either red from the cocktail of blood all over it or grimy brown from the dungeon floor.

She's crying with true terror while the old man looks on with awe.

I might feel sorry for her, too, if I were a better man.

Turning back to my guests, I see they realize I mean business.

I have one more shocker to pull from my sleeves before I tell them what I expect them to do next.

I open the box on the table and take out Felipe's head, holding it by the hair on top. A ripple of gasps rushes across the room and the princess heaves like she's going to vomit at the sight of her beloved fiancé. It shouldn't irritate me that she belonged to him, or was going to, but it fucking does. That's probably testament to how fucked my mind is.

Blood runs down my arm as I throw Felipe's head onto the table. It rolls toward the center, and the men look at it.

Felipe was to be their next leader. Now he is no more.

Fear keeps people in line. With men like these, you have to rain down a taste of Armageddon to show them you have the power. Everything I've done so far has added fuel to that goal. They'll know by now, even without me saying so, I mean to take charge.

They're not going to like having the Bratva control one of the biggest cartels in this world. But to truly take over Raul's empire, I want the men on board without the shit of a mutiny.

Either they sign the blood oath, or they're dead. It's as simple as that.

With my blood-smeared hand I taint her cheeks by running her father's blood over it.

I then turn back to the men and look each of them in the eye.

"I'm your ruler now. I, Mikhail Dmitriyev, will be your

ruler, and to make it official, I'll be marrying Adriana Alvarez one month from today." The princess goes limp on hearing my declaration. This will be an interesting twist of events for her, but something that must be done for me to acquire the cartel and ownership of all Raul's assets in his empire. "I expect you all to be there to witness our union, the same way I expect you to sign your allegiance to me. Those of you who are in, raise your hand."

All twelve raise their hand.

Good. Mission accomplished.

I signal for Sebastian to come over. When he does, I hand him Adriana.

"Take her upstairs to wait," I tell him. "Leave the old man."

"No, please don't hurt him," Adriana begs.

The shrill tone of her voice and the desperation in her eyes as she begs shock me.

She's a mess after seeing me kill her father and looking at Felipe's head, but it's now she really looks like she's about to lose her shit.

Now that I've threatened the old man's life.

"Please don't kill him."

"Get her the fuck out of here," I bark, and Sebastian, along with another man, hauls her out and carries my wife-to-be away.

I glance at the old man and wonder how deep her relationship with him is.

He looks like he's in his late sixties, but that's nothing these days. I'm not sure if the relationship is romantic, though. She screamed for him the way a child would for their parent. It was how I expected her to react for Raul.

I'll need to talk to him some more. Depending on what he says, I'll establish if he'll be useful to me or not.

Then I'll go and see her.

Chapter Four

Natalia

My head is still spinning.

No more from the pain I previously felt.

It's spinning from the answer of my fate and the worry over what might happen to José.

The guards took me to the bathroom first to clean off the blood from my hands and face, then I was taken to Raul's bedroom, which is where I currently am.

His room doesn't have an en-suite bathroom like Adriana's does. If it did, I would have bathed to get the scent of the dead off me. That mere wash I was allowed wasn't enough.

What's worse is that the room smells like Raul, and even though he's dead, his authoritative presence still lingers in the air, haunting the place.

I can smell him in the air, and the essence of his blood still clings to me.

I've never actually been inside here. I wasn't allowed on this side of the house, but I've caught glimpses from the balcony on the opposite side.

The room looks like it was made for the ruler Raul thought

himself to be. The king-sized bed in the center is covered in black silk that matches the wallpaper, and the pure crystals hanging from the chandelier are exactly what you'd expect royalty to own.

To me, however, he was always going to be a murderer.

I can't believe he's dead. Slain like an animal in a slaughterhouse. Adriana, too. Raul put so much effort into her safety and making sure people didn't know who she was that it backfired on him.

I've been in here for the last hour. Just waiting with only the echo of the ticking clock on the wall and the threat of the guards outside the door.

The door isn't locked. It's only closed.

I know not to be stupid, though, and think I'll get far if I braved trying to run.

That's the point of all of this. I can't run.

I could never run. Not from Raul, and not from my new captor.

Mikhail Dmitriyev.

That's his name. The name of my husband-to-be, who thinks I'm someone else.

Since meeting him, I've gone from worrying about him killing me, to worrying about when he's going to fuck me, to marrying him.

Marriage.

What the fuck am I going to do?

I keep trying to figure out if this is really happening, and I'm going crazy with worry. I also feel sick to my core because I know he would have killed José.

Why wouldn't he?

He killed everybody else. All those people who were unfortunate enough to be on Raul's estate, and then he killed Raul.

I'll never forget the way he killed him.

It was effortless, without any thought for compassion.

All the while, when Raul babbled what would have been indecipherable nonsense to everyone, I understood his garbling. I'm sure José understood, too.

That was possibly the first time we'd both seen Raul Alvarez show his love for his daughter. What we were seeing was a combination of the grieving father and one who was trying to take me down to hell with him.

After the way that scheme played out, I'm sure he would have been told Adriana was alive. So, when he saw me, in *her* dress, he would have known exactly what happened and what was going on.

By the same token, he wouldn't have wanted me to use the chance to survive.

When our eyes first locked, I expected him to scream the truth of who I was.

He did just that.

The bastard tried to, but he couldn't say anything with his tongue gone.

So much happened after that felt like redemption.

Raul's throat was slashed the way he cut my mother's throat after he raped her. She died as she tried to crawl away from him and back to Papa and me.

Tonight, Raul also got a bullet between the eyes, the same way my father went.

Redemption, yes. For those who are already dead, though.

Not for me.

I won't get anything like that. There seems to be a different plan for me. One I have no idea how to pick apart.

Right now, as I stand in this room, in this bloodied wedding dress covered in the blood of the men I've hated the most, I'm like the fly who flew straight into the spider's web.

I'm trapped, and now that I'm trapped, I'm not sure what is worse yet. My life the way it was yesterday, when I cried myself to sleep from worry over being a sex slave, or the version of myself now in the fucked-up present tense.

How the hell am I supposed to marry this monster?

What will my life be like?

Or, fuck...

How long until he doesn't need me?

I'm young, but the things I've borne witness to and heard have aged my mind well beyond its years. When shit is happening, the help are always the first to hear the hushed whispers of murder plots and witness those scheming plots unfold.

I've heard of enough wives who've died *accidentally*. Either their use had expired, they'd expired and their husbands wanted to trade them in, or they'd seen or heard something they shouldn't have.

In my case, I think I'll expire in use.

That's what's going to happen to me. This monstrous man is going to force me to marry him so he can rule the cartel, then kill me.

A tendril of panic seizes my body when the thud of heavy boots sounds on the other side of the door and the handle turns.

As the door swings open and I see him—Mikhail Dmitriyev—my heart leaps like a gazelle into my throat then beats like a harsh fist pounding against the walls of my chest.

He walks slowly into the room, and the door swings shut behind him. The dark intensity of his presence forces me to back into the wall as if the black silky wallpaper can offer me the comfort and safety I seek.

A mirthless smile spreads across his face, but it still animates his handsome features.

I notice he's clean of the blood that was previously on him, and he's changed his clothes. He's still wearing full black, though, in a shirt and slacks similar to what he just took off.

As he comes closer, sandalwood and sexy musk fill my nostrils, and I scan over the artful tattoos lining his fingers and climbing up his neck.

Everything is clearer in this light, including the solemn expression on his face.

Thoughts and questions collide in my mind.

Thoughts that do nothing to ebb my fears and questions he might not answer.

As he comes even closer, I think of two things.

One, he thinks I'm Adriana, which is what's keeping me alive.

Two, he needs me. Right now, he needs me, and even though I don't know how long the need will exist, I need to find whatever strength I can from that knowledge.

So, being this weak woman isn't going to help me.

I need to find strength although I'm afraid. Just like before.

"Are you afraid of me, Malyshka?" he asks, tilting his head to the side.

"Ma...lysh...ka?" I stammer.

"Baby girl in Russian."

That shouldn't heat up my body the way it does, but nothing about the last twenty-four hours has been normal. Should I be surprised if I've finally gone crazy?

God knows enough has happened to push me right over the edge. But since it looks like I'm still hanging on, I won't let go of whatever thread I'm gripping on to. I'll keep holding on for as long as I can.

"Did you kill José?" I manage.

Curiosity fills his face, and when he leans in and places his hands on the wall on either side of me, I think he might kiss me.

He towers over me, and my heartbeat doubles when I get that suffocating feeling again.

"Interesting, Malyshka. You showed more emotion for the old man than you did for your own father."

Shit.

I wasn't thinking. My mind and body were simply reacting as anyone would if they were watching their biggest enemy fall. I was being myself. Natalia de Leon. And I forgot to be Adriana Alvarez.

He's right. I barely showed an ounce of remorse for Raul. Anyone seeing their parent in such a way would have lost their minds. Having lost both parents in violent ways, I know exactly how I *should* have behaved.

The hysterics should have hit me the moment he told me he was going to kill Raul.

I, however, was so worried about Raul identifying me, I forgot the act.

This man is no fool, and what scares me is how he might kill me if he finds out I'm not who he thinks I am.

What do I do now?

Does he suspect I'm a fake?

I have to think fast and say something plausible that might explain my shock.

"That's not true. It all happened so fast," I lie. "You killed my father so fast. I barely had time to process what you were doing. You just killed him. You killed him right there in front of me."

My lips tremble on their own. I don't have to instill grief into my body. Neither do I have to pretend to cry. The tears are never far off. My soul is always weeping.

So, the tears I summon now are real, just not for what he thinks they're for.

"José is all I have left," I add. "He's been my bodyguard since I was a baby." That's true.

"You better hope that's all it is, Malyshka, or he's dead."

"So, he's alive?" I'm so eager for the prospect that I don't fully take in what he's saying to me.

"Are you screwing the old man? The answer better be no, and better not be a fucking lie either, because I want the cherry between your legs to be mine."

My body heats up again, and I'm appalled when I feel moisture beading between my thighs. Perhaps it's due to relief on some level that José is safe, because the wild images flooding my mind of this man fucking me against this wall are completely inappropriate.

Briefly, he presses his forehead to mine before he backs away.

"Answer the question, Malyshka."

"He's just my bodyguard," I reply. "That's all."

"Good, and lucky for you, I seem to believe you. Next question. Are you the virgin I've heard you are?"

A shudder runs through me when I detect the shimmer of greed in his eyes.

"Yes."

His smile widens. "I like virgins. I like being the first man to break them and train them to please me."

Them. I wonder how many of them he's had. He sounds like the virgin Pied Piper, and I'm just going to be another statistic in his catalogue of women.

"Were you serious about the wedding?" I risk asking and changing the subject.

A slow, easy grin brightens his face, and I know straight-away that I'm going to be some plaything to him. Another person who will think of me as a thing. A non-human being they can toy with.

"Yes. I was serious as fuck about the wedding." He cups my blood-stained face and presses his thumb into my neck. "Any objections, princess? You look like you have plenty to say. I'm interested in hearing it."

"We don't know each other. How can we get married? We just met."

"Shit like that doesn't matter to me, and definitely not when you were going to marry Felipe Naveed. I'll take you for myself and break you just for that."

Break me?

I could almost laugh.

I'm already broken. I just hide the pieces of my soul well.

I suppose, though, that's just a part of me. Something inside keeps me going. It's something stronger than hope. It exists deep within my core, right in the essence of what makes me, me. It forces me to keep surviving even when there seems to be nothing left to live for.

If that part of me breaks, I'm dead.

"Your marriage to me will seal the deal on my control of the cartel. It is formalities and the easy way to conquer your father's empire without rebellion. But I could do it the other way, princess. The harder, hellish way where I kill you and reign hell on Mexico. So, Malyshka, your choices are marry me, or die."

My mouth goes dry, as if someone has stuffed it with sand.

Marry him or die? Those are my choices. They both sound like the same thing to me. Like death. It's just that one might prolong my life a little longer.

"What's it going to be, Malyshka?"

"I don't want to die," I choke out, because that's the truth. I don't want to die, and anything I do now will be because of that.

He nods and brushes his lips so briefly over mine it's as if the mere kiss never happened.

"I didn't think so. Now that's settled, I'd like to see what's under this dress."

"What?"

He tugs on the edge of the bodice of the dress on a spot that's still white. That's when I remember his taunt to fuck me.

"Strip. Now. Take everything off, Malyshka."

Chapter Five

Natalia

Oh God.

       He's going to do it now.

       He's actually going to fuck me now.

My eyes bulge, and waves of terror crash against the walls of my soul.

I don't know what I'm supposed to do. I never thought it would happen like this, or that my first time would be rape.

What did I expect, though? I was to be sold in the virgin auction in a matter of days. Did I believe I'd magically have feelings for whoever bought me?

This situation is just as fucked up.

I'm owned in a different way.

Given the state I'm in, I thought I'd buy myself some time, but this man is clearly some kind of psycho. Maybe this is his thing, and the blood of his enemies on me will make taking me that much sweeter.

"Now," he adds with insistence, and steps back to give me space.

Swallowing past the lump in my throat, I lift one trembling

hand and pull down the little zipper on the side of my gown. Seconds later, the dress floats down my body, revealing my nude lace panties and matching bra.

"I said everything," he reminds me when I stall.

I struggle with what to take off first—my panties or my bra. Deciding either will still make me feel aware of him being the first man to see me fully naked, I start with my bra.

Obediently, I undo the little butterfly clasp in the front, and my breasts fall free. He watches them bobble, and I'm embarrassed when he looks at the taut, tight peaks of my nipples. When the cool air hit them, they tightened, but they're painfully tight because of him.

Despite my embarrassment, the heat flowing through my body rises when I take note of the hungry look in his eyes.

He's looking at me like he wants to eat me.

When I bend down to take off my panties, he catches my right nipple between his thumb and forefinger, giving me a gentle squeeze.

The sick thought of Felipe feeling me up pops into my head. He used to do it all the time. Sometimes, he'd allow his friends to do it, too. I'd fight, but they'd hold me down until they got what they wanted. They'd do whatever they could that didn't constitute as sex.

This mere touch feels just like that, but there's an air of difference that grates on my nerves.

The last thing to come off is the tattered plimsolls. Now I'm completely naked before him. All much to his satisfaction.

"Good girl." He smiles.

He releases my nipple but doesn't pull his finger away. He keeps his fingertips pressed to my skin and his eyes trained on my body as he takes a slow predatory walk around me.

My traitorous body absorbs the attention, and my pussy clenches as his eyes drink me in.

He runs his fingers over the flat of my belly, trails them around to my back, and runs them over my ass, where he takes a handful of flesh and squeezes before he lands a heavy hand down on the skin. I cry out from the stinging pain and try to move away, but he shoves me against the wall, spreads my legs with the top of his knee, and thrusts a finger right into my pussy. A place no man has ever touched before.

Fuck, as he strokes over my swollen clit, a burst of wetness flows from me, and he smiles. Arousal pushes fear aside when he leans forward and takes my nipple into his mouth. I feel like I'm going to lose my mind when he sucks my nipple and starts pumping into my pussy with his thick fingers.

"Dirty girl. You're so tight and wet for me," he husks. "You like my fingers in your tight, wet cunt, don't you?"

"No," I lie, and we both know my answer for a lie.

The wicked, sinful smile on his face tells me he does.

"Yes, Malyshka. Knowing you want me will make things easier for you."

"I don't want you," I argue. It's the wrong thing to say, but I need to tell him. It feels important to me that he knows I don't want him or any of this. "I would never want you."

Instead of looking offended, he looks amused.

"Is that right, Malyshka?" He speeds up his pumps and chuckles when I moan.

"Yes," I grate out. "Whatever you take from me won't be with my consent."

"Do I look like an honorable man to you, princess?"

"No."

"Good, so don't make that mistake of thinking I am. I don't care about such things, and I take what I want no matter if the person gives it or not. You, though, you're special. I'm going to break you so badly, you'll want me eventually. Then you'll beg me."

"Fuck you," I bark mindlessly, not being able to catch myself before the defiance tumbles from my lips.

He laughs again with surprise this time. "Oh, I do plan to fuck you, and you will enjoy it."

"No," I protest.

"Yes, Malyshka."

Before I can try to protest again, he adds another finger into my passage and pumps harder, assaulting my clit. Raw pleasure slams into me, robbing me of breath. The pleasure that roils within me assaults my virgin body, and I moan out so loudly I know the men outside must hear me. I'm so lost in his touch that I don't care, and I want the taste of insanity he's pushing me toward.

He keeps finger-fucking me, and I arch my back as I come hard on his fingers.

I writhe against his fingers, realizing only now I'm holding on to him. Gripping on to his wide, powerful mass of shoulders like I need him to survive.

Mikhail suddenly releases me, and I slump against the wall like a lifeless rag doll, my eyes landing on the big bulge of his cock pressing against his pants.

"On your knees now, princess," he orders. "It's time to give you your first lesson in pleasuring me."

As soon as he starts undoing his belt buckle, I know what he wants me to do.

"Have you ever sucked a cock before?" he asks.

"No."

"Fantastic. You can start with mine. I want those lips of yours around my cock. Get on your knees."

My fear and helplessness are what make me obey. My knees hit the floor, and I feel like I'm on autopilot.

When Mikhail shoves his pants down his hips, unveiling his massive cock, all I can do is stare at it.

It's not the first I've seen one because Felipe and his friends were all so disgusting. But seeing Mikhail's so thick, long, and erect with pre-cum beading at the tip of the bulbous mushroom head does something different to me.

It arouses me. And that's something that makes me feel

ashamed of myself. It's bad enough I just came at his forceful touch, and against my will.

But this...

I should feel nothing.

"Suck," he growls, and once again I obey.

The cold marble on the floor seeps into my knees as I grip the base of his cock and open my mouth to lick off the pre-cum first. I then take the rest of his length into my mouth, and he starts pumping. Slow then fast and faster, giving me a prelude to what it will feel like when he's inside me.

I don't know what the hell I'm doing or if I'm even doing it right, but I do it.

His fingers lace through my hair, and he cups the back of my head so he can fuck my face faster.

I suck his plundering length, feeling myself growing wet again and my nipples tightening from the wildness of this.

All the blood inside me heats to a boiling point when he groans and starts muttering whole sentences in Russian. He pushes deeper into my throat, and I gag. Instinctively, I pull away, but he fists my hair in his large hands and forces me back to take him. Tears tip over the edge of my eyes, but he doesn't stop fucking my face, and something primal calls to me from deep inside that craves his harsh treatment.

When his cock stiffens, a savage growl tears from his throat and the spray of hot cum hits the back of mine.

Salty and thick. That's what it feels like. And there's a taste embedded within it that I think tastes of sex—to me it does. Maybe I'm right.

I don't get the chance to mull over it any more than that because he catches my face and lifts my jaw up with his cock still set in my mouth and cum inside.

"Swallow," he commands.

I do, allowing the essence of him to slide down my throat. As it works its way down to my stomach, I feel like a mark of ownership has just been placed on me from having that piece of him inside me.

He pulls out his cock, and when I watch him tuck himself back into his pants, a sense of relief washes over me.

The moment of passion shatters, however, when his eyes darken and he reaches down to grab my arm so hard I think he might yank it off. His nostrils flare, and I gasp as he stands me up then shoves me against the wall, pinning my hands above my head so I can't move.

Jesus. What's he going to do to me now?

"Do not look so relieved, princess. I still plan to fuck your brains out, just not while you smell of the blood of my enemies."

My whole body starts shaking. I can't help myself. I don't think I could even if I tried.

The desire in his eyes that was there only seconds ago is gone, and what I see now is hate. Hate for the woman he thinks I am. He'd never know that Adriana and I were polar opposites, as different from each other as night and day.

"You reek of that blood, Adriana Alvarez. Inside and out." He gets up in my face. "It will be a reminder of who you are and what your father did to me. I will make sure you suffer for it."

"But I didn't do anything," I stutter. That's not fear talking this time; it's my instinct to survive.

"It doesn't fucking matter. You will still pay, and may God help you when I'm done with you, because I won't show you any mercy." He glares at me. "My rules are as follows, *Malyshka*: displease me, and I will punish you; defy me, and I'll punish you; try anything stupid like escaping, and I will punish you. However, if you fuck with me or my plans for the cartel, I will kill you. Do you understand me?"

My God, he's a ruthless animal. I'm shaking so much I can barely open my mouth.

"Yes."

"Good girl. Now go and get clean. Make sure you're ready to head to New York in the morning."

"New York?"

"Your new home."

He backs away, and I process his words—all of them.

I watch him go, and the moment the door closes, I sink back to the floor, naked and shaking.

This survival is only temporary. All I've done is bought myself more time on this earth.

But I don't think I'm actually going to survive this.

I don't think he's going to allow me to.

Chapter Six

Mikhail

New York

As I speed down the winding road leading to my father's house on my motorcycle, the ghost of the princess' touch lingers on my skin.

It taunts me like the frostiness of the weather. Like her, it's neither here nor there, but there's an unshakeable presence.

The marks her fingernails made on my shoulders are still there, too, imprinted on my skin although I never took my clothes off. She gave me those marks as I made her come and submit to me, giving herself over to pleasure.

The same pleasure I can't shake from my mind.

I haven't been able to shake her from my mind either.

I wanted to take her right there after I tasted her and took in her fear and arousal. The deadly combination was more potent than any drug I've taken.

Like a fucking addict, I fed off her fear and wanted more.

But all in good time.

Now we're in New York, we're in my world, and we can play by all my rules.

Last night, she was scared and caught up in everything that happened, but I expect her to be the spoiled bitch I've heard she is soon.

The princess would have landed an hour ago, and I'm assuming she's either still on her way to my house or already there.

I left Mexico last night because I didn't want to stay another second in that house. I didn't care how late it was or how tired I might have been, I planned to fly back home even before I left.

I take a right turn and slow down as the two mammoth-sized silver gates guarding the house I grew up in come into view.

The guards open them for me before I get there so I can ride right into the heavily guarded fortress that became home to the brotherhood more than two decades ago when my father became the Pakhan.

The stately home that emulates many of the chateaus and manor homes in Europe rises into view as I head down the drive.

It undoubtedly looks like the home it should be, but it also has that vibe that lets you know business is conducted here. My father always said he preferred business and home to be one and the same. Not because he's a workaholic. It's because he's a good leader who's immersed himself in his responsibilities.

Usually, there are three meetings here on a weekly basis between the elite group, the Brigadiers and the senior members of their brigade. The larger meetings are held at Dmitriyev Ltd., our family company, in the city.

Father used to attend all meetings, even when he was first diagnosed with brain cancer. By the time he became terminal, my mother insisted on him focusing on the meetings here.

I park, take off my helmet, and get off my bike. I then acknowledge the men guarding the doors to the entrance.

They bow their heads as I walk, showing me the same respect they give my father and brother.

I make my way inside, and as always, I take in the fervent atmosphere when I turn down the large hallway leading to the meeting room.

The atmosphere emanates from the décor and design my father chose for this particular section of the house. The Renaissance paintings lining the walls on either side are what does it.

This is the only section of this house where you might believe you're walking the halls of an Italian family home. It's the route our men would take and what they'd see on their way to meetings.

As an avid lover of great art works and an artist himself, my father chose the paintings that depict the most powerful images of war and death. As such, he favored Caravaggio for the emotion he evoked in his art.

The paintings serve as a reminder that although times change and so do the players, similar problems exist over time. Those who are in power will try to maintain power and gain more, and the weaker parties will either ally themselves with those in charge or overthrow them. Such was the case with many revolutions in history, and often what brought down the powerful are the things they overlooked or making the simple mistake of thinking they were invincible.

Walking down here is like taking a walk through the Vatican in Rome, where I've always felt the old mythological world had been preserved somewhat within that space. I have the same feeling here, but today, the images of war and death remind me of my own situation, because we are at war with an unknown enemy.

Raul Alvarez was only a piece of the puzzle that still mystifies me, and I need to get to the heart of what's going on before it comes back to screw with me and my family.

I walk into the meeting room and find the people I need to talk to are both inside.

At the head of the table is my father, whose face brightens when he sees me. Some of the life returns—a sign he was worried about me. Next to him is Ivan, my brother—my *half-brother*, but as Father keeps reminding us, the same blood flows through our veins. It matters not that we have different mothers or we're ten years apart. We're brothers.

I know he wants us to be the same kind of brothers he and his brother were, but unlike his brother, Ivan would never take a bullet for me.

The flat, emotionless look in his almost black eyes reminds me of that and is a tell he's jealous as fuck that I've just done something neither expected me to do.

Sophia, my aunt and my father's sister, walks into the room from the other side with a stack of papers in her hands.

When she sees me, she rushes over and hugs me.

She's the balance in our dark world. She's the closest thing I have to a mother now, and like my mother, she's always been there for me.

She was the first face I woke up to when I came out of the coma, and she's been on edge ever since worrying over my safety.

"Thank God, you've returned," she mutters, tears filling her eyes as she gazes up at me.

"Was there ever any doubt?" Father says in that same powerful voice he's used to command the legion of members in our Bratva and our allies. "This is my son, Sophia. Of course, he has returned."

"I'm just happy to see him return unharmed," Sophia says.

"Thank you, Auntie," I say. I only call her that in special

moments like these when we're together as a family. At other times, I refer to her by her name for business purposes.

Sophia might appear soft because of her good-natured ways, but she's the equivalent of a consigliere in the Italian Mafia to my father. Nothing gets past her, and she's the back-bone to our organization.

"And what news do you have, brother?" Ivan asks, running a hand through his dark mane of hair that has the same unruly style as mine.

That's perhaps as far as our similarities go.

I reach into my pocket and pull out Raul's ring. I walk right up to the table and hold it up so they can see it.

"We now have control of the Alvarez Cartel."

Father nods his approval. He's proud of me. "Well done, my son."

"Thank you, Father."

Getting control of the cartels in Mexico is a massive achievement to be proud of, but the key reason he looks like that is because of the justice I got for my mother and sister.

I put the plan together as soon as I could walk.

I left my hospital bed against doctor's orders and raced against time to find my sister. I already knew finding her would be a lost cause.

I never expected her to still be alive after I'd been out of action for three months with the truth of who took her locked away in my head. I still hoped to find her though.

The time spent looking for her, however, was to no avail. We just discovered what we already knew. That she was dead, but worse had happened to her.

By the time those bastards Raul sold her to were finished with her, we didn't even have her remains to bury. She was sold as a sex slave, raped, and killed. Then they burned her.

I was never going to find anything.

That revelation is what hit me only days ago, so my next move was to kill Raul and usurp his empire.

"Did you get the girl?" Father asks.

"I did. I plan to marry her in a month. The cartel heads will all be here to witness it. I have left Sebastian in Mexico, along with the only remaining lieutenant, to tie things up."

It turns out the old man was useful, after all. I kept him alive at first because I thought he'd be able to tell me who Raul was working with. Although I never knew his name, I'd seen him several times before and knew he was like a lapdog to Raul.

Last night, after I finished with the princess, I tortured him, too, and only decided to keep him alive because he was the last one left who would know the cartel dealings. He will tell me everything I need to know about the cartel and be the liaison between the other heads.

"Wonderful."

"And when do we get to meet the future Mrs. Dmitriyev?" Ivan gives me a stiff smile.

"I'm not sure yet."

"Bring her to dinner on Sunday," Father cuts in.

We always have dinner together as a family on the first Sunday of every month. This Sunday is that day. That gives me one week.

"Of course." I dip my head.

That dinner is going to be interesting. Fuck knows what kind of state I'll be in by then after being around Adriana. In the short space of time I've spent around her, I've flit continuously from being so hard I want to fuck her to being so angry her father was Raul that I want to kill her.

"Then we'll get to see if the rumors of her beauty are true," Ivan adds, cutting into my thoughts.

The devious flicker of mischief in his eyes speaks of his interest in her, which is a problem, because he's not getting her.

She's mine. I'm not going to allow him to play his little fucked up games to take her from me and screw with my plans.

"The rumors were very true, brother," I answer, giving him back the same stiff smile. "Her beauty surpasses the goddess Aphrodite herself."

"Good for you."

Yes, motherfucker. It is.

I'd say exactly that to him if our father weren't present. Father doesn't like the tension between us. Or the competition.

Everything has always been a competition between Ivan and me. He is my rival in every sense. Even now as I stand here, the competition is on as to who gets to be the next Pakhan of the Baranov. Him or me.

Ivan is the Sovientrik, and he got that title fair and square. He's been in the game longer than I have, and when the position came up, it was a given he'd get it. It was also a given that he'd be the next Pakhan.

Until our father changed the rules.

Like most of the brotherhoods in our alliance, in the Baranov the oldest son of the current leader becomes the next Pakhan when he retires or dies. It's only in circumstances where there are no heirs that the current leader chooses the next from the other members of the Brotherhood. If that happens, the Sovientrik usually gets the position because he's the closest to the Pakhan in leadership.

This is the first time that a leader has changed things up and practically created a competition between his sons.

A competition Ivan hates because now that he's thirty-eight and I'm twenty-eight, and we're both already part of the leadership, we're both on equal footing to get the lead. He's no longer entitled to a God damn thing.

Being the leader of the Baranov is not something I'm going to allow him to take, either, if what I'm doing is pushing me ahead of him. I singlehandedly brought down the Alvarez Cartel, and I own it. That's going to bode well for me.

"Well, it will be good to meet her in person," Father says. "I'm sure that will help keep her in line."

"I agree." Meeting everyone—essentially, more people like me—will scare the shit out of her. That will definitely keep her in line. But on to more important matters to discuss. My family meeting Adriana is the least of things to be concerned with. "We need to discuss the bigger picture. Eliminating Raul was just part of the problem."

"I think you're right, but one thing at a time, son," Father replies, and I tense. I knew he was going to say that to me. I think that advice is more about the intensity of the last few weeks than anything else. "You know what the cartel men are like. They aren't going to like us taking over. They'll be looking for a way out. Although the strongest element you have is marrying Raul's daughter, you will need to assert your dominance over them. It would be better to make use of your resources to do that."

"Father, we are being targeted," I point out, respectfully. You don't relax when that is the case. Fuck knows what could have happened during the missing time I was down. "What happened to Mother, Talia, and me was an assassination attempt. Now that everybody knows I'm back from the dead, the question is when they're going to strike again."

"Raul was a powerful entity, comparable to us, and you took him down. That's going to be a large percentage of the problem gone. It's also possible he was the *only* problem. Nothing else happened to any of us during that three-month span you were down."

"Maybe nothing happened because whoever was watching us knew not to strike, or they were waiting."

I don't believe for one second that we weren't being watched *all* the time. Or that my survival was kept a complete secret.

My safety while in the hospital was down to 24/7 surveillance. My father was also there most of the time and oversaw my care. That's what I was told. Even with all that regimented care, however, it doesn't mean we weren't being watched.

"Father, it was clear to me Raul was working with someone else, or other people. I think it's someone big. Raul refused to give me information, and he never shared the details of his plans with his senior lieutenant. I think if it were just him to worry about, he would have given me something more than his silence. Whatever he knew was strong enough to make him believe dying in silence was worth protecting his daughter. That is something we need to pay attention to."

"Ivan and Sophia, leave us," Father says, meaning he wants to speak to me in private.

Ivan and Sophia exchange glances, then leave. Once they've gone, my father stares at me with worried eyes.

As he motions for me to sit opposite him, the sunlight catches his white hair, making him look like he's already wearing a halo. He looks older than just a few days ago.

My father is eighty. He was older than my mother by thirty-five years, but I swear he looked to be about the same age as her when she was alive. Now, his age and illness are more noticeable.

I sit before him and drag in a sigh, knowing he's going to tell me something I won't like.

"Mikhail, you're going a million miles an hour, and it's going to get you killed," he points out.

"I'm taking care of our security."

"Of course, and there's nothing wrong with that, but you need to take a moment to deal with what's happened and with our losses. No one can keep going on a train of vengeance without stopping." He clears his throat.

"I feel if I stop, that's more time wasted. I was in a coma for months."

"Mikhail, you can't blame the time your body needs to heal. You almost died. Please remember that."

As if I could forget. Almost dying feels like a weakness I shouldn't have had.

For as ruthless and strong as I am, I was unable to protect my mother and sister when they needed me most. No one will ever know how that makes me feel.

"I do remember."

"While you were away, the team came back with the results of their investigation on Raul, and they didn't find anything we don't already know. Ivan worked with them personally, and they triple-checked everything."

This is the same team that was able to track down where Talia was taken to after I told them about Felipe and Raul. It was difficult to investigate before without names.

Our security team is thorough, and you can usually take what they say as gospel, but my gut tells me there's more to find and this is far from over.

"We were waiting to find out if you found more in Mexico to investigate. If you had, I'd say look into it, but there isn't anything right now," he adds, and I can't refute it. "So, I want you to focus on the cartel for the moment, because you will need to. But, of course, keep your eyes open. We have to always keep our eyes open. I'm not suggesting that just because we found nothing, there's nothing more to find, but it's a possibility. What I'm suggesting is to direct your focus on what you can see and control. Besides, with the upcoming leadership change, we're going to need to think of that, too."

"I know," I reply.

My insides always tighten when he talks about the leadership changes.

It's happening in a little under eight weeks.

As much as I want the chance to be Pakhan, the thought of losing my father aches my soul.

After the doctors gave him a year to live, he told us he'd be passing the torch. That happened two months before the accident, so he now has seven months by their records and will eventually begin to deteriorate in health and mental capacity. He didn't want to be around the men in that state.

Father has kept his sickness hidden for the best part of four years. We fought long and hard, but this is the end of the line.

"My plans to go back to Russia and die there are the same. I'll be leaving a month after the change of leadership. I just... won't have your mother with me." His hands shake at the mention of her, and I'm grateful he knows he can be real with me. "I can't believe she's gone, Mikhail."

"Me neither."

I might not have any regard for marriage, but my parents were the best examples of love to have.

In this dark criminal world we live in, it was different to witness the love they had for each other.

My mother wasn't Russian. She was American. It didn't matter where she was from, though; she loved Russia and would have loved to go there with my father to live out the rest of his days.

"My beautiful angel and my daughter are both gone. I'm going to be your father now, and tell you that I need you to be careful. It was a close call, and the way it happened was fucked up considering who we are. That's why I'm telling you to keep your eyes open and take things in their stride so you can focus. You hear me, son?"

"I do." I nod with assurance, but I already know I won't rest because of that feeling in my soul telling me I can't.

I understand the grief he must feel, but he's had three months to deal with it.

Everyone went through the motions, but to me, everything is still fresh.

It's three weeks fresh, and I'm the only one with the memory of that night I'll never forget.

I'm the only one who looked into Raul's eyes and knew the bastard was hiding answers I need to solve this mystery.

I missed my mother's funeral and buried what remained of

my sister last week. So the raging beast inside me forbids me to stop digging for answers.

The only thing I'll allow to soothe my inner turmoil is defeating Raul and taking his daughter for myself.

I'll take my pleasure in terrifying and taunting her to break her, then owning her body over and over again. More importantly, every time I'm with her, I'll remember Raul's agonized cries before I ended him. I'll remember I singlehandedly took away her father and her love for that bastard Felipe. I'll remember that I ruined her and the future her father wanted for her.

Her face will be a memento of my victory over the man who took everything from me.

I just hope like fuck that victory will lead me to conquering the bigger problem.

If I don't fix the problem, I'm still dead, and so is everyone else.

Chapter Seven

Natalia

"**M**r. Dmitriyev expects you to eat at the designated times. You are also to put in a request for anything you might need," Aleksander explains, straightening up as he cuts me a sideward glance. "Is that understood?"

"Yes. I understand."

I swallow hard to keep myself from groaning and keep up my pace next to him as we walk down the long, formidable hallway with barren gray walls on either side of us.

Aleksander is Mikhail's caretaker. His Russian accent is much thicker than Mikhail's, and I get the feeling he only speaks English when he needs to.

Aleksander was the first person I met when I arrived an hour ago at this fortress of a home that belongs to Mikhail.

The first things I noticed were that both Aleksander and the house are as cold and callous as Mikhail is.

At first glance, Aleksander would seem like a mash-up of Alfred from *Batman* and Mr. Belvedere because of the well-tailored suit he's wearing. However, his icy personality is nothing like either of them. I'd be more inclined to believe he was someone's idea of their evil twin version.

He's just shown me around the five-story mansion. I also got to meet the housing staff who so far seems to consist of three maids, two chefs, two gardeners, a pool guy, and a host of guards who all carry guns.

We walk out onto the third floor and stop by the balcony, where Aleksander motions to our surroundings and sets his hands by his sides.

"The only places in the house or the grounds that are off limits are Mr. Dmitriyev's office, unless he tells you specifically to meet him there," he says. "And the basement."

"The basement?" I understand why the office would be off limits, but for him to tell me the basement is off limits, too, makes me think Mikhail must have all kinds of shit in there. Just like Raul did. *Basement* would have been the fancy word he used for the dungeon. It's not the first time I've thought I traded one hell for another, or rather, I was drafted in. This basement issue is just one more example.

"Yes. Do you understand you aren't to go anywhere you are not permitted?" he checks.

"Yes, I do. Where is he?"

I can't even say Mikhail's name. I don't want to. I'm not likely to forget last night for many reasons. What he did to me will forever be burned in my mind.

I'll never forget the way he made me come as if my body was made to react to his command. It terrified me and that was bad enough. Seconds later, he had his cock in my mouth, fucking my face. I can still taste his cum in the back of my throat.

I'm sure at any point now he'll make his presence known. I was shocked, to say the least, that he wasn't on the flight this morning. I want to know where he is and what time I'm likely to see him so I can prepare my mind.

"Mr. Dmitriyev will see you later. Until then, you are in my care."

"Okay." That sounds like I might have some time but doesn't exactly tell me much of what I need to know.

"Did you need him for something?"

"No," I reply a little too quickly.

The look of scrutiny he gives me makes me wonder if my tone was harsher than intended. I'm trying to be careful, as careful as I can be; it's just hard when I'm so on edge. And I still have no idea what's happening to José.

I stayed in Adriana's room last night and must have bathed ten times until I thought I was clean enough, yet I still feel dirty.

I couldn't sleep either. Who could sleep after what happened? I also knew if I dared to, the nightmares would pick up where reality left off.

I kept hoping I'd see José, but I didn't. At the crack of dawn, two armed guards escorted me from Mexico. We left on a private jet.

Since I'd never been to New York before, I had no idea how long the journey was going to take, and being with them increased my anxiety. All I knew was that it would be a long journey, and I was right. It took six hours to fly here, and an additional half an hour to reach the house. So, I probably travelled for a total of eight hours.

I also knew the weather was going to be very different from Mexico. I was right about that, too. The furthest I've ever gone was San Francisco to visit my grandmother before she died. I also went to Florida when my parents took me to places like Disney World when I was little. Both places were as sunny as Mexico.

It's colder here. Cold like it might snow, so I was given a coat to put over the little dress I was wearing. I'm still wearing the coat, although the house is a lot warmer inside. The coat is more for comfort than anything.

The only good thing to come out of this crazy scenario of me impersonating a cartel princess is getting to take Adriana's beautiful clothes and shoes. I packed five suitcases, and the men are packing the other stuff to have it shipped here. It was anger that made me pack what I could. Anger for all the times she made me clean her shoes more than they needed to be cleaned and wash her clothes just because she wanted to keep me busy.

I left Mexico in the beautiful baby blue skater dress she told me was worth more than my life when she caught me looking at it sometime after she'd bought it.

"There are a few things Mr. Dmitriyev wants you to do before he gets back."

I don't like the sound of that.

"Like what?"

"A doctor will be here shortly to check you and administer your contraception injection."

The blood drains from my body. *That bastard.* "Check me for what?" I fume.

"I don't think I need to spell it out."

No, he doesn't need to spell it out, except I told that asshole last night that I'm a virgin. That means I shouldn't need any checks.

"The doctor will be here in about ten minutes," he continues. "We've sealed off the front living room for your examination."

"I already have a contraception injection." I got it last week in prep for my sale in the auction. Of course, I won't tell anyone that. Since it takes seven days to take effect, Raul wanted everything nice and ready for the *big day,* so he prepped me like a Thanksgiving turkey.

"You can speak to the doctor about that. He will test you and establish what medications you need."

"I don't understand why I need to see a doctor," I argue.

He gives me a narrowed look. "I'm certain you know by

now that you are to do as you are told without any exceptions or arguments. So, if I were you, Miss Alvarez, I'd make life easier for myself. Especially given who you are."

He looks me up and down with the same hatred I witnessed in Mikhail and the guards.

Of course, the hatred would be there. I keep forgetting everyone thinks I'm Adriana Alvarez. So, everyone hates me like they would her because everyone thinks my father ordered the killing of Mikhail's mother and sister.

The shitty thing about it is, if people knew who I was, they'd kill me. They'd kill me because Natalia de Leon isn't worth anything. Not even the dress she's wearing.

"Understood?" he asks, and I manage a nod. "You may wait in the living room if you wish, or the bedroom. Take your pick."

"I'll wait in the living room. I just need to go to the bathroom first."

"Very well. I believe you know the way. Do not keep the doctor waiting." He says that in the same commanding tone I remember Adriana using in regard to the seamstress.

"I won't."

The bathroom on this floor is to our left. I move away from him and head right in, locking the wooden door behind me.

I don't really need to use the bathroom; I just needed the break. These few moments are the only reprieve I can steal for myself. I've been stealing them since last night to gather my thoughts.

Right now, I just need to cry a little.

Just a little. Not too much to trigger the real pain that's cutting deep into me from the center of my core.

I look at my face in the mirror and notice the bruise on my cheek.

It's darker today in contrast to my skin.

I draw in a shallow breath and allow a few tears to spill

over my lids. These tears fall because I'm so fucking scared, I'm afraid to breathe.

I'm terrified, and I don't know what's going to happen from one moment to the next. I know Mikhail is not a man you mess around with, and I'm frightened someone is going to come up to me and blow my head off when they discover I'm not Adriana.

And fuck, what about the wedding?

He's going to marry me thinking I'm someone else.

Jesus. I've gone from the fear of being placed up for auction to getting ready to marry a Russian mobster.

How the hell did that happen?

Gathering my strength, I splash some cold water on my face, pat my cheeks, and leave the bathroom.

By the time I get down the stairs and walk into the living room, the man I'm assuming is the doctor is already inside setting up. At least Raul allowed me to see a woman. This guy looks just as unwelcoming as everyone else.

"Please sit here," he says, motioning to the armchair.

Like everyone keeps telling me, I do as I'm told and sit.

"I've had the contraception injection already," I inform him.

"When?"

"Last week."

"I'll ascertain that."

I say nothing more; I just go through the embarrassing motions.

I give him my arm to take blood and spread my legs when he first checks I'm a virgin. He then takes samples to check me for diseases. I'm sure one is likely to confirm the other, but what do I know?

He's probably just doing as he's told, too. Or maybe this is part of my humiliation.

The whole thing takes a little over an hour, and when he's

done, he barely says two words to me before he leaves, and I'm summoned to lunch in the dining room.

After that ordeal, I don't feel like eating, but I eat because I haven't since yesterday at breakfast. At least the maid who serves me the food seems more human, but she doesn't talk to me, and when she leaves and heads back to the kitchen, I hear her talking to the others in Russian. I don't know if she didn't talk to me because she was told not to, or if it's because she doesn't speak English and I don't speak Russian.

She served me a delicious-looking chicken casserole with boiled rice and a side of blanched vegetables. The meal smells and tastes as divine as it looks when I tuck in to eat.

It's definitely better than anything I've eaten in the last five years. Raul's servants like me were given the same thing he fed to the dogs—scraps.

It's been nine years since I had anything close to a home-cooked meal like this. That was before Raul took my family.

It was the eve of my tenth birthday when his men stormed our house. They came at night and dragged us out kicking and screaming. Black bags were placed over our heads, and we were taken.

That was when my mother and I knew Papa lost his job in the city and he'd not only been drug muling for Raul, but he owed him money. A lot of money.

I was never told how much, but I don't think the amount mattered. Even if it was ten Pesos, Raul would have still taken us.

We went to live on the plantation like the other men who worked the opium fields.

I was allowed to finish high school, but that was as far as my education went, and my dreams for my future in medicine. I wanted to be a doctor like my mother was. That's what led her to Mexico and how she met my father. She was a diagnostician. She came to work in a research center in Cancun. I wanted to go down the same route, and if my life were different, that's what I'd do. I know that's nothing but a dream now, and I should force it out of my mind.

My mother was forced to give up her dream to work in the fields, and my father trafficked drugs and people for Raul. All for free. They worked to pay Raul back.

They worked night and day to pay back a debt that would never be paid.

Then, to add salt to the wounds, Raul always had his eyes on my mother. He just never did anything until his wife was killed by his enemies.

That happened two years ago.

Days after he buried his wife, he started making sexual advances on my mother, which she refused. His final attempt was what did it, though. It was like he'd had enough of her refusal. She managed to escape him and came home with her clothes ripped up and bruises all over her face. She begged my father to take us away. Before he could think of an answer, Raul came with Felipe and his guards.

Papa tried to save her, but Raul threatened my life if he intervened. They held a gun to my head and made him kneel execution style so he could watch Raul rape my mother, then kill her.

We both watched helplessly.

My world ended that night and I'll never forget it. Even when my father was killed, I didn't experience the same devastation. Not because I loved him any less than my mother. It was just that Mom's death broke me.

It was at that moment when I realized nothing was stable and nothing was in my control.

I was already in hell, and I expected bad things to happen. After Mom died, Papa vowed to get me out because he knew it was only a matter of time before I suffered the same fate. That vow is what killed him.

Something catches my eye through the floor-to-ceiling glass windows.

When I lift my head, I watch as wisps of snowflakes fall onto the ground.

I've never seen snow in real life before.

I focus on it, when out from the evergreen hedge runs a white snow dog with ghost-like eyes. I'm not sure, but I think it could either be a Siberian Husky or an Alaskan Malamute. I'm not exactly well versed in dog breeds, but I'm sure it's one or the other. And it's exceptionally beautiful.

Quickly, I finish the little food left on my plate, then grab my coat from the living room, where I left it after the examination.

I slip it on and venture outside through the sliding doors.

The dog is way down the path now, so I quicken my pace and go after it. I try not to run and frighten it away.

When I get close, it turns and sees me, and I realize then that its eyes are ice blue.

After being around Raul's guard dogs that were trained to kill if they thought you were escaping, this creature is a breath of fresh air, and breathtaking. I never expected to witness something so beautiful here. The snow falls and melts in its fur, and my hair, too.

I can't help myself. I bend down and touch the dog's soft fur, and when it dips its head for me to continue stroking, I do, savoring the feel of the softness and gentleness of the animal.

It comforts me somewhat.

When it moves to pick up a twig from the side with its mouth and hands it to me, I realize it must want to play.

I throw the twig not far down the path, and the dog takes off to retrieve it.

It does the same thing again, and I find myself playing in the snow as it falls a little heavier.

The dog starts barking at something behind me, and when I turn around to see Mikhail standing on the terrace, everything inside me freezes like the icy snow falling around us. I was able to stave off the cold before, but now I'm freezing from deep within, like the coldness is resonating from inside my body.

Mikhail is dressed in black again, and as he walks toward me in the brightness of the day, it feels like I'm in a surreal dream. Everything in my head is telling me to run away, but I know I can't run anywhere.

I'm not quick to forget the warning of what he'll do to me if I try to escape. I'm sure mere running away from him will garner the same shitty result.

So, I stay.

I stay right where I am, steel my spine, and watch him walking toward me like the angel of death.

Chapter Eight

Natalia

Mikhail's honey-colored eyes and the gold hoop in his ear are the only touch of color on him, along with the red cross on his left hand and the red writing on his other hand. Everything else is like a dark shadow billowing around him.

Every step he takes makes my heart gallop, and I need to take slow breaths to calm myself. The worst thing I can look now is afraid.

Mikhail says something to the dog in Russian, and it bounds over to him. He lowers to tap its head, then straightens up and returns his focus on me.

"Didn't think I'd find you out here playing with my sister's dog," he states, looking from me to the dog.

It's his sister's. That explains why it has a gentler presence.

"I was just ... well, I came out here when I saw it. And it was snowing. I've never seen snow before."

"Snow," he says, and the dog barks. "That's her name."

"Oh," I breathe and gaze at the beautiful dog. The name is

fitting even now as I watch the snowflakes mingle with the dog's fur.

I wonder what his sister was like. The only thing about her I know, apart from the way she died, is that she owned this dog and now it's his.

Another command in Russian has Snow running back down the path where I'd originally seen her. I want to ask if the dog just roams the grounds, but that's a question for normal people. Clearly, the dog is fine. I am not.

As I gaze into those eyes of his, I wonder what he's going to do to me now.

Is he going to make good on his word to fuck me?

Will he hurt me when he does?

I don't know if I could bear it. I don't think I could go through such violence and make it back with my mind already so fragile.

So, what do I do to make it easier? I can't think of anything.

"Relax, Malyshka. I don't plan to fuck you out here in the snow for all to see," he begins and leans so close to my ear he envelopes me with his aftershave. "Unless you want me to."

My cheeks heat up at his words, and the images of him taking me right here flicker through my mind, but I manage to gather my composure.

"No," I reply, and he smiles.

"I have business to attend to, but I came to give you the good news."

"What good news?" I'm not sure what shape that would take for me in regard to him.

"The doctor says you're clean, and it seems like your contraceptive injection meets my criteria, so you won't require any further medication."

What an asshole.

His smile irritates me so much I can't hold my tongue.

"Did you have to do that to me?" I ask.

"Do what? I like to fuck bareback and without the worry of

impregnating my enemy's daughter. I see no harm in making the necessary checks I need to establish certain truths."

"I told you I was a virgin, so you should have known I was clean."

"I know no such thing, and you would be surprised what shit people get up to so they can still pass for a *virgin*. I like to be careful. I'm curious, though. Weren't you planning on having children with Felipe?"

I try to control the bile rising in my stomach and force myself to look like I'm grieving.

"I don't think that's any of your business."

He leans close again and looms before me with a mocking smirk. "Everything is my business, *Malyshka*."

He says Malyshka with emphasis this time, and I realize for the first time—and with annoyance because of the meaning—that it's easier if he calls me that or princess than Adriana.

It's easy because it's new, and he's new to me.

"In any event," he adds, "you're clear for me to take you at anytime and anywhere I want."

"What about you? How do I know you're clean?"

He chuckles, and the sound ripples through me. He lifts a lock of my hair and twirls it around his tattooed forefinger. I risk glancing down to see if I can make out what the tattoo means, but I think it's in Russian. I also think the tattoos on his hands are prison tattoos. José taught me a few things like that I needed to be aware of.

He just never went into depth. José cautioned me and said if I ever saw a Russian Mafioso man with the type of tattoos Mikhail was sporting, I should avoid them at all costs. *Run if you have to*. He actually said those words.

Now look at me. I'm waiting for the said Russian Mafioso man to confirm he's clean enough to fuck me bareback.

Christ.

What hell dimension did I fall into?

And why the hell did I think it was a good idea to ask him that?

The corner of his lips turn up into a sinfully wicked smile that tightens my insides, and a spark of arousal coils from my belly right into my pussy.

"Baby girl, I'm clean because I say I am."

Baby girl. It's clear he didn't call me Malyshka just now to make a point.

"Anything else you want to know about my dick?" he asks, crude and crass.

"No, thank you. There is nothing." I bite down hard on my back teeth and will myself to concentrate. Now that he's here, I can ask the burning question on my mind and try to steer clear of any talk of sex. "Where is José?"

"José Diaz is no longer any of your concern."

Panic turns my knees to water. "What does that mean?"

"It means exactly what I said."

"Did you kill him?" I stutter. Tears prick the backs of my eyes as I imagine him taking pleasure in telling me he has.

"Not yet, Malyshka."

"Is he in Mexico still?"

"Yes."

At least he's answering my questions.

"Is he going to stay there?"

"No."

"When will he come here?"

"That's enough questions about the old man," he cuts me off, and I catch myself when curiosity flickers deeper in his eyes.

Although it's infuriating, I see why he thought José and I were involved. It goes back to that fact that I'm showing more emotion over him than Raul—my supposed father.

I need to be Adriana again and think the way she would in this situation.

"What about my father's body? What did you do with it?" I ask in a fake breathy tone.

"Wouldn't you like to know," he taunts.

"Of course, I do. He was my father. Did you burn him like you did my fiancé?"

At the word *fiancé*, he gives me a look of indignation.

"Yes, I did. I burned your bastard father's body the same way I burned your beloved fiancé. I wished I'd hacked his head off, the same way I cut off Felipe's. I should have fed their heads to the dogs before I left."

"You monster," I gasp.

Before I can say another word, his hand snaps out and clamp around my throat. He squeezes so hard I see stars and my breath cuts off completely.

"I'm a monster? Really? I guess that's what I look like to you, princess. Did you know what your father and fiancé were like? Do tell me. Did you know?"

If I say no, it would be another lie he'll be able to spot from a mile away.

Everybody knew what Raul and Felipe were like.

I don't think he's assumed me to be some naïve princess locked away in a tower. He would have heard the rumors about Adriana. The whispers were either about her beauty or her evil. In fact, I'd say there was a good mixture of those rumors, so I can't say no.

"Yes," I choke out, and the moment I do, I regret it because now he looks like he's going to kill me.

"Did you love Felipe?" he demands.

Again, I have to give an answer I know Adriana would have to say. It's unfortunately, another answer that will infuriate him.

"Yes."

"Then you're just as much of a monster as him and your fucking father. You are just as fucking evil. Your fiancé shot my mother right in front of me. Shot her right in the head with a rifle. She had no hope. Then he sold my sister to sex slavers who abused her until she begged them for death. That's what your fiancé did to my family. At your father's orders. Those are the men you love, Adriana Alvarez. People who steal lives and kill souls."

I wish I could tell him I understand exactly what he means, but I can't.

I wish I could tell him I hate Raul and Felipe more than he does, but I can't.

He would just kill me now.

When he releases me, and I take in the disgust on his face, my priorities shift.

I stagger backward and catch my breath as the person inside me who's still Natalia de Leon fights against the thought of him believing she's as evil as those devils.

The feeling is so strong that I shake my head and allow instinct to guide me.

"I'm not like them," I blurt. "I'm not evil. I swear to you, I'm not. If you knew me, you would see."

I don't know if what I say has any effect at all because he doesn't answer. He just walks away and leaves me standing there in the cold.

It's a repeat of last night, except I feel he hates me more than he did then.

Chapter Nine

Mikhail

I *'m not like them.*
I'm not evil.
Her words seep into me as I walk away, leaving her in the snow.

I never allow anything to linger in my mind longer than necessary. Or people to get under my skin the way she has.

Nothing about this woman, however, seems to be following my usual set of rules. Of course, it wouldn't, because essentially, she's my captive and I'm forcing her to marry me.

I'll have her ring tomorrow, and in two days, I'll give it to her. That's when things are going to feel stranger than they already are. Especially since I hadn't seen marriage in the cards for me any time soon. Or at all. As to what we'll do once we're married, I don't know, but I'll cross that bridge when I get there.

I expect Sebastian to be back with José in a few days. I am, however, going to leave a few of my other subordinates there to keep things under control.

That's Mexico taken care of for the moment. After the

wedding, I'll head back there to see how things are going, and I'll take the princess with me—as my wife.

Aleksander meets me in the same businesslike manner I like him for when I walk into the dining room.

He's worked for me for the last eight years and does what he's told to do without expressing an opinion. Unless I ask for it. I trust him enough to ask sometimes.

I can tell he's wary of Adriana and cautious of the situation here. I am, too, if I'm honest.

The whole Raul situation has me on edge. When I left my father, I put things in motion to continue my own personal investigation. I have my street guys checking things out, and a friend from the Voirik Brotherhood is meeting me tomorrow morning. He's the last ace up my sleeve. If he investigates and tells me there's nothing more to find, I'll follow my father's orders and focus on the cartel but keep my eyes open.

"Was the girl any trouble?" I ask.

"No. She doesn't seem to be. Sorry the dog got loose. It doesn't like being left alone."

"No apologies necessary."

"I just wasn't sure if you'd be okay seeing her play with Talia's dog."

"I'm fine. Let her play with it. It's not a problem."

He dips his head. "Are you heading out again?"

"Yes. I have work to finish up at Dmitriyev Ltd." That's my work Ivan was taking care of while I was out of commission.

"You've had a hectic time. Are you sure you want to get back into the office today?"

I nod firmly, and he knows not to push me. "Yes. It's best I go."

Most things are in hand, but my brother is a man who will do anything to make me look incompetent. I'm not going to allow that to happen. I only wanted to touch base at home for a few minutes to make my presence known.

Ivan has been dealing with the high-profile clientele and

investors Father entrusted me with when he first made me the Obshchak of the brotherhood. In that role my primary duty is to take care of all the money coming into the business.

Even though Dmitriyev Ltd is our family business, the company has served the brotherhood for many generations and has been the primary source of income.

As such, the Obshchak has always had the position of chief financial officer.

I've two meetings to attend and paperwork that will take up the rest of the day. I don't want anybody questioning my capabilities in any way.

"I'll be back around ten, or a bit later," I tell him. "Make sure she eats. If she causes trouble, let me know."

"Of course."

I don't think she's going to cause any trouble today, but I have to prepare for it.

What I've done has caused a massive upheaval to her world and dragged her into mine. The conversation just now was intense.

I was intense, so I think she'll be compliant for the rest of the day.

Pulling on my leather jacket, I leave him, and head out again to my bike.

As soon as I pull out onto the winding road that will lead me back to the city, her words come back to me. They continue to swirl around in my mind, screwing with me. It's an odd feeling I want to shake, but I can't because part of me believes her.

Part of me believes she's not evil, and it goes back to what I first felt when we met. I sensed purity in her but couldn't explain it because of who she is.

I felt it again just now as she spoke, and I saw it while I was watching her play with Snow.

Men like me are like fucking sharks when it comes to anything like that, for the simplest reason of being around something we shouldn't have. In my case, Adriana Alvarez feels like a woman who is automatically off limits because of the darkness perpetually residing in me.

And that's what's screwing with me, because I can't figure her out.

Seeing her with my sister's dog grated on my nerves at first, but not because she was playing with it. It's because of the memories she conjured of Talia.

I took the dog to remember her by, but the memories are also a curse.

My father kept Snow at his house while I was in the hospital, but I took over her care when I got out. It was me who bought it for Talia on her twenty-first birthday. That was only four years ago and after she first got accepted at the New York City Ballet.

My sister was the prima ballerina, and before she was killed, she'd just gotten the assistant choreographer position after being with the company for three years.

The dog was like a long overdue present, and she loved it to no end.

So did my mother.

That nightmare night when disaster struck, Mother was the first to get hit. One bullet to her head signaled the attack. Another went straight to her heart before I could even turn my head to figure out where the bullet came from. When I did, I saw Felipe on the rooftop of the opposite building accompanied by a bunch of masked snipers; I just didn't know it was him until I came up against him face to face.

That night transpired two weeks before Christmas, so they never saw the new year.

Talia had just finished her first performance of the season in a ballet she helped choreograph.

The attack happened just as we stepped out onto the theater parking lot. We were one of the last to leave. Someone knew that.

Someone who was watching us.

Someone who knew where we'd be and what time we'd be leaving.

Talia screamed when Mother went down, and our bodyguards started dropping like flies. All I could think of was protecting her. We weren't anywhere near our car to get away from the danger. With so many bullets flying I couldn't risk her getting hit, so I shielded her with my body while I got her to what I thought was safety behind a hedge.

I pursued the snipers and found Felipe. From the sight of him I knew Raul sent him and what was going on.

That was also where I went wrong. When you're under attack and ambushed like we were, the chances of survival are next to nil. It's like flying blind while your enemy has you in a trap under their thumb.

Although I took down a lot of the snipers, I got shot twice before I made it to Felipe. He was trying to escape, but I gave him a good chase. I reached him when he jumped into his truck but couldn't get close enough. I didn't notice the detonator in his hand until it was too late. He released the trigger on a bomb that should have killed me.

It was a miracle I survived. I was told one of our allies found me in the debris. After that, while my father was investigating, he kept my survival quiet to allow everyone to think I died.

Of course, no one found Talia. Felipe's men would have taken her while I was down. That's the part that broke me. I couldn't have done anything to save my mother. Part of me knows I couldn't have done anything to save Talia either, but because I had a chance, I keep wondering what I could have done differently—or what I could have done better.

That night, Father, Ivan, and Sophia were supposed to be with us but weren't because my father had a bad reaction to some medication and couldn't make it.

Sophia was taking care of him at the time, and Ivan had to

go to the office to cover meetings my father couldn't attend during the day.

The ballet was one of the only times we would have *all* been together out in the open. That is why I think the assassination attempt was on the whole family. If we were all there, we would have all been gunned down like animals, which would have wiped out the entire Baranov leadership.

With no heirs to the Dmitriyev fortune left, Ivan and I are the last men left in the bloodline. Sophia never remarried after a tragic car accident years ago that claimed the lives of her husband and three kids.

If we'd all died that night, the result would have been chaos. It would have opened the door for Raul and whomever to take control over our brotherhood and the extensive wealth linked to our company.

Things are chaotic now, and they will continue to be so until I get to the bottom of this shit.

Chapter Ten

Natalia

As the sun's rays spill through the window, I wake up and glance at the clock on the wall.

It's six o'clock, and the space next to me is as empty as it was when I went to bed. I can't sense anyone else in the room with me.

Mikhail didn't come back last night before I went to sleep, and from what I can tell, it doesn't look like he slept in here.

I think I'd know if he had.

I gaze through the long French windows at the radiant sun, my first New York sunrise. Beautiful as it is, I have no idea what's going to happen today.

I already feel like I've aged a hundred years over the last few days. It's morning again, day two of me being in this house, my new prison.

Last night was the first night I slept in Mikhail's room, in his bed.

Thankfully by myself.

I was so sure he was going to make good on his word to

fuck my brains out, and after the way he handled me yesterday, I imagined him to be violent and cruel.

I figured after I ate dinner by myself and night fell, I may not see him again for the day. Again because of our encounter. When he didn't return, I was grateful for the small mercy.

At the same time, the worrying part about not seeing him means not knowing what's going on.

When you can see your enemy, you can keep your eye on them and be ready when they strike. When you can't see them, you have no idea what sort of ammunition they'll be gathering against you to wipe you out.

My guess is he probably came home and slept in a different room.

Or maybe I'm being naïve again because the alternative for men like him is the possibility he spent the night in another woman's bed.

Why would he sleep in another room in his house because of me?

What I need to do is get my head together and keep on my toes.

I wish I knew when José was coming here. Having him around would help.

Right now, I don't know if I'm going to see him again. If I don't, I'll be flying blind, never knowing when the other shoe's going to drop, and my secret will be out.

Not only that, I'm worried about him, too.

He's like family to me, and I have to face the very real possibility that this disaster could take him away from me.

I slide off the bed and make my way into the walk-in wardrobe. Yesterday, one section was cleared for me to put my things in.

The other section—basically the other half of the room—holds Mikhail's clothes.

I dare not look at his things. I thought of looking around to see if I could gather more than the bare minimum of information I have on him. But I thought better of it.

I realized he wouldn't have anything like that lying around. So, I know nothing more than what I've seen and heard.

I'm supposed to marry this man next week, yet I hardly know anything about him.

I don't even know how old Mikhail is. His ruggedness makes him look older, like a man's man, but that beauty in his features suggests he's in his mid- to late twenties.

Yesterday I spent most of the day putting away my commandeered clothes. What I'm after now is the only thing that belongs to me. It's a little shoebox I managed to take care of over the years.

Inside the box are my trinkets. I've hidden it under some jumpers I placed on the bottom shelf. There's nothing much inside to give me away, but I'm keeping it there for the simple reason that I don't want anything to happen to it.

I don't want the last few precious memories of my parents tarnished.

I sink to the floor and press my back against the wall before I open it, reaching for the one thing that will soothe me.

It's a picture of my parents and me when I was ten. We're in San Francisco at the beach, and we're happy.

Mom's blonde hair is sparkling against the sun, and her bright blue eyes are beaming. My father has a protective arm around us, and he looks proud.

It's a happy picture, of happier times, and a great memory. But it makes me sad because none of these people exist anymore.

Not even me.

I can't be the girl from this picture anymore, or I'm dead.

I must sit there for over an hour staring at the picture and trying to recapture my calm by looking at the trinkets in my box. I lose track of time and only regain my awareness when there's a hurried knock on the bedroom door.

Quickly, I put the box away, grab my robe, and rush out.

I don't know who that is, but I'm guessing it's not Mikhail. He doesn't seem like the kind of person to knock, and why would he on his own bedroom door?

The knock sounds again just as I open the door.

It's Aleksander, and he has the same tight lipped, displeased expression on his face he wore yesterday.

"Good morning," I greet him.

"*Miss* Alvarez, breakfast will be served in ten minutes," he replies, not even bothering to return the pleasantry, or even offer up some fake warmth. "I suggest you get ready and make your way downstairs. Mr. Dmitriyev does *not* like to be kept waiting. Breakfast is served at eight because he has to leave at eight thirty sharp."

"Okay. I—"

He doesn't wait for me to finish. He just marches off, automatically dismissing anything more I have to say.

What a prick.

He's just as abrasive as Mikhail.

I groan inwardly and backtrack into the room before I close the door.

I guess if *Mr. Dmitriyev* doesn't like to be kept waiting, it means Mr. Dmitriyev is sitting at the table. Waiting. Mikhail is here. I'm going to have to face him.

I shower quickly and change into a long-sleeved T-shirt and a little wrap-over skirt. Neither are really appropriate for the cold New York weather, but they're the best I can find. Adriana didn't wear pants. Her signature clothing was short shorts, dresses, and skirts. This one is knitted, so it will at least provide some warmth.

I plan to go outside today and play with the dog if I can. Then I'll try to stay outside as much as I can and only come in to eat.

I pile my hair on top of my head in a messy bun, then make my way downstairs to the dining room.

That's where I find my husband-to-be sitting at the head of the table looking like he's the king of the castle.

His face is expressionless, and it doesn't change when he sees me.

Not even a little bit.

He's serious, always serious.

How am I supposed to live with this man?

Even if I manage to pull off this stunt of mine and truly be Adriana Alvarez, what kind of life would we have?

Would it be like last night, where he's gone and I'm wondering if he's sleeping in some woman's bed? Would he be gone for days?

Would I care?

There's nothing normal about us, but I'd at least hoped if I were to ever get married, it would never be to anybody like him. A symbol of everything I loathe. He's death and captivity rolled into one. The complete antithesis to life.

"Sit here," he commands, pointing to the chair opposite him. Like Aleksander, he doesn't say good morning to me either.

I walk around to the chair and lower to sit, but the way he scans over my body before I do doesn't escape me.

I steady my mind and gear myself up for him, hoping I'll survive today's encounter.

The maid I met yesterday who seemed nice but didn't talk to me walks out of the kitchen with a tray of coffee and gorgeous-smelling pastries. It smells like you'd imagine breakfast to smell. Inviting and delicious, with everything nutritious.

When two other maids join her with more trays of food, I feel like I'm at one of those exquisite vacation getaways in Europe I've seen on TV.

They set the table with everything. There are three different styles of eggs, crispy strips of bacon, two different types of sausages, French toast, normal toast, and an assortment of spreads.

There's so much food I wonder if this is for the two of us or if more people are joining.

As the staff leave and no one else enters the room, I get my answer.

The feast is just for the two of us, and it seems this is what they do every day. I'm probably used to eating this much food over a week. I'm still full from yesterday.

The main maid I've seen—whose name I can't remember—returns and pours Mikhail's coffee. I notice he takes it black. No surprise there. But he does take two sugars.

She pours me some, too, then focuses her attention on Mikhail as they start speaking in Russian. All the while Mikhail keeps a straight face. I have no idea what they're talking about, and I can't figure it out. For all I know, they could be talking about the weather. Or me.

I start eating but continue to watch their interaction, wondering why he'd have such an in-depth conversation with his maid.

I notice how comfortable she looks with him, not like when she was with me. It's then the thought occurs to me that she could be one of his women.

Maybe he spent the night with her. She's quite pretty in an English Rose sort of way and is either the same age as me or slightly older.

She makes the simple maid uniform she's wearing look good with her shapely figure and has her long blonde hair up in a ponytail. It's also quite obvious from the blush in her cheeks that her interest in Mikhail is more than professional.

She likes him. And I guess from the flow of that conversation he might like her too.

Great. This is another snapshot of what our mornings will be like. I'll have to sit here and watch him flirt with his maids. I wonder if I'll catch him doing anything else with them. Something more unsavory.

After a few moments, she leaves us, closing the dining room door behind her, and the tension returns.

Mikhail looks at me as he takes a sip of his coffee. I stare back at him, not knowing what to say.

Clearly, from the sharp gaze he's giving me, my final plea yesterday fell on deaf ears and he thinks I'm evil.

What does he consider himself to be, though?

He massacred everyone at Raul's house. *Everyone* except me and José.

There were people there who didn't deserve to die. What qualified their death was their mere presence on the property.

How does he explain that?

In my book, that is evil.

Maybe he doesn't care.

My gaze drops to his knuckles, and my attention goes right back to all those tattoos. I'm sure now they're prison tattoos.

He's killed many over the last few days. Who did he kill to make him ink his conviction on himself?

"Ask me," he says, startling me.

Confused, I meet his hard gaze.

"What?" I don't know what I'm supposed to ask him or if I was concentrating so hard on his tattoos that I missed something he said.

"You're looking at my tats and trying to figure me out. Princess, if you have a question about me, just ask."

I stare back at him, knowing that's obviously some backhanded trickery to scare me. He knows I'm not going to like any answer he could give. So, I bite back my curiosity and shake my head.

"I don't have any questions about you," I lie, and the million questions I have just about *him* go crazy in my mind.

"No? Last chance to ask me, Malyshka. Don't you want to

know more about my tats? They seem to interest you so much."

"I'm good, thank you."

"All right. Case closed. Any other questions?"

I look him over and decide I might try for some basic questions.

"How old are you?"

He smirks. "Twenty-eight."

I was right about his age. I'd bet he'd look younger too without the fullness of his beard.

"Anything else?" he steeples his fingers on the table and stares deeply at me.

"Where do you work?"

"The family business, Dmitriyev Ltd. Just think of me as the accountant. Anything more?"

That was as basic as I can get. Everything else in my head will get me in trouble.

"No."

He finishes his coffee while I focus on eating my food. I'm eating way too much, but eating is giving me something to do. It's my *anything-but-looking-at-him* thing.

He sets the mug back onto the table and clears his throat.

"I want you to go shopping later," he states.

"What for?"

"Clothes. You need warmer clothes for the weather here, and I don't particularly like what you're wearing." He looks me up and down.

"What's wrong with what I'm wearing? These are nice clothes."

"Yes. It's sexy as fuck, but I'm not the only one who's going to think so." His gaze settles on my cleavage, and I swallow hard against the spark of arousal threatening to push its way through me. "I have guards patrolling the grounds who will think so, too. That's just one thing wrong with your Malibu Barbie look."

Malibu Barbie? Is he being serious? I couldn't look any different to Malibu Barbie if I tried.

"What's the other thing?" I challenge.

"Your father bought them for you, so the less I see of them, the better. I'm sending you to the store to get a whole new wardrobe. Aleksander will go with you. Think of your old stuff as keepsakes. Is that clear?"

"Yeah." I can't exactly complain. Getting new clothes is probably a good thing. At least I get to pick them and will feel less like I borrowed someone's life.

"The seamstress is also coming by tomorrow to discuss your dress. You only have tomorrow to pick the style you want. So, make sure you do it, and don't give her any trouble," he states.

Seamstress.

For *my* wedding dress.

Me.

God, this is actually happening. We're really getting married.

I'm going to be in my own dress, and we'll be married.

It won't be the fairy-tale wedding I dreamed of having when I was a little girl. It will be like some nightmare.

And who will be there to see it happen?

His people. All people who hate me and nobody for me. Unless José will be there.

Or not. What if I don't see him again?

I was told yesterday he was none of my concern, but I have to ask the question just so I know.

"When am I going to see José?" I say quickly and pray he doesn't go crazy on me. "Am I going to see him again?"

He sets his elbows onto the table, and I can tell I've taken this conversation in a direction I didn't want.

"I already told you, he's none of your concern anymore."

"I know, but I just wanted to see him. Is he still coming to New York?" It would be a cruel joke and a sick twist of fate if

I'm sitting here asking these questions while Mikhail has already killed José.

"I'm going to say this one more time, Malyshka. José has nothing to do with you anymore," he informs with emphasis on every single syllable. "And just so you know..."—he touches my face and lifts my chin, so I meet his gaze head on—"I'm a very jealous, possessive man, and I'm not exactly a fan of your interest in the old man."

"I told you; he's my bodyguard. This is the longest I've gone without seeing him."

"I don't fucking care. In my mind, you look like you want to fuck him."

My mouth drops, and I don't know how it doesn't hit the floor.

"You bastard," I hiss, backing away from his grasp, different to yesterday when I allowed him to hurt me. I'm just so appalled by what he said it's enraged me, and I can't calm myself back down.

He bolts up, squaring off with me with his nostrils flared and eyes blazing.

Sensing he's about to go ape shit on me, I stand, too, but back a few paces away to put some distance between us.

He's too big. Too tall and formidable. I'm sure he wouldn't hesitate to crush me in one move before I could think to get away.

"What did you just call me?" he demands, balling his hand into a tight fist.

"What is the matter with you?" I snap, answering his question with a question. Surely, his behavior isn't normal by anybody's standards. It's not by mine, and I can't believe what he's implying. He implied the same thing back in Mexico, but I was so worried that I couldn't fully address the matter. "How does asking for a man who's like a father to me make me look like some kind of whore?"

"What. Did. You. Just. Call me?"

"You heard what I said, and I gave you an answer."

"Lady, I call it like I see it. If you look like you want to be the old man's whore, then that's not on me. It's on you. Fuck, maybe the doctor got it wrong, and you've been fucking the old man this whole time."

"Fuck you, you fucking asshole. How dare you say that to me!" The moment the words leave my mouth, I regret them. Every one of them.

Jesus, who told me to say that?

Why did I snap back like that?

I don't get to think any more because it takes a split second for him to lunge for me, and I swear I see my life flash before my eyes. Everything rushes me, the good and the bad.

When he grabs my arms, I scream and do the only thing I can think of to break free. I send one hard kick to his knee.

I was aiming for his balls. I just never reached.

I make an impact, though, and he loosens his grip on me in an instant.

However, I think the only reason he lets go is because I catch him off guard. I shock myself, too.

I don't, however, waste time mulling over it.

I run.

Chapter Eleven

Natalia

My heart leaps into my throat, and I summon all the strength I can gather to run away from him. But Mikhail is only paces behind me, cursing me in English and Russian.

I dash through the door as fast as I can and bolt down the hallway without knowing where I'm going or what the fuck I'm doing.

God, I fucked up.

I fucked everything up, and now I don't know what the hell Mikhail is going to do to me when he catches me.

I reach a dead end and it's game over. It would have been anyway, because who am I kidding? Did I really think I was going to run away from him in his own house?

One strong arm secures my middle and lifts me off the ground while I'm mid-flight.

My screams and pleas to let me go ricochet off the walls and carry down the hall. It's to no avail, but I do notice that no one comes to my aid. Not even to check what the commotion is about.

I know the maids at the very least can hear me, but all I hear is myself whimpering.

"I'm going to teach you a lesson you will never forget," Mikhail growls, flipping me around so he can toss me over his shoulder caveman style.

I'm little more than a rag doll to him, or maybe less than that.

Uncaring and more than the monstrous man he was yesterday, he carries me kicking and screaming back down the hall and into a room with double wooden doors. It's one of the libraries.

The lights pop on, one at a time, as we enter.

That stifling dominance ripples off him in waves as he marches me over to the table with a stack of encyclopedias and sets me down.

"What are you going to do to me?"

I get my answer when he bends me over the table and lands a hard slap across my ass. My body jolts like it's being attacked by an explosion of electricity, and I cry out from the impact.

That hurt like hell. He's not done with me yet, though. He yanks down my skirt and panties at the same time, exposing my bare ass.

I attempt to protest, but he grabs the back of my neck and pushes me down on the flat of the table.

Three hard slaps come down on my ass so hard stars speckle my vision and tears blind me.

"I told you what would happen to you if you defied me," Mikhail reminds, giving me another three slaps.

My skin stings like it's on fire, and as the pain rushes over my body I see stars.

"Stop, please!"

"No, you fucking stop asking me about *José*. Or maybe it would be better for both of us if I killed his fucking ass."

"No! Please no." My God, he is crazy, and I've truly

fucked up. I can't let José die because of me. I can't. "Please don't kill him."

"Then stop pushing me."

Two more slaps make me feel like I might vomit, and another makes me scream out loud.

"Stop it, Mikhail. You're hurting me." I sound so foolish to say such a thing. He knows he's hurting me. That's the purpose of punishment.

Hurt me so I'll feel, break me down so I'll obey and bend to his will.

Be a *thing*.

Or *nothing*.

But he stops. He stops at my anguished cry, and I almost think I imagine it. I question myself when I feel his thick fingers running over my burning skin in soft strokes. The strokes smooth right down to my pussy, and I couldn't be more appalled at myself when my body reacts to the flutter of his fingers.

He strokes my clit, and the cacophony of pleasure and pain rushing over my body is a complete juxtaposition. I don't understand what the hell is wrong with me, or why I'd be so turned on by him after what he just did.

"Bad girl, you like this," he taunts.

"No," I choke out on the edge of a moan.

"Liar."

He turns me around to face him, and I gasp when he picks me up again, setting me on the table this time. That's when I feel the intensity of my pain.

And how wet I am.

Shit. What the hell?

"Open your legs," he orders.

I open my legs, but my brain is so twisted I can't wrap my head around whether I'm doing what I'm told because he terrifies me or because I want more of what he's giving to me.

I spread my thighs, and he holds them apart so he can bury his face in my pussy, and Jesus Christ, I'm seeing stars for a whole other reason.

I don't even feel the pain rushing over my ass anymore. All I feel is him and his tongue as he pushes into my passage.

No one but him has ever touched me here before, and right now, I don't care that he's a monstrous villain. Every thrust of his tongue over my clit pushes me higher into the arms of pleasure and over the edge of reason into madness.

I find myself writhing against his face, allowing the scruff of his beard to scratch my skin, and I squeeze his shoulders again when I come.

I come differently to the last time. Most likely because he's giving me his tongue and not using his fingers. Last time was nothing in comparison to this, and all I can think of as the waves of pleasure crash through me is what his cock will feel like when he's inside me.

For a moment, I lose myself and give in to it, give in to him.

I allow myself to be the prey and let the predator take me over.

Mikhail eats out my pussy, drinking every last drop of my arousal, and when he's done, he straightens and catches my face, shattering the moment.

"Malyshka," he whispers the exotic endearment he's christened me and leans close to my ear. "I told you not to fuck with me. If you hope to survive being married to me and want to keep *certain* people alive, you'll do what you need to, to please me and not piss me off."

A menacing smile taints any beauty in his features, reminding me Mikhail Dmitriyev hasn't stopped being my enemy and never will. And on top of that, he just threatened José's life.

What have I done?

Now I really have something to worry about.

"We will finish this later," he promises.

I watch the monster bend down to retrieve my panties. He shocks me further by sniffing them. He then pockets my panties and walks away, leaving me again.

Shaking from the inside out.

Chapter Twelve

Mikhail

As Eric Markov walks into my office, I force my mind back to reality and stop thinking of the woman I've been trying for the last few hours to get out of my head.

I managed to tamp down my rage yesterday by staying away.

I worked late to finish up the paperwork and prepare everything in advance for the week ahead, but I didn't need to. As much as I wanted to bury my cock deep inside the princess, I was in that place again where I needed to shake off the shit and cool off.

I was doing a good job until I tasted her sweet pussy.

The taste of her is still in my mouth, and I don't want it to go.

Eric's presence is important, but I'm so hyped up on lust for my wife-to-be that I can't think straight.

A quizzical smile settles on Eric's face when he looks at me, and I push the last thoughts of Adriana Alvarez out of my mind.

This man is my last ace. He offers the kind of help no one else will be able to give me to solve the rest of this mystery to protect my family and legacy.

We met a few years back just after he'd joined the Bratva. It's always good to see him because we get on so well. It could have to do with the fact that we hold the same positions in our brotherhoods, or that our temperament is quite similar. He, however, has a more lackadaisical approach to life that I lack.

I'm always serious. Always. With a brother like Ivan, I've had to be.

Eric is from the Voirik, who are based in L.A. There are five brotherhoods in the States that have had a longstanding alliance that goes way back to the early days of the Vory. The Voirik are one of them. His Pakhan, Aiden Romanov, however, has ties to my family that go beyond that because of their logistics company and similar business interests. We both mine diamonds, but we also mine and refine uranium. *That's* what Dmitriyev Ltd specializes in, with the diamond mining activities forming a subsidiary. That's where we made our fortune.

It's also where the logistics company comes in handy and why Eric meets with us on a regular basis. Like me, he looks after the money going in and out.

Today, his visit will work in my favor, because he's possibly the only person I can confide my worries in.

"Hello, old friend," he says, taking the seat before me.

"Hey. Thanks for coming."

"No worries. How are you doing? Last time I saw you, you were attached to tubes."

This is the first time we've seen each other in months. He would have been one of the few select people in our alliance to know I survived the assassination attempt. And because he's one of the few people I call a friend, he would have come to visit me while I was in the hospital and dead to the world.

"I'm okay." I'm probably not by medical standards, but I have to be.

"Well, it's good to see you on your feet."

"Thanks. It's good to be back."

"Looks like you're back in action, too," he observes.

"I am."

"Should you be?" He inclines his head, and his longish dark blond hair falls to the side.

I give him a firm nod. "I need to be back in action."

"Your message sounded important," he states.

"It is."

Instantly, his bright blue eyes cloud with concern. "Has something else happened?"

"In a way, yes, and I need your help."

"You have it. What's going on, Mikhail?"

Apart from knowing I woke from the coma and the confirmation of Talia's death, no one knows what's happening yet. My father is going to hold a conference call tomorrow and inform the members of our alliance of Raul's treachery. He'll also let them know we have control over his cartel.

Eric, however, will be the first to find out the full details.

I drag in a breath and tell him everything. I tell him much more than I did my family because I can be real with him, and the moment I started talking about Raul, I knew he was on the same page.

"Fuck," he breathes and runs a hand over his beard when I finish. "Mikhail, I get what your father is saying, but there's definitely something more going on that needs to be addressed. It sounds that way."

"Yes," I agree. "But now that the investigation team can't find shit, I don't know where else to look."

"So, you want me to do it?" He smirks, and I nod.

Eric is a computer wizard and has a habit of being able to dig a little deeper than everyone else.

"Yeah. I'm at a loss. Other than what I'm already doing, I don't know what else I can do."

"That's fine. I'll take a look at what the team found, and I'll go over everything."

"Thank you." I'm already at ease.

"And you're getting married next weekend?" He raises a brow.

"Yeah, marry the princess and take control of the cartel," I reply, and he gives me a nonchalant smile.

"And show their alliance you own them forever."

"Exactly."

As much as he loves his wife and fell in love the vanilla way, he's as ruthless as I am, so he won't question me any further about what I think about what I'm about to do.

He'll know Adriana Alvarez is a means to an end and an emblem of defeat.

"Congrats on your conquest." He smiles. "Having control of the Alvarez Cartel is no mere thing. I'm sure that will add to your good favor regarding the upcoming decision of leadership."

"I hope so."

Like everyone else, he's aware of the animosity between Ivan and me, and the increased tension between us now that we know my father's plans.

"I'm sure it will," he agrees. "Well, leave investigating Raul to me. If there's anything more to find, I'll find it."

I don't doubt that.

"Thank you."

Now all I have to worry about is the princess.

* * *

I manage to finish everything I have planned for the rest of the day.

When I get ready to leave, I think of the princess again. It's just past ten, so I'm guessing she could be in bed by now.

I haven't received any calls from Aleksander, so she must

have been the good little lamb I thought she'd be. After this morning, I am interested to see what I'm going to come home to.

Since I have access to the house's security system set up on my computer, I decide to take a quick look.

I find the camera in my bedroom and see her sitting in the corner of the room by the window. She has her knees hugged to her chest and her head resting on top of her knees.

Curled up like that, she looks smaller and helpless. That childlike position illustrates her defeat and makes her seem younger than her nineteen years.

It's then I remember she's barely a woman.

Seeing her in my room feels strange, but she's a pretty sight I can't wait to explore again and stake my claim on.

Poor thing. She will have anxiously waited all day, wondering what was going to happen to her. I have her daily schedule regimented, but the times when she's by herself must seem like an eternity of torture for not knowing anything about me, or what I plan to do to her next.

I know she's fucking worried about José, too. I don't care what relationship she has with him; I don't like it. I am a possessive prick, but there's more to them that grates on my nerves. More I can't put my fucking finger on.

When she lifts her head, I realize she's crying.

I have no sympathy for tears. They don't work on men like me, but something about seeing her like that gets to me, and I remember her words from yesterday.

Is it true?

Is she really not evil?

She sounded sure I wouldn't think she was evil.

Would it matter?

Maybe. Maybe it would matter in terms of how I treated her. Or maybe it wouldn't.

I don't know either way. What I do know is, regardless of where she came from, I'm attracted to her.

So, what would I think of her if I knew her?

The word on the street in Mexico is that Raul's spawn is just as ruthless as him. I've heard of her doing terrible things to the house staff. Shit you wouldn't expect a woman of that age to think of.

People from all over fear my family as much as they revere them and would never fuck with us, but there are different categories of evil. We wouldn't kill for fun, or some fucking shit like kill just to see what a person looked like dead. That's what Raul was like. He was fucking crazy.

People tell tall tales and say all manner of shit to keep others in line, but that stuff about him and his daughter would have been mostly true.

I don't think I have enough information to make up my mind about her, but what my eyes are showing me is something entirely different to what I've heard.

What I detect in her eyes is pain.

I see the deep pain a person would feel when they've suffered great hardship and loss. She has the sort of look most often associated with a person who's lost everything. Like the poor and the destitute. It's not what I expect from a cartel princess.

The pain in her eyes would almost mirror my own pain for my loss. And at the same time, it doesn't. Her pain seems to run deeper.

That makes me even more curious than I already am about her. Particularly when something in my core tells me the pain I'm witnessing isn't due to her loss of Raul and Felipe, and it's not the situation with me either. Or her worry over José.

If it's not any of those things, then what is it for?

Who could have hurt her?

Who hurt her more than me?

She gazes right at the camera, and while I know she has no idea I'm watching her; she's looking at it like she can see me.

Looking at me with those bright hazel eyes that add more

to her ethereal beauty. I've had many beautiful women on my arm, and beneath me, in my years.

Adriana Alvarez is no less beautiful than any of them. There's something about her, though, that prevents her from just being another face in the host of beauties looking to be attached to me because of who I am and what it means to be mine.

This woman wants nothing to do with me. If I were to open the gates, she'd run far, far away from me, never looking back.

Knowing that makes me want her even more.

She belongs to me now. She's as much mine as the cartel and the Alvarez empire will be once we get married.

I own her, and there's not a damn thing anyone can do to stop me from doing whatever I want to do to her. *Whenever* I want.

I close the link when she sets her head back down onto her knees and finish packing up.

By the time I reach home, my cock is so hard for my fiancée I nearly blow my load just thinking about her tight pussy. The bulge presses against my pants and only grows when I walk into my room and find her asleep on the bed. The main light is off, but the lamp on the nightstand is on.

I take a quick shower in the en-suite and head back into the bedroom with a towel wrapped around my bottom half.

When I stop by the window to pull the drapes closed, I look at her again and notice the change in her breathing pattern. I know she's no longer sleeping and is aware of my presence in the room.

I smell her fear, and all it does is entice me.

I smell her arousal, and all that does is make me want to fuck her even more.

"I know you're not sleeping, Malyshka," I say, breaking the blanket of silence settling over the room.

A visible shudder ripples over her skin, moving the sheet

that's pulled over her shoulders, then she turns to face me with those beautiful eyes.

They're puffy and swollen now from crying, but still beautiful.

And now that I'm looking at her, I want to be inside her even more than I did before.

Chapter Thirteen

Mikhail

"**I** heard you in the shower," the princess mumbles, looking me over cautiously.

Always careful.

She takes in my muscle and the tattoos I know freak her out. I'm not sure if she knows all their meanings, but I saw her looking at my knuckles this morning. If she guessed the tattoos of rings on my fingers were prison tats, she was completely right.

The tattoos she needs to be afraid of aren't my prison ones, though.

It's the Bratva leadership ones on my shoulders and chest which tell her what kind of monster I am. I'm covered, so that should give her a good guess.

Or maybe she knows. Monster was what she called me yesterday.

She wasn't wrong.

"Why didn't you join me?" I taunt. As expected, she looks thrown by the question, and even in the dim light I can make out the rosy flush in her cheeks.

"I bathed already, thanks."

She swallows hard when my eyes drop to her heaving breasts in the camisole top clinging to her body. The left strap slinks down the smooth skin of her shoulder, inviting me to touch and taste her.

I accept the invite, but when I move closer, she sits up defensively, her delicate hands clutching the sheet to cover her chest as if she can hide those tits from me. I almost laugh, and few things amuse me.

Does she really think a bedsheet can protect her from me?

Or stop me from looking at her body?

Or maybe she's hiding because she wants to conceal the arousal evident in her tight little nipples. The razor-sharp peaks are pressing against the flimsy bedsheet.

Even if her body weren't betraying her, I have the memory of this morning and the way I made her body bow to my touch and command. Like it or not, she's attracted to me, and she's just as screwed by that ripple of attraction between us as I am.

The difference between us is, when I want something, I take it. I don't fight against my natural primal desires.

"You look like you were crying," I state and give her a curious look.

"I'm fine."

As I take in her long fingers, I think for the first time about what must have happened to her engagement ring. I never saw one.

I don't remember her wearing one when I first saw her, and not when the guards took her to the dungeons. I would imagine that's something she would have been required to wear since the engagement was announced months before the assassination attempt.

"What happened to your ring?" I ask. The question sounds weird considering we weren't talking about that.

"What ring?"

"The engagement ring Felipe gave you."

Her cheeks flush. I'm not sure if it's because she's scared or embarrassed.

"I lost it a few days before... before the incident. I was going to get fitted for another one after the rehearsal."

"Is that so?"

"Yes."

I keep my gaze trained on her while I take the towel off me. Her eyes drop to my dick, erect and ready to fuck her.

"Stand up and take your clothes off," I tell her.

With trembling hands, she slides off the bed and obeys. I know the quickness in her movements and her willingness is down to being scared of what I might do to José. It fucking irritates me, but I tamp down my rage.

She lifts her top over her head, unleashing the beautiful heft of her breasts.

The pajama bottoms and panties come off next, and just like in Mexico, she stands naked before me. This was what I wanted this morning.

Her just like this.

I still can't get over how perfect she is. The only differences between us being in Mexico and tonight are that she doesn't smell like death and the moonlight shining down on her skin is mine.

Not hers in the land of her father.

"What are we doing?" she asks.

"What do you think we're doing, Malyshka? I told you we'd be finishing what we started this morning."

She doesn't answer, but the tremor in her hands is all I need to see to know how afraid she is. Her body is humming with fear.

That's not enough to stop me from taking what I want. I feed off fear and crave it.

Pain, however, is something else entirely.

The pain in her eyes does something to me I never expected. Seeing it right in front of me instead of through the lens of a camera has more of an impact on me, and nothing usually does, because it grips me.

My fucking mouth is watering to taste her, and arousal is clawing through me, begging me to claim her.

But... the pain I witness tamps down the desire of the villain in me and beckons to the parts of me that are still human.

I want to fuck her and get the fantasy out of my system, but I don't want to take her like this.

When I take her, I want to be the master of her body, not fear or pain.

But that doesn't mean I'm going to act like a saint and do nothing. Definitely not after the taste I had of her.

I have no shortage of things to teach my virgin bride.

There are plenty of things to train her in.

"Lie on the bed and spread your legs for me," I tell her. Her eyes dart nervously back to the bed.

She looks like she wants to say something but thinks better of it.

Good girl. She's learning quickly to obey and not defy me.

Bringing her hands together, she gets back on the bed, and a spike of heat ignites low in my gut.

I turn the light brighter so I can get a good look at the beauty as she lies back on the stack of pillows and spreads her legs for me.

I swear I see heaven when I rivet my eyes to her pretty, pink pussy and trail my gaze up the length of her body.

Everything about her begs me to touch her. From the silkiness of her skin to the ripe peaks of her delicious mounds.

So, I do, appeasing my hunger for her.

I position myself between her legs, and I commend her for not taking her eyes off me.

She shouldn't. It's not smart to take your eyes off a predator. That's the moment you get caught in his trap and he'll fuck you over forever.

I move to the side of her neck and press my lips to skin softer than I imagined. Filling my hands with her breasts, I squeeze and roll her nipples between my thumbs and fore-fingers.

When I kiss my way down to her breasts and take her left nipple into my mouth, a low moan slips past her lips. It's a helpless sound speaking of her inner battle to resist the pleasure I know I'm giving her.

I suck harder and start alternating from one breast to the other, unleashing a chorus of ecstatic moans she tries to force back, yet fails miserably.

I give her a wicked smile she hates. As she moves her hand to cover her mouth, I grab it and pin her hands above her head.

"Fucking stop acting like you don't like what I'm doing to you," I grate out.

"I don't."

"Liar."

One hard thrust of my fingers into her pussy makes her come undone and come all over my fingers, writhing against my touch.

"I've barely touched you, and look at you. You like this."

"I... don't."

"You like *me* doing this to you."

I pump in and out of her pussy, loving the suction sound her juices make around my fingers.

"Ahhhh.... Stop... I can't. It's too much."

"Too good," I correct her.

"Mikhail." Her back arches off the bed, and she presses into my fingers, her hips moving against my hand as I give her more pleasure. "Mikhail!"

My name on her lips sounds like music to my soul. I want to hear it again and again.

She says it again, and I release her hands so I can go down on her.

The moment I slip my tongue past her pussy lips and slide

into her passage, I get drunk on the taste of her. The scent of feminine pleasure fills me, and I lick up her arousal, taking as much as I can get into my mouth.

Fuck, she tastes amazing. And I realize she's not resisting anymore. She's taking the same way I am.

As I eat out her pussy, licking and sucking her clit, she takes it, and I feel her desire for me to give her more.

I give her more and more until I have her coming again all over my face.

Her scent and her arousal drive me insane.

This is my kink. I love smelling the awakening of a woman's body to pleasure and the taste of how stimulated she becomes.

With virgins, though, the scent is somewhat different. There's something primal in the scent that makes it feel like it belongs to you *forever*.

Nothing will change the fact that I'll be the first man to touch her, and her scent and arousal in this moment all belong to me.

The princess is so receptive to my touch, I can't wait to see how she responds to my darker tastes.

When my dick hardens to the point of bursting, I know I need to finish. No fucking way am I going to embarrass myself like some teenaged boy.

She looks at me as I release her and stroke my cock.

"You know what comes next, baby girl," I say, fisting my length. "Get on your hands and knees and suck my dick."

Her eyes round, and embarrassment flushes her cheeks again, but she doesn't argue.

She moves toward me, settling down on her hands and knees, and takes my dick into her mouth.

I know I'm not going to last. I've been hard all day, and her mouth on me feels too good.

I don't allow myself to savor the feeling of her sucking me

like she did nights before. Instead, I unleash the beast and start fucking her face.

I pound into her mouth, grabbing a fistful of her hair when she holds on to my thighs and sucks harder, and still I want her to take me deeper. I thrust in deep. Tears run down her cheeks, but she takes what I give her.

"Harder," I groan, and she sucks harder and faster.

Pleasure sets my body on fire, and I come. A white-hot climax rips through me, and I roar like a beast devouring its prey.

My cum sprays into her mouth, and she continues to suck. Tonight, I don't have to tell her to swallow it. She automatically does, milking every last drop of cum from me, then licking me off.

We're both breathing hard when she finishes.

I let go of her hair, and she straightens. We stare at each other, both uncertain of what to say or do next.

It takes me a moment to get my head together and regain the shift in power—regain my control over her.

Fear returns to her eyes, and she reaches for the sheet to cover herself as if we didn't just devour each other like animals. Me on her and her on me.

She tasted me like she needed to. Now that the sexual haze has cleared, she's remembering she needs to be wary of me.

"Lie down," I tell her.

"What?"

"I said, lie down."

She lies down, rolling onto her side with her back facing me. As her hair shifts across her back, something on her skin catches my eye. Something I never saw before.

It's a few faint lines across her back. They're pale and barely there, but still there. I count three like that and another possible one underneath, but half of it is so blended in with her skin it's hardly noticeable.

I just notice things like that. I didn't notice the marks in Mexico because her hair covered them up.

I know what they look like, but I find it hard to believe what they are.

Whip marks.

Would Raul have done that to her?

Whip her?

They're old scars, so I can't imagine Felipe did it.

"Who hit you?" I ask outright.

"What?" She glances over her shoulder.

"Who did this to you?"

Her lips part when I run my fingers over the lines I can see.

"It's from an accident when I was younger. I fell into a hedge and scratched myself."

She's lying. I can tell she is from the unsteadiness in her eyes, but I don't allow her to see I know she isn't telling the truth.

The only reason she could be lying is to protect something. And that something must be her fucking dead father.

It could only be him who did that to her. I just don't know why she would want to protect his name.

Maybe it's not that.

Maybe it's something else.

Something I'm not going to figure out tonight.

"Oh, right," I answer and decide to put her out of her misery, and myself, too, when I switch off the light.

Now all we have is the sliver of moonlight shining through the crevice of the curtains. I can just about see her. I lie next to her, reaching for the covers to pull them over us.

Knowing it will jar her nerves, I slip my arm around her tiny waist and pull her closer to me so her back is pressed against my chest.

"Relax, Malyshka." I press my lips to the shell of her ear.

"How can I relax when I don't know what you're going to do to me?" she mumbles in the dark.

"You relax because I tell you to. I'm not going to fuck you tonight unless you want me to. Your body feels like you want me, but your eyes tell me something else."

"I'm tired," she whispers after a moment's pause.

It's a good answer, because she's not sure what I'll do if she says no. Our encounter earlier changed things up a little, and she's more afraid of me than she was before.

"Then sleep, Malyshka."

We lie just like this in silence until she falls asleep.

I don't sleep, however. I barely sleep most nights, anyway. The days of being in that coma put me off sleeping.

I'm not normal, I know I'm not, and I know I never will be. It's situations like the one I'm in that make me the way I am.

Right now, I hate how vague everything is.

The only thing that's not vague is the attraction I feel for the beautiful woman lying in my arms.

We feel like a surrealist painting where nothing makes sense. And yet it does to those who know how to make sense of it.

I just can't make sense of her.

Chapter Fourteen

Natalia

I feel like he's getting closer to figuring me out.

Closer to knowing I'm not the real Adriana Alvarez.

Like yesterday, I woke with the sun. Thankfully, Mikhail wasn't in here, so I got some much-needed time to myself.

I spent the whole day walking on eggshells with my ass aching and my mind a disaster.

My ass is still aching and the nerves in my body are tingling from a deadly cocktail of worry and arousal.

Worry, however, is the dominant ingredient to that mixture, and it will either make me sick or kill me.

The worry over what's going to happen is making me crazy, and what's worse is I'm alone in this.

I'm all by myself, and I have no idea what's happening outside the walls of this home.

What clues will give me away?

I keep thinking of what it will be.

There are bound to be many things.

The house staff might have been killed, but what about other people Raul couldn't have hid Adriana's identity from?

People like her doctor and her friends.

There are no extended relatives to worry about on either side so I'm okay there, but there would have been other people they were close to.

Adriana also went by many aliases. She had a different name for when she was at school, to when she went out on the town. She also had a different name when associating with her friends, but I can't trust that she kept her identity a complete secret.

What if she didn't?

Or, fuck? It doesn't even need to be a person. It could be pictures.

Raul had pictures in his house of his late wife and daughter, who looked nothing like me. I didn't even remember those until now.

What if Mikhail's men find something there?

Now that a few days have passed, it's all sinking in that I don't know if I can keep up the charade.

How am I supposed to live the rest of my life as someone else?

How do I do that?

When Mikhail calls me Adriana and I stall because that's not me, what do I do?

That's on a simple level. But on a larger scale, something more could happen to give him clues that something's off with me.

Last night, he picked up on two things I hadn't even considered. He asked about the engagement ring the real Adriana wore all the time even when she was screwing around. He also asked about the marks on my back.

The men in the cartel are ruthless bastards, but most of the ones with sense like Raul don't mark the bodies of the women who will earn them money. He wouldn't have dared hit Adriana anyway because he loved her. By the same token, Felipe wouldn't have cared if she was covered in bruises and looked like the creature from the black lagoon because of all he stood to make from getting control over the cartel.

Raul stopped hitting and knocking me around when he decided he was going to sell me. That was my get-out-of-jail-free card.

I keep wondering what's next.

What will Mikhail notice next?

This is the start of my third day here, and I'm a mess again.

To add to my debacle, I don't like the way my body reacts when I'm with him. Being told to please him in order to survive and keep José alive is one threat that will keep me in line.

He found my kryptonite. But what do I do when I no longer feel like I'm being forced?

What does that say about me?

I don't know what the hell happens to me when he touches me, but it's not something good. Or something I should get used to. Last night, I found myself craving more of what he gave me, but if I'm being honest, I've felt like that since his first touch in Mexico.

Maybe I have gone crazy, indeed, and I'm on a different level of fucked up.

At seven thirty, I get ready and make my way downstairs for breakfast. The last thing I need is for Aleksander to come summoning me like he did yesterday.

I notice him on the way to the dining room, but I don't greet him the way I did yesterday, and neither does he, which is fine. It's clear he doesn't like me.

I'm used to being disliked, so that works.

I'm surprised when I walk into the dining room and don't see Mikhail there.

The same maid from yesterday serves me, but again doesn't talk. Her name is Irena, and the other, who assists the chef in the kitchen, is Shelly.

Both are quite pleasant, but it's weird they don't say anything at all to me at any point of the day.

Ten minutes pass with still no sign of him. I don't know if that means he left the house early or if he's just late. I eat because I'm nervous.

It's better if I don't see him. It's easier, but nerve wrecking.

The sound of heavy boots connecting with the wooden floorboards has me turning my head. I know it's him and not Aleksander even before I look around.

I'm right, and the moment our eyes lock, I remember everything he did to me last night.

An unwelcomed blush rushes over my entire body, making it come alive with the memories of how he touched and tasted me.

It doesn't help that he looks even more gorgeous than he did a few hours ago since we last saw each other. He's wearing full black again, just like every time I've seen him. The wild locks of his hair glisten in the bright morning sun, the longest strands curling under his ears, and the gold hoop in his ear reminds me of the pirate again. Not just because he looks like one, but because of how he raided my body and pillaged my sense of logic from my mind.

What is logic, though, when you have to do everything you're told?

Those golden eyes lock on mine, and he doesn't look away when he walks up to the table and sits next to me.

"Good morning, Malyshka," he says.

He didn't greet me with any form of pleasantry yesterday. Now that he's doing it, I wonder what's happening.

"Good morning," I reply, keeping my eyes on him.

Like yesterday, the maid walks in to serve his coffee, and as they indulge in a full-on conversation in Russian, I still don't know if they're talking about the weather or me. Whatever it is, I don't like it, and I'm finding everything harder to deal with because my mind is already such a mess.

When she walks away back to the kitchen, he takes a sip of his coffee and turns back to me.

"You look like you have something to say, Malyshka."

"You speak Russian and English interchangeably," I state because that's a safer conversation than anything else I want to ask him.

"I do. My mother was American, and we always spoke English at home."

That was the same for me—*me, Natalia.*

Adriana's parents were both Mexican, but she went to a private boarding school in L.A. until she was eighteen. That's why she spoke English.

"You seem to speak more English than Spanish," he notes.

"I do. I went to school in L.A." I'm grateful for the little key bits of information I know about Adriana's life.

"I had to learn Russian because of who my father is," he informs me, and that instantly makes my nerves spike. I'd never given any thought to his father. Who is he? People say the son is worse than the father. If Mikhail is how he is, what is his father like?

"Who's your father?"

He smiles, and I don't know if that means I should worry. "You get to meet him on Sunday."

"Sunday?"

"We have a family dinner on the first Sunday of every month. We're going."

So, I can be the center of attention and hatred. The fork that was barely dangling between my fingers drops onto the plate. The sound makes me jump.

"Don't worry, Malyshka. They won't bite unless you give them cause to."

I think they have enough cause to loathe me just for being

Raul's daughter, and I can't think of anything worse than sitting around a table with a bunch of people who will hate me. *Oh wait... I can think of something much worse. Death.*

What the hell have I gotten myself into?

I glance down at the unfinished scrambled eggs on my plate, and when I flick my gaze back up to meet his, he takes me in with that curiosity again.

"My father is the Pakhan of the Baranov Brotherhood," he announces, as if I'm not frightened enough.

"Pakhan?" I mumble, and he nods. "And what are you in the Bratva?" I know what his day job is, but what I'm asking about is so much more.

"I am the Obshchak, and hopefully next in line to be Pakhan, if my brother doesn't beat me to the finish line."

I don't know what to say or think other than I'm in more danger than I previously thought. As witnessed, people like him won't just kill you. They annihilate and show no mercy. I should have known what kind of monster he was from the get-go.

I knew from the tattoos on his chest that some of them must mean something about leadership in the Bratva, but I never imagined my husband-to-be was so high up the ladder.

"Have I scared you, Malyshka?"

"No," I lie.

He leans closer. "If you're going to lie to me, you could try a little harder and not looks so guilty. It gives you away."

I wonder if he can tell *I'm* a lie. Maybe if he asked me for my name, I'd give myself away by looking guilty and he'd know.

He reaches into his pocket and pulls out a little black velvet box. At first, I wonder what it is but, when he flicks it open, I glimpse the stunning diamond engagement ring inside. It steals my breath away.

"Give me your left hand," he says in that deep baritone that works its way inside of me.

I stretch out my hand, and he takes it. He pulls the ring out of the box and slips it on my finger. I instantly feel different.

I've never had anything so beautiful or expensive on my body. If Adriana considered that piece-of-shit dress I wore from Mexico as worth more than me, what would she think of this?

It instantly shows a difference in wealth. Adriana's ring did not look like this, and I would not have expected Mikhail to have bought a ring so breathtaking for someone like me.

I'm speechless.

He takes my hand again and holds on to it.

"Do not lose it, Adriana," he says, calling me by her name. It sounds so weird. "If you lose it, you will not like what happens if I find out. I am not like Felipe. I will not understand why it's lost, or how you lost it. To be on the safe side, it's probably best you don't take it off. At the very least, keeping it on should remind you of who you belong to."

Who I belong to.

"Like I could forget."

"Don't smart-mouth me." He shakes his head and tightens his grip on my hand.

"I'm not smart-mouthing you."

"Then don't talk back."

"I'm simply saying I wasn't smart-mouthing you. Do you have to keep reminding me that I'm a thing and I belong to you?"

The corner of his mouth lifts into that sexy smile. The sight makes heat spark in my core with those memories of last night again.

"Yes. Speak to me like that again, and I will spank that tight pussy of yours. But maybe you want that." A dangerous smile dances across his lips.

"No," I say quickly.

"Are you sure? You seemed to enjoy your punishment last time."

"I didn't."

"Liar. You keep lying to me, Malyshka."

My entire body goes rigid at the accusation, and I pray with everything in me that this won't be the moment he sees straight through the lie I am.

"I'm not lying," I mutter.

"Yes, you are."

As he leans closer and closer, I become wrapped in the taunting scent of him, and the glow of primal desire lurking in his eyes tells me I'm safe from the truth.

Safe for the moment, and safe from the truth of who I am.

I'm not safe from everything else and whatever this thing is I feel between us.

That's what he's talking about.

That thing that almost feels forbidden.

Sandal wood and musk envelope my mind, luring me to temptation when he runs a finger over the edge of my jaw.

I'm forced to level my stare with his. Then, without warning, he lowers his lips to mine. Not for the faint kiss he gave me in Mexico, but something else that sends shivers through my body.

He pulls back an inch for a few beats, just to stare into my eyes, then his lips come back crashing down on mine again for a cruel, punishing, delicious kiss.

It's a kiss that mirrors what he does to me.

Hurt me and please me.

Enchant me and terrify me.

Frighten me and captivate me.

All of it, all at once.

My body burns with the pleasure, and my lips part with shock when he slips his hand behind my head to deepen the kiss. He forces his tongue into my mouth, and that's when I taste him.

The true, raw essence of him. The darkness and death. The power and dominance. The want and need.

Everything is there in this all-consuming kiss. I never knew I craved him until I tasted him.

Mikhail Dmitriyev tastes like delicious sin. Like everything I'm not supposed to have but want.

The pleasure of the kiss fades into the ether when he pulls away, leaving me breathless and greedy for more. Another shocker to my brain.

He stands, and I stare up at him as he licks over his bottom lip. Then, without another word, he walks away without looking back.

He disappears through the door, and I stare at the empty trail he leaves behind.

I stare, once again in shock by my reaction to him, but this time I'm also shocked because I realize I'm drawn to his dominance over me because it brings out my inner desires and everything I've always suppressed for one reason or another.

I'm drawn to him because he lulls me into a false sense of freedom.

Something I've never had but always wanted.

Chapter Fifteen

Mikhail

"**E**verything is in order in Mexico," José says.

I temple my fingers and acknowledge him with a nod.

We're sitting in my office at Dmitriyev Ltd. He arrived in New York with Sebastian an hour ago and came straight here to see me.

"That's good to hear, amigo."

"The men have also informed their workers of the new leadership change and who they're to report to from now on."

"Were there any problems I should be aware of?"

"No."

I didn't think so.

I ordered my men to burn Raul's house to the ground once they'd removed all the important things. The same way leaders of the past sent a message to the people by burning what they revered, I wanted that house torched as a reminder to all in the alliance of Raul's downfall, and a threat not to cross me. Ever.

Everything should be ashes in the wind now.

"That's good. Everyone seems on board."

"They are."

I give him a crude smile, and he shuffles nervously in his seat.

The man is right to be nervous because he's not sure yet if I'm going to allow him to live past the next hour. I haven't given him a guarantee either.

He knows I don't trust him. He hasn't done anything yet to even begin to earn anything like that from me, and he knows he walks the thin line between life and death.

Now that we're on to phase two—managing the cartel—I need to decide what more I'll need him for. Since nothing has been resolved in relation to who was working with Raul, and I won't be able to focus completely on the cartel until it has, I might still need him for something, so he's safe for now.

He wouldn't like to know that *vague* possibility of needing his ass is the only thing keeping him alive. And the only thing that's kept him alive up until this point.

Seeing him face to face now makes me want to kill him because I'm not exactly sure I believe he knew nothing of the assassination plot. It doesn't make sense that he wouldn't know.

His two black eyes and broken nose, however, are reminders of how I tortured him, yet he couldn't tell me anything. He already knows Adriana is safe with me, so he has nobody to save but himself.

But I also want to kill him because I'm jealous over whatever feelings Adriana might have for him—no matter what they are. I know it's absurd because she clearly sees him as a father figure, but I don't want her having any heartfelt emotions toward anybody who worked for Raul.

It's harder for me because obsession is taking over my mind. I can feel it working its way into every cell in my body. Like poison.

That kiss earlier was supposed to be a taste.

I wanted to taste her purity. The thing that was out of reach to a devil like me.

I got my taste, and she was the most delicious thing I ever tasted.

Then I saw that look in her eyes. The look of the same desire I felt begging me to take more. So, I took more than my fair share, and she left me starving for more.

She left me starving and wanting.

I know it's because I haven't fucked her yet. All I've achieved is fanning the flames of fantasy.

"Raul's files are also in order for you to further investigate," he states, cutting into my thoughts.

"And you got *everything*, right?" I'm double checking. I had my men keep a close eye on him, but there's every chance he could have concealed stuff. I felt if there were ever going to be any clues, they would be in the house.

"I did. I also downloaded all of Raul's files from his computers at work and at home. When I checked, there was nothing in there in relation to what happened to you and your family. I presume you've already looked at them, but I still got them in case anything was missed."

"That's fine. It has been looked at, but we can keep them for reference." The investigation team hacked the system before I went to Mexico and found nothing. I'm sure Eric will want to take another look at them because he's thorough.

"Everything else we brought over was physical, like the contracts he'd signed with the allies. It's all in the storage unit downstairs."

Sounds like he did a good job and I do have everything. I'll personally go through the files, then contact Eric if I find anything. Sebastian will be on the street if I need him to check anything out. I just hope all of this won't take too long. It's never good to be left in the dark when your enemies have a head start.

"All right. That's sufficient for now."

"Is there anything else you'd like me to do?" he asks, eyeing me with that caution again.

Clever, clever. The conversation has now come to an end, and that's a subtle way of asking me if I'm going to kill him.

"I want you to continue to do what you did for Raul with his contracts. But you'll be managing it from here in New York."

He furrows his brows. "Wouldn't it have been better for me to be based in Mexico?"

"Of course, but I want you where I can see you. I can watch you better this way." I give him that ruthless smile again, and he looks like he's ready to shit himself. This guy is no weakling. Raul did not have weak people working for him. What he had were strong, intelligent men. So, the good thing about José is he knows when his knees should bend to someone who has more power and authority than him. That's his survival mechanism. Nothing more.

"I can assure you, Señor Dmitriyev, I have nothing to hide."

"I'm not some idiot, José. You have *all* the access to the workings behind the biggest cartel in this world. That's some type of power." This motherfucker knows things I don't even know. He's just as good as Felipe was and a good replacement. That's one reason I killed Felipe right off the bat. "I'm not about to allow you to give the *others* the same access so they can try to screw with me."

"I wouldn't do that."

"I don't know you well enough to believe that, José." I shake my head, keeping a sharp gaze on him. "And I'm not a man who takes risks with his fortunes. So, I want you to stay in New York and help me manage everything from here. Understand?"

"Si, Señor." He dips his head reverently, and the snake tattooed on his neck bows, too.

"Good."

A flash of apprehension flickers in his eyes, and I know from that he's about to ask me about Adriana.

"Is Señorita Alvarez okay?" he asks. I give him credit for the balls it took to do it.

"She's fine. I'm taking good care of her needs."

It's clear from the indignation swallowing up the nerves I previously witnessed in his eyes that he doesn't miss the innuendo.

He presses his lips together in a thin line of displeasure, but we both know that as mad as he might be about what I'm doing to the princess, he's not going to say anything to me about it.

I wonder how he'd feel if I told him she was enjoying how I take care of her just fine.

"Okay."

"You can leave now."

"Is it possible to see her?"

"I said you can leave now."

"I just—"

I pull out my gun. That silences him. "Last chance, José Diaz. You can leave now. I told you everything you need to know about my wife-to-be."

"I apologize, Señor." With another dip of his head, he rises to his feet and leaves.

I return my gun to my pocket and release a heavy sigh.

I need to calm the fuck down.

It's just that my patience is wearing thin. My patience for everything is dwindling into the ether, and I'm not known to persevere for anything.

I hate anything beyond my control, and this situation is exactly that. As the days go by and I'm nowhere close to getting things resolved, I'm pushed to that place where I feel like I'm going fucking crazy.

It all started when I realized how sick my father was and culminated in this.

Deciding I need to take a walk, I leave my office and head out to the garden in the atrium.

The garden was one of Sophia's stress relief ideas because of the long working hours we clock in here. It runs all the way from the fifteenth floor to the ground, and because you can see it from the outside, it sets our building apart from the other multi-story buildings in the city.

I head to the water fountain and grab some water.

The moment I down the cold liquid, I feel slightly better, but my brain is still unhinged. The doctors said that would happen sometimes, especially if I didn't rest, and I haven't.

I've been all over the place, and I don't even know where I've found the strength. What caused me to slip into a coma was knocking my head when I fell after the bomb blast. I remember being launched into the air from the impact. That must have been the thing to knock me out, because I don't remember anything after that.

When I found out what happened to Talia, it pushed me over the edge. Days before I set out to Mexico, we held a memorial for her. It was hard to accept my mother and sister were both dead.

Dead and gone forever.

Nothing, not even me, could ever bring them back.

I have family, but I couldn't feel more alone with their passing. Father will go next, and as much as I love Sophia and she takes care of me, she's always tried to keep the balance between me and Ivan. Doing so often means she tends to be with him more.

It's understandable given the way we came into his life.

Father married my mother months after Ivan's mother's death. They were having problems and weren't even together in the end. Ivan was a child who saw that, and his resentment stems from my mother, sister, and me being the new family our father fell in love with.

At the family home, there were hardly any pictures of his

mother around when I was growing up, and now that he has his own home, he probably has the ones that exist. It was like she was erased from existence and our lives.

Sophia is sensitive to that, and I guess I am, too, but only to some extent and only for business. Even my pursuit to get down to the bottom of this assassination plot is about business, and protecting Father and Sophia, of course.

In regard to Ivan, though, it was clear to me long ago that the only emotion I would ever feel for my brother is hatred.

Hatred that started after he tried to drown me in the river when I was only eight, and many other *accidents* like that one.

Bastard.

The door to my left opens, and in walks the devil.

Think of him, and he appears.

Ivan sees me straightaway, and he comes closer, walking with that authority every leader exudes. It's obvious he already thinks he's Pakhan and I'm going to be his eternal subordinate.

I straighten and get ready to hear whatever shit he has to say to me.

He gives me a fake-as-fuck smile and stops paces away to look at me like I'm shit he's trying to avoid stepping in.

He's lucky the same blood runs through our veins. Any other man who dared look at me like that would be dead before they could think to do it.

He knows that, though. That's why he's pissing on me.

"You look happy, brother," he states. "Seems like all is well in the nest."

"It is." I'm always either vague on purpose with him or blatant. There are never any in-betweens with him and me.

"Have you fucked her yet?"

"Why? Why's that important to you?"

"Just curious. I didn't think you'd be waiting for the wedding night. I also figured you'd use her as a fuck toy and throw her away when you're finished."

"So you can have her?" I'm not stupid. This interest from the other day is continuing.

He's probably also pissed as fuck he didn't come up with the idea to take Adriana and control the cartel.

That vengeance was mine, though. Mine alone.

"What if I did want her?"

Normally when he pushes me on women, I don't really care. I shouldn't care this time, either, but something inside me snaps at the confirmation that he might want her.

"We're not having this conversation. So, you can go back to fucking whichever whore it is you're fucking this week and leave me and mine alone."

He laughs. "Touchy, touchy, brother. You can't blame a man for being curious about a beautiful woman who's been forbidden to every man for years. None of us have seen her besides you, so my curiosity is understandable."

"I guess so, but you can take it elsewhere. She belongs to me, so she's still forbidden to every man."

The edge to his laugh now suggests I've pissed him off.

"When I become Pakhan, you do know I can demand your wife if I want to."

I move forward so fast he barely has time to register I've moved. I'm up in his face now, ready to knock his teeth down his throat.

"I'd like to see you fucking try," I seethe.

Ivan doesn't move, doesn't blink, doesn't even flinch, even though we're not equally matched in stature. I'm all muscle and height, while he's got the height but lacks in muscle. So, basically, he's a fucking dead man if I get my hands on him.

"You think you could stop me?"

"You are not Pakhan yet, *brother*," I spit. "If I get the job, there'll be one hell of a shake-up."

The one thing Father stated when he dropped the bomb on us about his plans was that we get to restructure the leadership the way we want. Ivan knows if I get the job, he's not going to be anywhere near the elite.

I even plan to break tradition in every sense and appoint Sophia as the Sovietnik, not Ivan. In the Bratva, women don't usually hold leadership roles, but she would have earned it. I think Father would want her to have it, too. Sebastian will be my Obshchak, so there would be no place for my brother except in one of the brigades. He won't like that, so he'd most likely leave the fold.

"Stupid cunt. I'd bet you think that's what's going to happen."

"Boys," says a dainty voice from behind me before I can answer him.

It's Sophia.

We both turn to meet the disapproving glare she's casting our way. Her arms are folded over her chest, and her pale blue eyes narrow with displeasure.

"That's enough," she adds. Her Russian accent is always thicker when she's furious. "It is inappropriate to behave like that right in the open where your employees can see you."

"Mne zhal', Sophia," Ivan says sorry in Russian and walks back the way he came without any further conversation.

Her face softens the moment he leaves, and she fixes her attention on me.

"Mne zhal', Sophia," I say as well.

"Mikhail, I truly wish things were different between you and your brother. It's not good to have family pitted against each other the way you are."

I won't bother to tell her the tension stems from him, not me. It was always him. It has been since we were children. Years from now, we'll be old men fighting with our walking sticks and the fucking tension will still be there.

She's a peacemaker looking to heal broken bonds, so I get it. This is just one bond she can't heal.

"You know what he's like, Sophia."

"I do. But I try with the both of you." She sighs. "All things aside, your father has now set up your individual meetings for the week after the wedding. You're first."

That meeting is about the company, not the brotherhood.

Right now, our father is the owner and Ivan and I have roughly the same responsibilities as joint C.E.O.s. That's going to change, too, regardless of who gets to be Pakhan.

"Mine's first?"

"Yes. He wants to speak to you first. Your brother last. Your meeting will be at the lake house. He didn't give me a reason for that."

I give her a narrowed look. The lake house was the place he and my mother used as their getaway. I've only been there a handful of times. It's odd he wants to meet me there.

Very odd.

"I guess I'll find out."

"Yes, I suppose. Your father is quite an unusual man. Remarkable in every way, but unusual. I guess he has his ways of doing things for a reason."

"He does." Nothing is truer than that.

"How are you holding up?"

I nod. "I'm okay."

"My dear boy, there's no way you're okay. How can you be? You've been in a coma for the last three months, and you've woken up to a world where your mother and sister are dead. I'm not going to believe you're 'okay.'"

I pull in a deep breath. "I have to be okay." Because I can't fall apart. That's not me, although my insides have already collapsed.

"Please try to take it easy." She rests her hands on my shoulders and gives me a reassuring squeeze. "You won't help yourself if you burn out."

"No."

She releases me and gives me a smile. "I'm heading out to

your place now, so I guess I'll be the first to meet your bride-to-be."

She sorted out the seamstress. I didn't think she'd go to the fitting, though.

"You're actually going to the house?" I raise my brows.

"Yeah. I thought I might get there a little early and meet Adriana properly. Is that okay with you?"

I'm not sure if it's a good thing for Adriana to meet Sophia. Sophia has a gentle way about her that eases the tension, and I don't exactly want that yet in my home. But, Sophia knows I won't say no to her.

I never could.

"That's fine."

"Great. Well, I'll see you later."

"Sure."

When she's finished with my wife-to-be, I'll take over. I need the distraction of Adriana's body.

Right now, she's the only thing keeping me sane.

Chapter Sixteen

Natalia

I t's been hours since Mikhail left. Yet my lips are still burning from his kiss.

I can still feel the spiral of ecstasy and the hunger that coursed through me for more.

Both are still very much there lingering, like a ghost in my head haunting me.

It's just before lunch. I've been outside with Snow, taking a walk on the extensive grounds of my new home.

It's much bigger than Raul's fortress in Mexico, and while I love the idyllic view that came with living on the coast of Mexico, there's something enchanting about walking around a winter wonderland.

It's been snowing again. Not as heavily as it did on my first day here, but near enough.

The snow's settled now, so everything is pretty, like a scene from *Frozen*, except I'm stuck in a dark fairytale. A dark parody where everything is flipped in reverse, the villains reign, and there's nothing called a happily ever after.

Snow runs into the patch of snow by the hedge, and I smile

because she's the same color and all I can see are her eyes and pink tongue. Next to the backdrop, she's so fluffy she looks like a cloud floating by on the ground.

She's been a good companion to me. I don't know what I would have done if she wasn't here. Lord knows I would have gone crazy inside the house, where there's nothing to do but watch the clock.

I was told I could watch TV, but I don't like watching TV when I'm not comfortable. Aleksander is always walking around and the maids always cleaning and talking, just not to me. I don't want to be anywhere where people might be talking about me behind my back.

At least in Mexico, Adriana was a bitch enough to talk to my face.

Since I'm more of a thriller or mystery novel girl and not a big fan of the classical literature books here, going outside was my only option and seems like what I'll be doing for a long time to come. I do have it on my to-do list to pick up a few novels when I'm next allowed to go to the store.

But that's the lowest thing on my list of priorities.

In my current state of flux, I don't think I could sit down and relax my mind long enough to get lost in a novel.

Every day is worse than the last, and I'm left wondering what's next, or what's going to happen to me.

The seamstress is supposed to be here in a few hours, so at least I have a heads-up on how the day will go. It's the part after that I'm worried about.

Since I don't want anyone to come looking for me, I make my way back when it's close to lunchtime, and I'm surprised to see an elderly lady talking to Aleksander on the terrace. She has lily-white hair and screams of wealth in her white mid-length fur coat, a brown leather skirt, and ankle boots.

Something tells me from the respectful manner Aleksander is looking at her that she can't be the seamstress.

When I get closer, she notices me, and her crystal-blue

eyes twinkle when she offers a kind smile. It's genuine and not forced like most of what I've seen so far in this house.

She looks back at Aleksander and says something to him in Russian. I catch the mention of Snow's name, but that's all I recognize.

Aleksander then comes up to me and takes the dog while the woman makes her descent down the steps to meet me.

"My dear, you are as lovely as I've heard," she observes, her smile brightening.

"Thank you." It's a great compliment any girl would love, but it gets under my skin because everyone who says it is talking about Adriana. Although they're looking at me and observing what I look like.

"I am Sophia Dmitriyev, Mikhail's aunt," she introduces herself with an elegant dip of her head. My stomach dips at the same time, twisting into more knots.

Mikhail's aunt?

God. Now what is she going to be like?

My lips tremble at the worry of more backlash from someone else.

I can't imagine she's going to welcome me with open arms when my presence here is due to Raul killing her sister-in-law and niece.

"Nice to meet you," I answer, carefully. I'm sure it's not supposed to be nice to meet her, but I say it because I don't know what else to say.

"Please do not look so worried." She holds up both dainty hands. "I mean you no harm. Mikhail asked me to make the arrangements with the seamstress to see you today. I thought I'd come by and meet you before she gets here. Maybe even help you pick out your dress. That's all, I promise."

"Oh, I see. Thank you," I mutter, feeling somewhat at ease for hearing she's not a threat. I am still wary, though. It's prudent to be on guard.

"Come, let's go inside. I asked the maids to serve us lunch in the sunroom for a change of scenery."

"Okay."

We walk into the sunroom and take off our coats. Today's spread has already been laid out on the table and looks delicious, as always.

Sophia sits first and motions for me to sit in the wicker chair opposite her.

I do, and she reaches for the cafetière filled with strong aromatic coffee to pour some into my cup first before filling hers.

"Thank you," I say, taking a little sip. The jolt of caffeine and warmth gives me a boost. Just what I need right now to keep my head above water and my awareness.

"You're welcome." She focuses on me. "It's good of you to play with Snow. I worried she'd be cooped up in this house while Mikhail was at work."

"I like animals. I never had a dog."

"Me too. My brother is allergic, so we never had one growing up. Of course, that meant Mikhail grew up without one, too. His sister, Talia, was in love with dogs. She adored huskies." She smiles, but a touch of sadness pinches my heart.

"They're beautiful dogs."

"Absolutely. Mikhail got Snow for her when she joined the New York City Ballet."

"Wow, she was a ballerina?" I'm impressed.

"The best. She was prima ballerina, and her love for music was something that touched everyone. She took after her mother. She was a dancer, too."

"I see."

"What do you like?"

It's been so long since anyone asked me that, I don't know how to answer the question. My heart remembers, though.

"Anything to do with medicine. I... wanted to be a doctor."

She looks genuinely impressed. "That's quite extraordinary, dear."

"Thanks." I almost give myself away and tell her my mother was a doctor, but I catch myself before I make that mistake and hang myself.

"What kind of doctor?"

"I wanted to go into diagnostics."

"Very impressive, but...I suppose that's changed now," she states, looking around us, taking in my situation.

"Yes. It changed a long time ago." I don't have to try hard to play the part of the girl robbed of her dreams. I am that girl. "I knew after high school things were going to be different."

I knew well before then, and the bastard Raul only allowed me to finish school because he'd get more money for me at the auction if I had some education.

"Well, we run a medical research charity and are based at the local hospital. After the wedding, when things settle down, I'll see if I might be able to arrange for you to do something there. If it's okay with Mikhail and you decide to go back to school, I'm sure that would be some experience you could gather toward your career."

I simply stare at her. That sounds like a dream come true. Something I'd never imagine for myself. The closest I got to the medical world was helping my mother tend to the workers on the planation who'd been injured. That's how Raul made use of her medical skills. She taught me everything she could during those times and helped me find a love for something I never knew I could find such difficult times.

I should be thrilled at the suggestion and possible offer. Instead, I find myself thrown off-kilter because such a thing doesn't feel becoming of someone like Sophia, who should hate me.

As nice as she's been, I feel awkward for the same reason, and I'm compelled to ask what her angle is, even if asking will get me in trouble.

"That would be great." I prepare myself to ask the question. "I don't mean to be rude, but why... why are you being so nice to me? Not that I'm ungrateful. I just want to know. I am Raul's daughter, after all."

I try to still my racing heart while she keeps her focus on me.

"A lot of terrible things have happened recently. Your father being the cause of great pain and suffering. He did unspeakable evil no one can forgive or turn a blind eye to, but I don't believe it's going to help anyone if I treat you badly. Not when you're going to be a member of this family."

I press my lips together briefly then take a measured breath. "So, you don't think I'm to blame, too?"

A speck of hope flutters inside me at the possibility of this woman being my ally in some way. Or maybe it's the fact that I have no one on my side. I don't know how much power she might have over Mikhail. Nevertheless, the fact she's here, says something. Even if it's something small, it's something, and something I might use. If only for some level of comfort.

"No. I don't blame you. Unless my eyes deceive me, to me you're just a young girl who got caught up in a war. Am I right?"

War. That's a good word for it.

I stare at her for a moment, thinking how true that is of my entire life. War has always been on the horizon for me, and I've always had to suffer in some way for being caught between disagreements. My youth has made me helpless, and I'm still at the point where I have no power. Things have been like that for so long I can't remember what it's like to be normal.

"Yes... that's what happened to me," I answer.

She nods. "That's what I thought."

"I'm so sorry for what my father did." I feel like a hypocrite saying that to her after she's been so reasonable. At the same time, someone needs to say sorry for what Raul did, and I am sorry. On behalf of myself. I do wonder what exactly happened. I haven't been given complete details and dare not ask.

It would be so inappropriate, although I am curious to find out.

"I accept that, and thanks. Eat before the food gets cold." She offers me a kind smile I appreciate, and we both eat.

She talks about the hospital a little more, and I listen, finally getting absorbed in something that interests me. I even find myself wondering about the possibility of working there.

It feels outlandish because I know I can't think of such things now or even plan to do anything that will place me in these people's lives. Or my dreams.

Dreams for me are something which will have to either wait or stay in my head.

All I can focus on now is getting myself out of this situation.

Whenever that may be.

There's nothing I can do right now or in the next week or the next month. But I can keep my eyes open.

Before I know it, the seamstress is here, and Sophia takes me into the hall to where a hundred beautiful dresses await me.

The designer's name—Maria Artois—is someone I recognize from TV. I heard some celebrity wearing her dress for their wedding on one of those reality shows Adriana used to watch.

I can't believe I have a hundred dresses to choose from, all made by her.

Her seamstress looks to be around the same age as Sophia, with a similar style, and is a nice, well-mannered lady. Not like the one in Mexico who loathed the sight of me because I was the help. She couldn't stand the fact I was putting on such a fine dress and even told me nice things weren't made for people like me.

This seamstress told me the dresses were made for me.

It's nightfall by the time I get through the last batch of dresses, and I almost yield to the enticement of believing this is really my life and I'm the doting bride.

The temptation intensifies when I spot the perfect dress.

The dress I would choose if this were truly the wedding of my dreams.

It's a timeless ballgown plucked from a fairytale with swirling beaded patterns on the sleeveless lace bodice that complements the plunging, scalloped neckline.

Cascading ruffles trimmed with sequins run down the endless length of the flowing skirt, which seems to float over the floor. Saying it's beautiful doesn't feel like it's enough of a word to describe it.

"You need to try that on now," the seamstress says with a firm nod.

When I try it on, I hate that I love it. I shouldn't love anything about this day, this moment, this feeling.

It's the first time I don't feel like I'm wearing someone else's skin or am in another person's mind. I feel like me, like this is me, and I realize it *is* me.

I might be pretending to be someone I'm not, but that doesn't mean this isn't me.

Sophia walks up to me, lifts my hair away from my face, and nods.

"This is the dress, my dear. I think you look truly amazing," she says with a smile.

"Thank you."

"I think she looks truly amazing, too," comes a prevailing male voice from the door. A voice I would recognize anywhere, asleep or awake.

We all look toward the door as Mikhail walks in, moving with an air of authority.

Out the corner of my eye I note how Sophia straightens and no longer seems to take charge.

She's not afraid of him the way I am. Her reaction seems

more respectful than anything else. The seamstress, too, takes notice and looks cautious.

Mikhail comes closer and walks right up to me. It only takes a second before my mind summons the intimate kiss we shared this morning. A kiss too intimate for us, for him, for me.

My first kiss was from one of Raul's drunken soldiers trying to force himself on me. I was barely fourteen and he was nearly fifty. My father luckily got me away from him. If he hadn't, God knows what would have happened to me. There were many underaged girls on the plantation with children. Girls as young as twelve. All impregnated by Raul's guards.

The myriad of kisses that followed after the first were from men who'd forced their lips on me and would have forced me to do more if not for the forbidden mark Raul placed on me. Touching me meant death. Felipe barely got away with what he could, but he knew Raul would have killed him, too, if he lost him the business opportunity I was.

Mikhail is the first man I gave my kiss away to willingly.

"I think we can agree this is the dress," he states, glancing at Sophia, who nods and smiles.

"Apart from your mother, I don't think I've seen a more beautiful bride," she states, and then she says something more to him in Russian.

He returns his attention to me and looks me up and down before talking again.

"Spasibo, chto byli zdes'. YA by khotel pobyt' seychas so svoyey krasivoy zhenoy."

He's speaking to her but looking right at me, and, of course, I have no idea what he's saying. Unlike when he's talking to the maid and I'm not sure *what* they're talking about, I know he's talking about me from the way he looks at me.

"Of course, that's no problem. We'll be done in about fifteen minutes," Sophia replies.

"Great." He glances back at her then leans close to my ear in an openly seductive manner, uncaring of who is watching us. "Come upstairs when you're finished." His voice is low enough for my ears only, but I'm aware of the two women watching us. "Don't wear any panties."

Our eyes lock, and my breath hitches. I swear I turn every shade of red. My skin is hot with the seductive rush that heats my body up from the inside out. I remember the panties he pocketed yesterday morning and the way he sniffed them before tucking them away.

"Or a bra," he adds, deepening his stare.

I know what he wants.

I know what going upstairs with no panties or a bra will mean and what's coming next.

He wants me, and he wants me to give myself to him now.

He doesn't wait for an answer, doesn't need to.

Mikhail knows as much as I do that the word *no* will never be an option for me.

Chapter Seventeen

Natalia

I make my way up the stairs on shaky legs.

Sophia and the seamstress just left, and the house has quieted down. Even though tonight shouldn't be that different to any other night, the house seems extra quiet, so quiet you could hear a pin drop from the other wing.

Aleksander has retired to his quarters, so the only people inside the main section are Mikhail and me.

The only good thing about that is the fact that I don't have to feel so aware walking up the stairs with no panties on.

I'm wearing a woolen tunic that just brushes the tops of my knees.

I'm also aware of the moisture gathering between my thighs, and I'm not sure if I should lie to myself and believe I'm not aroused, because I am.

It doesn't make sense to think I could be aroused for anything other than him, and I hate my body for betraying me. It's like the years of being around the worst men known to man have done nothing for my common sense. What good is common sense here, though?

What fight do I have?

What power do I have?

I don't need common sense to tell me what I already know, and being aroused is just one problem.

The other is that this is my first time with any man. I have no idea what to expect, or what being with him will be like after.

How will I feel after?

I've done more things with him than anyone, and he does something wicked to me. Something sinfully wicked to make me lose control. It's like allowing madness to make you walk off the side of a cliff. You know, of course, you're gonna die, but you still do it. You still allow madness to take you. That's what he is to me.

I find him in the bedroom shirtless and leaning against the wall between the long French window and the sliding doors. He's opened the window, and the cold night air is wafting in as he puffs on a Cuban cigar.

I didn't know he smoked, but it doesn't surprise me.

It suits him now that I see it.

He drags on the cigar and lets out a ring of smoke when I enter the room. His eyes are on me now. All over me, drinking me in, stripping me so bare I already feel naked and exposed.

As the door clicks shut behind me, he puts out his cigar, but he doesn't close the window.

It's too cold to have it open, but I'm thankful for the contrast it provides to the heat coursing through me.

I bite down hard on my back teeth and will myself to concentrate and think about why I'm doing this. It's not hard to remember when I recall what he told me about surviving.

Those words are what ran through my mind last night as I spread for him.

.   .   .

"Wise selection on the wedding dress," he states, being the first to break the silence.

"I guess as long as you like it, then it's fine."

"Do you like it?"

"Does it matter?"

"Do. You. Like it?" He comes closer and wraps me in his masculine scent.

"Yes. I like it."

"Then we don't have a problem, Malyshka, do we?" He quirks a hard brow.

"No. We don't," I agree and decide to change the subject. "What did you say to Sophia when you were looking at me?"

His lips tip into the beginning of a smile. "I told her it was time to leave because I wanted to spend time with you. Speaking of which, the time has just begun."

So much for the subject change. All I've done is gone in the direction he wanted me to go.

My back goes ramrod straight when he reaches for the hem of my dress and lifts it so it rides up to my hips and exposes my pussy.

"Good girl. No panties. So obedient." He cups my bare sex and strokes over my pussy lips.

"As if I have any choice."

"You always have a choice, baby girl. It's just a matter of which you like or what consequence you wish to pursue or avoid."

That's sounds like bullshit, because we both know it's his rules or nothing.

He angles himself closer, and my heartbeat races. Closer and closer he comes until he's a breath away from my lips. He runs his tongue over my top lip, tasting me while he keeps his eyes fixed on mine, and in that moment, I feel like I'm in the devil's lair again, right in the den with the beast, and he's sampling me before he takes me whole.

"Kiss me," he breathes.

"What?" There's no way he called me up here with no panties on just to kiss me.

"Kiss me, like this morning."

I don't want to, and I don't want to do the other thing, either.

"Why? Why do you want me to kiss you?"

"Because this morning, you gave yourself to me."

"No." I shake my head.

"Liar."

"I didn't—"

His lips crash down on mine, stealing away my denial. The thing is, I don't know if I'm lying to myself or if it's the truth.

It's hard to assess the validity of either when he's kissing me like this, like he wants to take everything from me. My ability to focus has gone to hell, and all I feel is him.

He pulls away like he did this morning, and I'm left feeling like all my energy has been syphoned from me.

"You want me." He considers me with a cold glare and cups my face.

"I don't," I answer firmly.

"I told you, I don't like lies. I'm curious as to why you think you should keep lying to me when your body constantly betrays you."

"I don't want you, and whatever you take from me tonight won't be with my permission or me giving myself to you. It's force. The same way you're forcing me to marry you." I'm losing control again, and he notices.

When he slides his fingers into my pussy and smiles as he feels how wet I am, I know he can see the truth through my words.

"Your cunt is soaked, Malyshka. Fucking soaking wet, and once again, I've barely touched you." He starts pumping and tightens his grip on my chin.

I have no words. What the hell am I supposed to say? And

what the fuck can I say when I'm trying so hard to hold back the moans building in my throat.

He presses his cheek to the shell of my ear and blows his hot breath over my skin.

"Have you been a dirty girl, thinking of all the filthy things you want me to do to you? Is that why you're so fucking wet? Have you been thinking of all the ways you want me to touch you? Or maybe it's what we've done before." He speeds up, finger-fucking me now. "Maybe you loved feasting on my dick so much you can't wait for me to fuck your brains out and have my cum inside your tight little pussy."

"Stop it."

"No, Malyshka." One flick over my clit has me moaning, and the devil smiles upon me, relishing my defeat. "Liar. Such a pretty little liar. But you know what? I like it. Your defiance just makes me want you even more."

I believe him. Why wouldn't I? I might have lied to him continuously right from hello, but he's never lied to me.

"You're about to feel how much I want you," he warns, moving over to the wall with me. As he shoves me up against the hard surface, panic assails me, along with a gamut of emotion.

He rips the dress off my body, and all I hear is the fibers tearing before it's sailing through the air and I'm naked.

I gasp, but then he's undoing his belt and shoving his pants down his hips.

"Wait," I beg when he takes out his cock.

"Fuck no," he growls.

Before I can protest again, he lifts my leg and guides his cock to my entrance.

As he pushes into my wet passage, I know any hope of escape is gone. He's going to do this whether I want it or not. It's like he said before. He takes what he wants. Nothing else matters.

He holds me against the wall and pushes his cock deeper,

forcing his way through. His length inside me is so painful and thick it hurts like hell, but I feel a strange combination of pain and pleasure.

I cry out but can't form words. The slight edge of pleasure cloying to the pain forbids me from stopping him.

"Shhh, baby, it will only hurt for a little while, just a little while."

I look away and wince, but he catches my face and guides my gaze back to his.

"Look at me," he commands as he pumps in and out of my passage slowly. "Look at me while I fuck you, Malyshka."

"I hate you," I whisper while he forces me to stare at him.

He gives me a ruthless smile and pulls out of my passage just for a moment.

"Liar."

He thrusts back in, impaling me and taking away my innocence.

Forever.

I feel the moment my maidenhead snaps because my walls stretch, and I cry out from the pain of his massive cock tunneling into me.

It continues to hurt, until it doesn't. It's when he begins to move faster inside me that I feel good, and I hate myself again for the thought.

Shit. It feels really good. So good I start moaning.

He feels good, and I'm slipping away again into an unknown pleasure that calls to me with the promise of freedom.

How the hell can this make me feel free?

How can *he* make me feel free?

Yet he does.

Seeing I've passed that awkward stage of newness, he starts fucking me harder. Faster.

Faster and faster until we both fall into a rhythm.

The echoes of our bodies slapping together and the sounds

of us having sex reverberate off the walls of the room. His deep groans and my moans combine in a forbidden symphony of sin, and the raw pleasure he gives me makes my body bow to the sweet sensation of being claimed. It sends my mind tumbling into surrender, and I let him take me.

I give myself to him, knowing I can't fight this entity that has this power over me. It hooked its claws into my soul right from that first moment we met and possessed me, so all I'd do is obey his every command.

The truth is, I'm not sure if I'd want to fight because a sick part of me wants him, too. I got a taste of that yearning yesterday after he spanked me, and once again this morning. Now I have the full meal of what he has to offer, and my body wants it.

I want it.

The moment I accept that, I come. I come so hard, the wicked sensation sends me right over the edge.

I writhe against him, hot and wild like I've lost my damn mind.

"That's right, Malyshka, give yourself to me," he growls as my walls clench around his ruthless cock.

"Mikhail," I cry.

"Fucking perfect." His next words are in Russian and sound like he's cursing, then he kisses me hard and cruel, and he comes, too.

The spray of his cum hits my walls then floods my passage, hot and virile.

So hot it radiates all over me and my skin tingles from the sensation.

He holds me against the wall as we calm from the explosion of pleasure, and I watch the pleasure on his face.

I take it all in. The chisel of his handsome face, his high exotic cheekbones, his honey-colored eyes with a twinkle that disappears so quickly it was like it was never there.

Then the moment shatters when he pulls his cock out of

me and I slump forward, feeling like he's stolen a part of my life-force.

He's still holding my face. He loosened his grip while he was fucking me. Now it's tight again.

Something wet and sticky runs down my thighs, and I glance down in horror at it.

It's a mixture of blood and cum, evidence of what just happened and what it means. I watch his cum overpower the blood, a metaphor for us.

He looks down at it, too, and taps the edge of my chin so I look at him.

"That means you belong to me now, Malyshka. You're mine. My woman. No matter what happens, you will always remember I was the one who took your innocence."

He releases me, and I slump against the wall, too weak to stand, too weak to breathe or do anything besides look at him.

"I took your innocence, and I know your secret," he adds with a pensive stare.

My eyes go wide. "What secret?"

"You wanted me to take you." A wicked smile lifts the corners of his firm lips. "I felt the moment you gave yourself to me. Now you know that I know."

I can't even feel relieved he's not talking about my bigger, darker secret because what he's saying is true.

He backs away, and I watch him walk out the door, never looking back as he leaves me naked again, feeling ashamed and cold, broken on the floor.

I should be used to him leaving by now. This time just feels different.

Every day here has either ended or begun with something to jar me.

Tonight is no different.

I just have a new problem.

Chapter Eighteen

Mikhail

She's wearing clothes now.

A dusty pink camisole top similar to what she had on the other night clings to her body. The tiny straps have slinked down her shoulders and expose the huge swells of her breasts.

I can just glimpse a nipple poking through the thin fabric.

If she were awake, she'd fix her top straightaway, even though I've seen her naked several times.

But my princess is fast asleep, and she looks like a life-sized doll lying on my bed with the silk sheets barely covering her.

Ebony hair is sprawled out over the silk pillows while the moonlight kisses her skin the way I want to.

I'm as envious of the fucking moon for touching her as I am of her feelings toward José.

It's late—after midnight late—so I knew she'd be asleep. She was already exhausted. I just stole the last traces of her strength.

I like watching her sleep.

I like watching her awake, too. More so when she's in the height of her fear and doesn't know how to figure me out.

She can join the club because I still can't figure her out, either.

I couldn't stay in here after I fucked her because I wanted to do it again the moment I pulled out of her, but she wouldn't have been ready for the hard fuck I wanted to give her.

I went to work out for a few hours and to swim.

Anyone would think I was crazy for swimming in the freezing cold pool, but I like it. The cold wakes me up and keeps in touch with my feelings. It makes me feel nearly the same as the fire I feel within me when I'm with her.

My cock is twitching to be inside her again, and the memory of seeing my cum swallowing up her virginal blood is playing over and over again in my mind.

It's something I won't forget. I never forget. I don't think most men would.

There's something primal in taking a woman's virginity that stays with you, and I've never been with a woman who made me want to take her again after that.

Not that I've only ever been with virgins. I've just never seen the point in pursuing anything with them after because the enticement was to be their first.

This woman makes me want more, and my obsession pushes me to want to know more about her, too.

I chance moving the sheet from her back so I can look at those scars again. I can barely spot them in the moonlight, but they're there.

She's so tired she doesn't stir as I run my finger over them, touching her silky skin as I wonder what the fuck she must have done for Raul to whip her.

There are no other visible marks on her body. Just those. And there's something about them that summons me to pay attention. I just don't know to what. Other than what they are and the lie she told me when I asked her about them.

I look at my ring on her finger and remember her in that dress earlier.

The dress looked like it was made for her. As if the designer had created it with her in mind. When I saw her in it, I couldn't take my eyes off her. I must have stood there for a good five minutes before I spoke, announcing my presence.

Adriana is a mystery to me, one that keeps enticing me, and now that I know her secret, I want to know her others. The ones she's got buried deep beneath.

When she stirs, I run my fingers over her skin again, and as her breathing changes, I know she's awake and aware of me. I decide to be a selfish bastard because I want her all over again.

I'm sure her pussy got a good break from me. It's time to take her again.

"I know you're awake, Malyshka," I say. It feels like déjà vu from the other night. The only difference being that I had more control that night.

Now that I've had a taste of her body and I liked it, I'm ready to feast.

She rolls onto her side, and I tug at the top.

"Why did you bother to put clothes on?"

She glares at me. Her eyes hold a flame of anger, but the state of her nipples pressing against the thin fabric says so much more.

"I wear clothes to bed."

"That changes tonight."

"That is ridiculous."

I press down hard on her arm, and she catches herself before she can say anything else to defy me.

"Do I need to spank that ass of yours again. Just give me a reason."

"No."

"Good, then obey me and do as you're told. Take off the top." I pull down the sheets and see her panties. "All of it, take it off. I want to fuck you again."

Her skin turns that sweet color in the silver moonlight. The trace of color in her cheeks against the dark surroundings reminds me of a neo noir painting, and she herself is a work of art.

Biting down hard on her bottom lip, she takes off the top and panties then tries to cover herself with the sheet.

I pull it away. She winces.

"What is the matter with you? I'm cold."

"You won't be in a minute. Get on your hands and knees."

A flicker of apprehension washes over her face, but she obeys. I feed off her nerves. She would be nervous. This is a different position for her, and the best. I can't wait to hear her moans of ecstasy.

When she turns and settles onto her hands and knees, my eyes settle on her ass. She has the perfect shape. Her ass is full and round, perfect for spanking and fucking. That will come very soon. Right now, I'll enjoy the sight.

I take off my clothes, too, and she glances behind her to look at my cock. When she catches me looking, however, she looks away.

"Feel free to look if you want, princess."

She doesn't answer. I didn't expect her to.

I'm ready to go, and when I run my fingers over her sweet pussy, I feel she's ready for me, too.

Fuck me, she's wet and so responsive to my touch.

Unable to resist the taste of her delicious nectar, I lean in and lick it up. I savor the taste and take more, licking over the little bud of her clit.

She can't resist any more than I can, so when a little moan falls from her lips, I give her more and move closer to play with her nipples.

"Mikhail..." she moans.

"Yes, baby, I plan to give you more."

I straighten, grab her hips, and inch into her tight little pussy.

She's nearly the same as she was earlier, and it feels just as good being inside her.

I speed up when my body takes over. I can't control myself when the enticement to fuck calls to me. I just go with it and allow desire to guide me where it wants to take me.

I can't even force myself to slow down so I can try and last longer because she feels too good in this position. Too fucking good.

Pleasure short-circuits my brain as I drive into her perfect body as she climaxes. Her pussy clamps onto my dick like a vice, and I blow into her.

The force of my own climax has me roaring like a beast, and when I pull out of her, the same obsession grips me again to take more from her body.

She slumps down, breathing hard, and the sight of my cum leaking down her thighs is another stamp of ownership on her body.

Quickly, I walk into the en-suite and clean off. I then grab a towel and warm it with water from the hot tap for her. She looks surprised to see me return with it, and more surprised when I clean her off, too. There's blood again, and I wonder if I hurt her. I know I was rough.

"Did I hurt you?" I ask, but she looks away.

"No."

It's another lie, but I let it slide.

"Lie on the pillow."

She lowers onto the silk pillows, looking nervous again.

I set the towel down and lie next to her, slipping my arm around her waist.

"What do you really want with me?"

Her voice sounds small in the dark.

"What do you mean, Malyshka?"

"I get the marriage. Marry me and rule the cartel, but why are we doing this part? Why are you doing it?"

It's a good question. One I should be asking myself, but I

don't care to because the answer is obvious.

"Because I want to," I decide to tell her.

There's another beat of silence before she draws in a small breath.

"What happens when you stop wanting to, Mikhail? What happens long after you get the cartel and don't need me anymore?"

I don't know.

The answer is, I have no idea. She's asking me what we'll do after we get married. That's the bridge I haven't crossed yet. And I won't be crossing it tonight.

"Go to sleep, princess."

I can't see her face, but I know she's hurt by my lack of an answer. She's probably thinking all sorts of shit. Maybe even wondering if the time will come when I decide to kill her and her precious José. We come from the same world, and she's not naïve to the darkness that exists within our sphere.

With a father like Raul, she wouldn't have been innocent to the thoughts and plots of bad men like me who only know death and darkness.

Marriage alone is all that's required to take over Raul's empire and assets. It doesn't mean I have to stay married to her. Or that she has to stay alive or in my life.

We stay like that in the silence until she eventually falls asleep. I wanted her to drift off first, but I still watch her long after with her question ringing through my mind.

It hasn't even been a full week since she's been in my life, yet I feel like this.

We'll be married next weekend. How can I be worried about what will happen after that when I'm stuck in the in-between?

When my eyelids droop, I give in to sleep. It feels like I'm only out for a few seconds before I hear screaming.

My eyes snap open, and I know I couldn't possibly have been sleeping for seconds because bright sunlight beams through the windows. And the screaming is coming from next to me.

Adriana thrashes on the bed, lost in a nightmare, lost to me. She shakes her head side to side and screams again, louder this time.

"No!" she cries. "No, please, please don't kill her. Don't kill my mother!"

"Papa, save her, *please* save her. Don't let him kill my mother."

What the hell?

Seeing her distress, I get up and take hold of her shoulders, trying to wake her.

It takes her a full minute before she opens her eyes and tears are streaming down her cheeks.

She's breathing like she's just run a marathon, and her skin is as flustered as it was yesterday when I left her.

Her beautiful eyes are riddled with fear, which doesn't change when she spots me.

She tries to calm herself, but it doesn't work. She's breathing too hard and in ragged breaths that remind me of my younger days when I was subjected to the shit Ivan used to put me through.

I get up and open the window to let in some air. It's only when the blast of cold air hits her face that her breathing calms and she gathers her composure.

"Are you okay?" I ask.

"I'm fine." She barely looks at me, and when she does, it's with that same caution she exerted days before.

"You were dreaming about your mother?"

Her lips part, and she trembles. "Yeah. It was just a nightmare."

"Or a memory?" I know the difference between night-mares and memories.

My nightmares are of bad memories, and they're of my mother, too. Of her dying. I keep seeing the bullet lodged in her head and another in her heart. I keep remembering the helplessness I felt as I watched my mother, a woman who was my everything, dying right in front of me, and there was nothing I could do to save her.

"Yeah... A bad memory," Adriana mutters.

I narrow my eyes. I wasn't aware she'd seen her mother's death. The way I heard it, she would have been at school here in the States. Raul was meeting with an ally when it happened. They killed his wife because of a drug deal gone wrong. Unless that was a lie, Adriana wouldn't have been anywhere near the incident.

If she has memories of it happening, then someone lied somewhere along the line.

"What happened?" Curiosity is getting the better of me. I know this doesn't matter to me one way or another, but I'm curious because of how shaken she seems. For some reason I also find myself thinking of the scars on her back.

"I don't want to talk about it."

Of course, I don't like her answer. It's not what I expect when this is the closest she'll get to *niceness* from me.

"When I ask you something, you tell me what I want to know."

"You don't need to know everything," she snaps.

I bare my teeth and rush her, catching her throat to put her back in line.

It's the teardrop tracking down her cheek that curbs my rage for her defiance. That's definitely a first for me.

"Like I said, when I ask you something, you tell me what I want to know."

"You took my body and crushed my soul. My mind belongs to me. I don't have to tell you what's in my head, or my heart."

I stare at her for a long moment, thinking of what to say, when I realize her mind and heart are things I can't steal.

But... I want them.

I want them both. I want everything, and I shouldn't because this thing between us is just feeding my obsession. Nothing good can come of it.

More tears run down her cheeks, and when hate fills her eyes, I hear her words from last night ringing through my mind.

Right there against that wall, paces away from us, as I staked my claim on her body, she told me she hated me, but her eyes never looked like this. Like if she had a gun, she'd shoot me.

I think she would.

Why wouldn't she? I'm her biggest enemy, and if given a chance to take me down, she'd take it. I wouldn't blame her.

The buzz of my phone on the nightstand breaks the deadly silence and I look away from her.

That's a message I already know will be important. No one contacts me at this time of morning unless they have news. I expect it's either going to be Sebastian or Eric.

I back away from Adriana and retrieve the phone.

I was right. The message is from Eric.

The preview tells me all I need to know.

I got something for you. Meet me at the restaurant in the Hamptons at nine. It's important.

I know which restaurant he means. It's an Italian bistro called La Roux. That's the only restaurant we meet at when we're in the Hamptons, and we don't go there often.

It's nearly eight now, so I need to get going if I want to beat traffic.

I return my gaze to the princess and a visible shudder runs through her.

"Be ready for me when I get back," I say. "If you're not, I'll punish you."

That's all I say to her, and I don't look back as I leave.

Chapter Nineteen

Mikhail

I arrive at the restaurant just before nine.

When the maître' d leads me to the tables on the top floor, I know Eric wants us there for a reason.

I find him sitting at the back in an elegant booth eating a continental breakfast.

He nods at me when he sees me.

"Get him the same as me, please," he says to the maître' d, who nods and saunters away to retrieve my order.

I sit in front of Eric and look him over. "I take it me eating means I'm going to be here awhile."

"Yes, and you need to blend in," he answers. "The place is going to be busy in a few minutes. I expect the people I need you to see will be here roughly around that time. Their reservation is for ten past, and we're sitting up here so we can watch them."

This sounds promising.

"What did you find?"

"I'm not really sure yet. I found a piece of information, and this is us following it through to fill in the blanks." He clears his throat. "Do you know a guy called Tony Iglesias?"

"Never heard of him."

"He's one of Raul's... what the hell do I call this guy? For the purposes of today's discussion, let's just call him a middleman with some above-board tech skills. I took a look at Raul's emails from his office and found something interesting I haven't seen in a while because it takes a special kind of person to do this shit."

My interest piques. "What?"

"Put simply, your investigation team missed a few key things."

Jesus, this is all I need to hear now. "What did they miss?"

"A lot of Raul's work emails were encrypted with what my guys call ghost files. It's a file with a secret encryption that allows it to be hidden within another. To read it, you need to either know how to spot it or use a certain code to reveal it. It looks like your people completely missed those files."

"Fuck. Does this mean everything needs to be rechecked?"

"Yes, it does. I scanned the files for secret encryptions because I thought things on Raul's system looked way too clean for a cartel king. That's how I got intel about this meeting here in ten minutes." He straightens. "Raul arranged for Tony to meet someone called the Red Fox, to sign the Dmitriyev Ltd. contract."

The blood drains from my face. "The Dmitriyev Ltd. contract?"

"Yeah. I don't know what that's about yet, but I'm interested in knowing who Red Fox is code for. That's why we're here. We look and see, then take action."

I don't know what the hell to think other than that I was right.

"Eric, if they're meeting about the Dmitriyev Ltd. contract, it must mean the plan is still in motion."

He nods. "I think so, Mikhail. Forgive me for saying this,

but I'm not sure yet if the files were missed by accident or if it was done on purpose, so I think we should keep this between us. At least for the moment."

The suggestion of missing the encryption on purpose opens another can of worms I've considered when I thought of who could be watching us and how. But I placed the thought at the back of my mind until we sorted through everything else. Now it's resurfaced.

"You don't have to ask me for forgiveness, Eric, and of course we can keep this between us. To be honest, I think I prefer it that way." I do. I'm sure my father won't like to hear I've been doing something he told me not to do. That was an order, however, he gave me as my father, not as my Pakhan, so it's different.

"Good, because often times when shit hits the fan and no one can explain how it got there, the answer is closer to home."

He's right, which irks me even more. And if he is right that the files were missed on purpose, that means someone from inside our Bratva was working with Raul and wanted us dead.

"What makes you think it could have been done on purpose?" I need to know. I'm aware that as open as he's being with me, he's also respectful.

"I assume the skill set your people have must be close to mine, or the people in my alliance. I don't fully believe something like that would have been missed. The dead giveaway was everything looking too clean. But that's just my opinion. Your people were handpicked by your father. I would not disrespect a Pakhan by suggesting the people in his decades old system is flawed."

"I appreciate you pointing it out to me."

"I know you do. That's why I'm going to recheck everything. It's going to take me some time to go over it all thoroughly, but I'll get it done."

"I owe you for this."

He chuckles. "Next time we go to Vegas, play me a hand of poker, and we'll call it even."

I laugh. "I beat you fair and square last time."

"I don't like being beaten."

"Neither do I, but I'll play you again."

"Good man." The smile recedes from his face when the door opens, and he glances over my shoulder. "Tony's here. Now to see who the Red Fox is."

I look and watch a well-dressed Mexican guy walk in. Like when I entered, the maître' d approaches him quickly and gives him the VIP treatment.

They walk to the far corner of the room but stay in our line of sight.

Tony looks like Raul did, like a sophisticated businessman in his Armani suit, but his presence gives off the dark vibe all men from our world carry with them. A moment later, the waiter returns with my food, and Eric and I eat.

I'm more anxious than hungry, but I eat to blend in.

At ten past nine, the door opens again, and who I recognize walk in has me setting down my fork.

The middle-aged man who walks in is called Barabbas Ponteix.

He's a black-market trader who works for high-level politicians and men with money older than dirt. There's no question over whether he is Red Fox. That's the type of code name he'd use to conceal himself.

I glance at Eric, who's already looking at him the same way I am.

We watch him until he's ushered toward Tony before we look back at each other.

"Mikhail, whatever happened months ago is definitely still happening," Eric states. "Whoever hired Barabbas Ponteix is someone big. My guess is they want your company, and you are all still in danger."

All I can do is look at him, because seeing Barabbas

confirms my worries. Someone still wants us dead, and from the look of things, it could be someone right under my nose.

I seethe inwardly when I remember how Raul kept his silence to save his daughter. A man as powerful as him would only worry about a threat if the person he feared was more powerful than him.

Someone he knew who could still get to his daughter even after his death.

Who is it?

Who the fuck is it?

I reach for my gun, getting ready to go down there and to end them. When I think of my mother and sister, I want to kill them.

Eric, however, stops me with a heavy hand on mine.

"No, old friend. Calm the fuck down," he cautions.

"Why, when they're right there?"

"You have far too many loose ends to tie up, and those two guys there are foot soldiers. Fucking pawns. In the same breath, don't believe a man like Barabbas is here by himself."

Damn it. I hate that he's right. This is so frustrating.

I glance around at the people in the restaurant who all look so normal. A man like Barabbas is going to have backup. I can handle a showdown, but not if I don't know who's who and where they might fire from.

"I suggest we keep to the element of surprise and you start small by talking to Tony," Eric says. "We can then track Barabbas' movements. Sometimes, you have to watch things play out to get all the pieces of the puzzle before you strike."

"Okay, I'll send someone to get Tony later so we can have a little chat."

I just hope for more luck than during my interrogation with Raul.

Chapter Twenty

Natalia

Today is the first day since I've been here when going outside hasn't helped me cope one way or the other.

I opted for being by myself because I couldn't even muster my usual energy to get the dog. Part of me felt it was unfair to subject Snow to my sullen mood. I've heard dogs pick up on things like that. I thought it was best to stay away since I couldn't even begin to try to fix myself.

Two things were on my mind right from the moment I opened my eyes.

The first hit me the instant I saw Mikhail. I remembered how ruthlessly he claimed me last night and how I gave myself to him.

I'm not a virgin anymore.

That part of me is gone and I feel different—changed. I feel like my body has changed in a way I can't quite describe and the light of innocence I carried has disappeared.

He took my virginity, and I feel exactly the way I feared I would. *Lost.*

Lost in the wind and lost in my emotions. Which is what spurred on the second thing. My nightmare.

I dreamt about my mother's violent death the same way I used to after it happened. A person doesn't witness such evil and walk away unscathed. I went through everything from nightmares to severe panic attacks and anxiety because I was sure Raul was going to kill us next.

Time lessened the sting, but the worry didn't go away.

Now the nightmares are back to haunt me. I'm terrified I'm going to say something in my sleep that'll give me away.

The difference between years ago and now is that I don't have my father to take care of me, and I don't have José, either.

All I have is myself. While I might be able to control my thoughts when I'm awake, what do I do in my sleep?

God knows what I said this morning. I don't. I only guess it couldn't have been that damning because Mikhail didn't look suspicious. He knows Adriana's mother was killed, but I don't know what he knows regarding the circumstances of her death. It's not something Raul would have given full details of. So, I don't know if the bare minimum I told him damned me today, or it might in the future.

I might damn myself again tonight.

Tonight... My chest tightens when I think of tonight.

Mikhail told me to be ready for him when he got back.

I already know what set off the nightmare is everything happening in my life. And *him*. Since everything else is a result of him, the real problem is Mikhail.

What the hell am I going to do?

I gaze out at the rippling waters of the lake before me. I've been out here since after dinner just biding my time. It was already dark when I came out for one last walk.

Now it's getting darker. I know I need to head back. Aleksander told me to be inside the house by eight unless I was supervised. As if I'd really try to escape or something.

I make my way back inside the house. The moment I reach the bedroom door, I know Mikhail is inside.

The door is closed, but I sense him, and my body awakens at the prospect of his touch.

I don't know if I can handle another night like last night. I can't handle what he does to me yet be nothing but a toy to him. What am I thinking, though?

That I want to mean more to him?

I don't want that.

I can't have that.

I dare not think that because it would mean factoring in more on my part, too, and I don't want to do that.

I don't want to yearn after a man who's wrong for me in every sense.

So, I'll be the toy.

Another toy in his game. Another pawn.

Pulling in a deep breath, I decide to open the door and walk in.

Like last night, cold hits me first, but it's not the window that's open this time; it's the sliding door.

It's only partially open, but it's enough to let the cold air in to drop the temperature in the room.

I'm guessing he's out on the balcony, but I don't know if I should go out there.

He's going to know I'm in here. He would have heard me.

Maybe this is part of tonight's game where I have to guess what he wants me to do with the clues I see. The opened sliding door suggests he wants me to meet him outside, and once again, I have no choice other than to follow his rules.

I keep my coat on and walk out onto the balcony. Then I see him.

He's smoking again. Smoking the same type of cigar he did last night.

He's got his shirt sleeves rolled up his thick forearms, and the muscle looks more pronounced with him leaning against the stone railing.

Mikhail continues to gaze ahead at the clear night sky for a few awkward moments before addressing me.

The same way I sensed his presence before I entered the room, I know something's not right when he looks at me.

He looks like something is on his mind. I have no idea what it could be. I can't even guess. All I hope for is that it's not something to do with me.

"Either you need to come inside before it gets dark or get one of the guards to accompany you if you want to stay out later," he says.

"I thought I could stay out until eight."

"Rules have changed."

"Why?"

"I don't want my wife-to-be wandering around in the dark woods by herself."

Something has happened. I can definitely feel it now.

"What's going on? Is something happening?"

He chuckles, dark and cruel.

"You think you get to ask me something like that when you won't even tell me details of a nightmare?"

"That's different," I retort, feeling my stomach twist. I can't talk about that nightmare for my own sanity even if I were to lie about it; and if I'm to lie and pretend I'm upset over Adriana's mother's death, I can't get that wrong.

"Baby girl, how is that different?"

"It just is. I don't want to talk about my mother's death." That's true, so I can speak from the heart. I never spoke to anyone about it because those who were close to me saw what happened to her. José wasn't there, but Papa told him everything. "You hate me and mine. My mother meant everything to me. She had nothing to do with what happened to your family, so I don't want to talk to you about her just so you can taint her memory, or her."

He continues to stare at me for a few moments, then takes a long draw of his cigar before he puts it out and sets it down in the ashtray.

My nerves spike when he walks up to me and rests his hand above me on the doorframe. Inching closer, he stops a kiss away and hovers before me with a menacing smile.

"Did I tell you I hated you, Malyshka?" he mutters in a deep baritone.

I narrow my eyes at the question because it's so weird. So weird I have to wonder if he's screwing with me.

"I'm not stupid."

"Then fucking pay attention, princess." His large hands cup my face with a softness that's almost creepy because I'm not used to him being gentle.

Whenever his hand goes anywhere near my neck, I always wonder if he's going to snap it or crush my windpipe. I'm wondering the same now, even with the soft stroke he gives my cheek.

His touch sends a shiver of arousal through me, and I instantly remember how we were last night.

"I am paying attention."

"No, you aren't." He leers at me. "If you were, you'd know that when a man tells you he wants to fuck your brains out, it's not because he hates you."

His crass words make my mouth go dry. Heat skitters down my spine, my cheeks flush, and I know I'm blushing.

When he notices my reaction, his eyes gleam with desire. They smolder with it and come alive with seductive fire.

Another stroke along my cheek kicks my heart rate up a notch, and my mouth waters.

This is not good. I shouldn't react like this. I want to pull away, but I can't make myself. The part of me that craves him overpowers my ability to think straight, and I can't move.

"When a man calls you his, it's not because he hates you, Malyshka." He runs a finger down the edge of my neck and lingers over my cleavage. "But allow me to show you how much I *don't* hate you."

Paralyzed by the intensity of his words and those eyes, I don't move when he leans in to kiss me. I receive the kiss like I'm starving for it and he's giving me an undiluted dose of life.

The kiss sends a rush of pleasure through my body, and the enticement lures me to kiss him back. The moment I give in to the wild call screaming at me to give myself to this man, the first thing I notice is how different we feel. *I* feel different.

I feel free. No longer unhinged. And that itself is crazy. As our kiss turns hungry, my body bends to his will and prepares itself for his, prepares itself to *be* his, and I don't feel the hatred I spoke of. All I feel with each touch and kiss he gives me is desire and need. The need for more and more.

Chapter Twenty-One

Natalia

Mikhail picks me up and carries me back inside the room.

Setting me down on the plush cream carpet, he pulls away from my lips momentarily to gaze at me. The molten heat blazing within the honey depths of his eyes melts me and traps me.

"Take your clothes off for me, princess," he husks, his voice thick with arousal.

This is it. We're doing this again.

I'm doing this again, and again I'm scared of how I'll feel after. If I feel like this now—barely able to think past his touch —what's going to happen to me when we go to that place he took me to yesterday?

That place he unlocked and gave me everything I never knew I needed.

I take off my coat and follow with everything else until I'm naked.

The way he looks at me—like I'm the most beautiful woman he's ever seen in his life—is something I'll never forget.

I know I can't be. All I need to do is look at him to know I'm not going to be anything close to the women he's been with. However, there's something triumphant in watching him look at me like I'm what *he* needs.

And it's already harder to convince myself I'm just a toy to him when he looks at me like that.

"Get on the bed and lie down."

I crawl onto the bed and watch him take off his clothes. As I lie there, I allow myself to stare at him, to really take him in.

My eyes travel over thick muscles inked with tattoos. I'm not paying attention to the ones on his fingers that scare me or the Russian-looking ones that indicate his leadership. I look at the others, like the eagle taking flight on his lower abs and the Japanese characters running down his hips.

My eyes move to his erect cock as he takes off his pants, and I notice the pre-cum beading on the thick head.

He's perfect and he knows it. And he knows I know it, too. Standing there like that, he reminds me of a Greek god. Just one look is all anybody would need to confirm the potency of his power and strength. More intense than that, though, is the power and strength he has over me.

When he grips the base of his cock and fists himself, the heat raging inside me turns to liquid fire.

A wicked smile spreads across his face, and he intensifies his stare.

"Still think you don't want me?"

I bite down hard on my back teeth, praying he doesn't push for an answer.

"You should see your face, princess," he adds with a wild smirk. "You should see your body the way I do, ripe and aroused for me."

I believe him. I can feel my body pleading for him to return to me. My nipples ache, my skin is buzzing from the kiss, and I'm wet, probably soaked.

My pussy is clenching with the need to have him and I'm hungry for him.

He pumps his length harder, so more clear pre-cum drips out of his cock, then he swipes his thumb over the head and wipes it off.

Holding out his finger, he gets on the bed, too, and places his finger to my lips so I can lick off his cum.

I do, tasting the saltiness of need and sex.

He smiles and runs the same finger over my pussy, pushing into my wet passage and smiling wider when he feels how wet I am.

"Wet again, Malyshka. This is going to be interesting."

"Why?" I mumble.

He answers by pushing deeper into my passage. I moan out loud in response and grip his arm as he continues to pump.

"That's why. You keep filling your head with lies, and I want you to accept the truth. I want you to accept that it's okay to want me."

"No," I moan.

"Yes."

He pulls his fingers out of me and replaces them with his cock.

He cups my sex and rubs the head of his cock over my folds before easing into my pussy.

It hurts, but not as much as last night. I feel more pleasure than pain.

I wince at the strange feeling of both, desperately seeking the pleasure. When I grip the sheets, he pulls out and lowers to my ear.

"It will hurt as long as you fight me. You need to stop and give yourself to me."

"I don't want to," I moan mindlessly.

"You need to, Malyshka. Make life easier for yourself. I'm going to fuck you either way."

He moves down to lick my clit, and that's when I lose any

trace of resistance. It snaps, and the pleasure I crave comes, forcing away the pain.

His tongue thrashing over my swollen clit feels so good, so damn good I feel like I might come. He licks for a few minutes then returns his cock to my entrance and slides in easier than before.

"That's better. Good girl. Allow me to take you, and you won't feel the pain."

Hyped up on the need for pleasure, I do as he says, but this time, I do it for me.

I do it because I'm right there at the place he took me last night, and that part of me just awoke and wants him.

He starts moving inside me, slow then fast as my walls tighten when they take him.

At that moment, an explosion of pleasure washes over me in rippling waves, slamming into my body with savage energy.

He starts to fuck me. Every secret part of me absorbs what he gives me and begs for me. Mindless, mind-numbing ecstasy sings through my veins. I'm so lost in him I can't find my way back. Nor do I want to.

The vein on the side of his neck thickens and pulses as he speeds up, driving faster and harder into my pussy. It's too much. He's too much. I've lost control.

Mikhail tunnels deeper into my body, owning me, and as he mutters a string of curses in Russian, my walls squeeze, and I come.

I arch my back off the bed and scream out his name as the greedy orgasm takes me.

I still have his name on my lips when he glides a hand to my throat and holds me down. Not in the threatening way he did before, but it feels like it. I'm so caught up in pleasure that my mind can't think past the earth-shattering sensations exploding inside my body.

"Tell me you want me," he demands, gritting his teeth as he drives into me.

My lips part, but I hold back, still fighting, still trying not to fulfill that last request.

Any hope I have is gone when he jackhammers into me, rutting into my body like an animal.

"Tell me you want me, Malyshka," he cries, driving harder. "Tell me."

"I want you," I hear myself say, and I realize then he's broken me.

He did it. He broke down my resistance and confirmed the secret in my heart.

As I look at him, I expect the conquering smile, but he doesn't give me that.

Instead, he pulls out mid-thrust and kisses me.

"I want you, too," he whispers against my lips.

Hearing those words at this moment does something to me I can't explain.

As he caresses my face, I find myself running my hands all over his chest, right into his hair. He does the same thing to me. Cupping my breasts with his large hands and kneading them before he smooths his hands up into my hair.

He breaks the kiss again and gazes down at me with a mixture of confusion and lust before he slides his hand back down to my pussy, then further to the tight rosette of my asshole.

I gasp when he pushes a finger inside, and I'm shocked when I think it feels good.

A deep chuckle rumbles within his chest when a small moan falls from my lips.

"Just like I thought. Interesting. This is going to be fun."

"What are you going to do to me?" I whisper.

"Fuck every hole in your body before the fucking night is out."

My mouth drops when I realize what he means to do. I rivet my gaze to him and swallow hard as he gets off the bed and opens the drawer on the nightstand.

His cock is still as erect as it was before, so I know he's not finished with me yet.

I've never opened that drawer. I wouldn't dare for fear he'd think I was snooping around.

When he takes out a black sash and a little tub of lubricant, I wish I'd looked. It would have at least prepared me.

"Don't look so worried, baby girl. I told you I have a lot to teach you."

He reaches for me and flips me onto my hands and knees.

"Are you going to hurt me?" I mutter.

"No. Never. Just listen to the sound of my voice, Malyshka."

The sash goes over my eyes as he blindfolds me, securing the fabric into a knot behind my head.

Panic threatens to break through because I can't see him, but when I feel his fingers glide down the length of my back, a smidge of reassurance returns to me. It's only there for a moment, however, and dissipates when he strokes over my asshole.

My nerves rush back tenfold, but the more he touches me, the more aroused I become. Raw arousal washes through me when I feel him rubbing what I imagine must be the lube in my asshole. Then he gathers some of my wetness and does the same thing.

"Relax, princess. Relax for me." The sound of his voice spirals into me. Being blindfolded heightens my senses. I feel him and hear him everywhere. Inside of me and out.

He presses his cock to the entrance of my asshole, and I suck in a deep breath.

It feels weird and like we're doing something we're not supposed to. Then he pushes in deeper. It hurts, but it feels too good to want him to stop.

I clutch the sheet and wince, moaning and groaning as he slides deeper inside me. An unexpected blast of pleasure jolts my body forward, and fucking hell, my mind feels like it's going to rip in two.

He grabs my hips and starts to pump inside me, splintering my mind with every thrust.

Every nerve in my body quivers as he takes me this way. It's an overdose of everything that takes me higher and higher until I feel like I'm flying with my head spinning.

He speeds up, and I feel his cock stiffen inside my passage. I come then, and so does he. A rush of hot cream pours into me. It feels different from when he came inside my pussy, but no less potent.

I also experience the same draining feeling I did last night, and like a rag doll, I collapse onto the bed.

He pulls out and removes the blindfold.

I chance looking at him because I want to see him. I want to know what he looks like after passion has taken us and he's not walking away from me.

What I find is the beautiful side of him pushing past the ruggedness and darkness he is.

Brushing the side of my face, he presses his nose to mine.

"I want more, and I want to give you more, Adriana Alvarez."

Adriana Alvarez.

This hits me hard, and I find myself desperate to hear him call me Natalia. As he holds me, I want him to know me, and I don't want him to think I'm her. It feels like he belongs to her even though I know he can't belong to me.

Desperation, different to my need for survival, clutches my insides, and I realize I'm so desperate for him, I'll be whoever I need to be for him to take me like that again.

"Will you let me, Adriana?" he whispers against my skin.

"Yes."

Chapter Twenty-Two

Mikhail

As the goddess bounces up and down on my cock, I lose my mind all over again.

Water splashes over our bodies and over the side of the hot tub as we have sex for the fourth time tonight.

I told myself when I first took her that I was using her for the distraction I've needed all day, but I knew it was a lie.

I also told myself I'd only have her once, but that was a lie, too, and I'm still lying to myself because I want her again.

I need her again, and yet I'm buried deep inside her.

I hate lies. I loathe them, so I'm not in the habit of lying to myself.

When I do, it's always for a good reason. This is the first time it hasn't been.

This is the first time I've allowed obsession to take me and make me reckless.

I'm buried to the hilt with her riding me with her gorgeous tits bouncing in my face, and still, I'm greedy to take more than I can get. More than what she's giving me. More than what she wants to give me.

Her mind and her heart. She said I broke her soul. I don't think I did, though, because I can still feel it. That's what's hooking me and luring me to her.

There's a light in her eyes, a fight to survive that draws me in.

It's something I never expected to see in her.

Maybe I looked too deep, deeper than I was supposed to, and listened too carefully to the voice that was telling me to pay attention.

I fucking am, and I can't stop touching her. I can't stop trying to take more.

That is the thing that's kept me distracted by her for the last few hours while I've digested the intel I learned today and waited for my men to get Tony.

I went to work after I met with Eric and tried my best to focus on what I should be doing next. Warning my family is the first obvious thing, but I need more information. I need to be able to give them some direction of who we should suspect if there's a fucking rat amongst us.

And to add to the shit, I need to think of her, too.

If the problem is still at large, she's in danger for being with me. She is the key to the Alvarez Cartel. Another bastard just like me will know that. He'll try to take her from me, and I can't allow that.

Not when I want her.

She moans as she comes hard, and I cup the back of her head to drink in the glorious sound I want to steal.

She kisses me back, and I love her submission to my dominance. She's not fighting anymore, and it doesn't look like she wants to. She's under the same fucking spell that holds me, and I don't want the enchantment to break.

We move from the hot tub back to the bed, where I take more, and she gives it to me.

We take until we're drunk on greed and can't move. I have no idea what time it is, but I'm not tired, and neither is she.

She lies in my arms, pressed up against me like we're lovers and this is how we usually end our night. I have the lamp on so I can see her, and she can see me.

Her head is resting on my chest, but I can tell she's looking at my knuckles, at my tattoos.

In my world, you're not fully part of the Bratva unless you've done time. I did four years of my twenty-five-year sentence for murder at Southport Correctional Facility.

When we ink ourselves in the Bratva, it's meaningful and a sign to others of who we are. All my tattoos are meaningful. Some for honor, others are reminders so I'll never forget.

Such is the case with my prison tattoos.

"I killed three men," I say, cutting into the silence.

Adriana lifts her head and looks at me with her beautiful eyes.

"Why?" Her voice is barely audible.

"They tried to rape my sister. One of them was a mother-fucking serial killer. It was his idea to drug her with a date rape drug after he met her at a club. He and his friends stalked her for weeks." At the time, I thought that was the worst thing that was going to happen to Talia. "If she wasn't who she was, she wouldn't have had the street smarts to escape them when they took her. She managed to get away and get herself to a hospital. The drug was poison and would have killed her. Which was their intention. They were going to rape and kill her. When I got the call and learned what happened, I went ape shit and hunted them down. I didn't care who saw me finish them. That's exactly what happened. Someone saw me."

"What happened after?"

"I went to prison. When the right people witness your actions, there's little you can do to avoid going to the big house, but I didn't care about that." I smirk, then my smile falls. "To me, the men who tried to hurt my sister were dead."

I got out early because my father pulled some strings when

he offered up information on some names on the fed's hitlist. I'll keep that to myself, though.

"Now she's gone and none of that matters. I slayed her demons after she died, but it won't bring her back."

We stare at each other for a few beats, then her eyes turn glassy.

"I'm sorry."

I stare at her and remember how she watched me kill Raul and never begged for his life. Since then, little things have cropped up to make me think her life wasn't as rosy as people said it was.

She's different from what I expected, and no one has ever managed to stump me for as long as she has.

"He hurt you, too, didn't he? Raul?" I gaze at her head on, and when she nods, some small part of the mystery that's her falls into place. If he hurt her in the way I think he did, then it's no wonder she never begged for his life. "The marks on your back... you didn't fall, did you?"

"No," she whispers.

"He whipped you?"

She stares at me for a long moment before she nods.

"Why?"

Why the fuck would Raul do that to her?

She shakes her head, and when a tear drifts down her cheek, I know whatever Raul did to her must have been bad.

"I can't. I can't talk about it."

That's the second thing she's told me she couldn't talk about. Both things had to do with her parents. Mother and father alike.

Any thought to prod or demand she tell me what happened to her is interrupted when my phone rings. We both look at it buzzing on the nightstand.

The message this morning was important enough. When my phone rings at minutes to midnight, I know I have to leave the house because this is the call I am waiting for.

I get up. Adriana sits up, too, pulling the sheet over her breasts.

It's Sebastian calling, and I answer the phone.

"Yes," I say.

"We got Tony, boss. I'm at the old meat locker near Main Street. José is with me, and so is Eric."

Perfect.

"I'll be there in ten minutes."

I hang up and look at my bride-to-be. The call is a reminder of the emblem she represents, but I'm prevented from thinking of her as such when I detect the worry in her eyes for me.

"You're going out at this time?"

"I have to."

"What's happening?"

"Go to sleep, Malyshka. This is where my world and yours don't cross."

I walk away but look back at her this time and wish I'd gotten to finish our conversation.

* * *

The old meat locker is the perfect place to interrogate a motherfucker because it has all the equipment ready for torture.

I've been using it for years for my own purposes. My father and brother use the standard dungeons under the building in the city that look more like police cells. I'm a little rawer than that, and old school.

I'd like my next victim to suffer in every sense, and I don't think they deserve the benefit of a cell.

I walk inside. It looks like a scene from the movie *Saw*.

When I see my men standing around a battered-looking Tony sitting on a chair, I'm reminded I'm here for something much more sinister than a psychological horror. I'm the nightmare.

Eric is leaning against the wall near my senior team of guards with a phone in his hands he is looking through. José stands opposite him with that uncertain look on his face.

Sebastian looks like he's been keeping my seat warm and moves away when I approach.

Tony lifts his head and looks at me. He knows who I am and knows I'm alive, so I decide to skip past all that icebreaker shit and get to the point.

I have very specific questions I need to ask him, and I've had all day to prepare myself.

"Tony, I'm going to spare you the grief of the bullshit and get to the point," I begin. "Tell me who you're working for."

"I don't know anything about who's in charge."

This is exactly what I hate about fuckers like these. I land a punch straight to his gut, and he doubles over, only to receive another punch to his face.

I pull my gun out next so he understands I'm fucking serious, that I'll kill his ass if he doesn't tell me what I need to know.

"Fool, you are a fool. You really expect me to believe that?" I roar.

"It's... true." He coughs. "I swear to you I don't know anything."

I glance at Eric, who is staring at him with keen eyes.

"You met with Barabbas Ponteix this morning about the Dmitriyev Ltd. contract. What the fuck is that about?"

His eyes go wide, and I know I've struck a nerve. I've touched something I shouldn't know about.

"The company. It's about the shares in the company and the agreement on who gets what once the takeover happens."

I grab his hair and hold his head up. "What fucking takeover? I never heard of any takeover, so, please, enlighten me."

He starts shaking. "Barabbas belongs to a crime syndicate."

"I know that part. What do they want?"

"They all banded together with Raul," he sputters. "The plan was to take over the company so they can have control over the uranium production. That's still the plan. I'm just writing the contracts. Barabbas brought his signed this morning, and I took it."

So, that's what's happening. Motherfuckers.

"Who's in charge, Tony?"

"That's not how it works. It was all set up in secret, so neither Barabbas nor I know who's in charge. We just meet to discuss the contracts. A message is delivered to my office with instructions, and I get my payment after the meeting. The last message informed me of Raul's death, and I was to continue my work as normal."

This is shit, but it's the kind of sophisticated shit I'll admit I expected. It's just worse because it's about me. I return my focus to Eric. He's looking at me now.

This isn't over just because this prick can't give me what I need.

I look back at Tony, who's shuddering now.

"How long has this been going on?" I demand.

"November. The end of November last year."

Right when my father announced his illness and his retirement. I believe even more now it has to be someone in our brotherhood. Maybe one of the Brigadiers. They were the first to find out. But so were all our subordinates.

"Who else is involved, Tony?"

"Only Raul knew that, Mikhail. He never even told Felipe or his other lieutenants. He told no one because he signed an oath in blood and the price if he went against them was his daughter's life. He would never risk Adriana's life for anything."

Now I glance at José. He nods at me as if to say he is telling the truth about Raul. I trust no one, though, until I have facts in my hands.

Fucking Raul.

That motherfucking dog. He would never risk his daughter's life, yet he hurt her. It's like I'm always talking about two different people.

"Let me go, please. I have told you all you need to know."

"Let you go so you can run back and squeal bloody murder?" I taunt.

Eric steps forward and hands me the phone. "That's his phone. I hacked it. I found the same code hiding some pictures. Nothing more." He shakes his head in disgust. "You need to look at them. You're not going to want to let him go after."

Tony looks like death in that moment, and I'm almost afraid of what I'm going to see.

"I didn't know she was your sister," Tony blurts before I can even look at the phone.

I don't meet Eric's eyes. I just take the phone. The first image shatters my soul. It's of Talia, naked and bound with ropes around her wrists and feet with five naked men surrounding her.

They're smiling while she's crying.

My sister went through all of this before they killed her, while I lay in a hospital bed.

I couldn't save her. I couldn't stop them from taking her.

This is what they did to my sister.

"She was a present—"

I cut off Tony's words with a bullet to his head, then another, and another.

And another.

I don't stop until I empty my gun.

And still, it won't bring her back.

Chapter Twenty-Three

Natalia

I glance at the clock on the wall for the millionth time, and my lungs constrict when I realize it's close to ten o'clock and Mikhail still isn't back yet.

I haven't seen him since last night. Another two hours will make it a whole day since he's been gone.

I'm not certain about his usual habits, but with the exception of the one night I didn't see him, he's been home well before this time every night this week.

That call Mikhail got at minutes before midnight broke the spell I was under and placed me in a different one.

One that had me wondering how I changed from being the terrified woman who was looking for a way out, to the woman who was worried about her captor's safety.

No one has said anything to me, and they've all gone about their day-to-day activities like normal. Maybe everything is normal, but I don't think it is.

It's bad enough I gave myself to him over and over again and the lines between us have blurred so much I can hardly see them. Last night, I forgot who he was, and I allowed him to take me in ways I never imagined.

I've spent the day flitting between thinking about how I lost control of myself and my thoughts when I was with him to worrying about where he is.

It's clear something is going on.

Something bad that's a continuation from Mexico. I don't think it all ended with Raul's death or taking me.

I have a feeling it's either to do with the cartel or the repercussions of taking it.

Or it could be something bigger. Something Bratva related.

I have no idea because I have no details other than what I've seen and heard so far.

Whatever is going on has me on edge.

I told myself I was obviously worried about what's going on because now that I'm Adriana Alvarez, I've set a bait on myself. Anybody could claim me and do the same thing Mikhail is doing to me. Maybe I'd just prefer the devil I know until I have a plan to escape him.

That's what I told myself, although I knew deep down it wasn't entirely true.

There was a moment when he opened up and didn't seem like the beast anymore. It was as he spoke about his sister and what he did to go to prison. I've had people who've loved me, but they were taken away from me in a way to show me they could never protect me. Mikhail seems to be a man who would die protecting the people he loved, and if he could, he would have died trying to save his mother and sister.

The only good thing to come of last night was talking to him about things that were true. I knew I was dancing close to danger, but it gave me an ounce of myself back.

He knew the marks on my back were whip marks, and things are playing out to look like Raul was the cruel father. A sort of blessing in disguise.

I don't know how long I can keep this up, but if he believes things like that, it will help me, especially during times when I can't act like the pampered princess I'm supposed to be.

"These shoes would look great with the dress, dear," Sophia says as she walks into the kitchen. I almost forgot she was here.

We were sitting in the sunroom looking through wedding shoe brochures when I came in here to get some water.

I needed a break. I got the water and got lost in my worries.

She gives me a smile as she sets the brochure on the countertop and points to a pair of delicate-looking embroidered three-inch heels. They look like an elaborate version of Cinderella's glass slippers.

I agree. The shoes would look amazing with the dress I've chosen, but so would all the others she picked.

"I like those, too."

"We have too many to choose from." She gives me an exasperated sigh. "Here, have a look at the ones I circled, just to make sure you've seen everything that might be suitable."

"Thanks for doing this."

I take the brochure to humor her. Looking at wedding shoes is the last thing I want to be doing right now, although it's giving me something to do.

She's been here since lunchtime. She came with the seamstress for the final fitting on the dress and to discuss accessories like my veil and shoes. I picked the veil. The shoes were the last thing left.

The seamstress left several hours ago, but I think Sophia detected my worry and decided to stay a little longer to keep me company.

"I'm going to pack up and head out," she says. "I've asked Aleksander to come back and sit with you for an hour."

"Oh, that's okay. I'll be fine." I really don't want him sitting with me.

"It's totally fine. I've asked him to come and make you a late supper. Mikhail might be back by then."

Although I really shouldn't I think of asking her what might be going on, she's the only one here so far who's talked to me like a person.

"Sophia, do you know if something is still going on in relation to my father?" It's so hard to call that devil my father. "I don't know anything. I apologize for asking. I know I shouldn't, but it's hard to be kept in the dark."

Her face softens, and a look of concern fills her eyes.

"Oh, of course. And no apologies necessary. It's a messy situation. I don't know anything myself, but there's bound to be repercussions in a situation like this." She drags in a deep breath. "I'm sure Mikhail is just making sure any threat Raul posed and anyone else who was working with him are completely eliminated."

"Do you think someone else was working with my father?"

She nods. "Yes. It would make sense. But what's worse is the destruction of trust. It's hard to accept that an ally you've known for over twenty years could switch sides on you and you have no concept of what happened or why."

Over twenty years?

My God, that's older than me. I never knew Raul had an alliance with them for so long, or at all. I just thought they were enemies.

Although... I have seen Russians at the house in Mexico and heard them talking. They wouldn't have seen me. I guess they would have come from Mikhail's family.

It is very strange Raul would kill the way he did and break a strong alliance with people who are obviously powerful. Unless he had assistance from someone just as powerful.

It would be just like him.

"You don't know why he did what he did?"

She shakes her head. "We have no clue. He's just ambushed us."

"When did it happen?" I chance asking.

"Weeks before Christmas."

"Christmas?" But it's now March. "Didn't you know my father was responsible?"

"We didn't. This has only come to light since Mikhail got out of hospital. The assassination attempt left him in a coma."

"Mikhail was in a coma?" I thought the attack was on his mother and sister.

"My dear, the attack was supposed to have been on the whole family. It was chance that half of us weren't there, and he survived. The goal was to kill us all. That's what this is about." She gets tearful. "That awful night of the attack, his sister was taken, and we hoped she'd survived, too, but it was not meant to be. Your father sold her to men who tortured and killed her. God knows what else they did to her."

A shiver runs down my spine as understanding blooms in my mind. I remember how he sounded when Mikhail spoke about sister last night.

She was sold and tortured. The same plan Raul had for me. To be sold means death. Those men do whatever they want to you and torture you until you beg for death, or they kill you. How do I know this?

I've seen it happen.

I've seen Raul buy girls for himself and kill them when he's done with them.

No wonder Mikhail behaved the way he did in Mexico and killed everyone.

No wonder he showed no mercy when he took me.

But what about now?

Nothing has changed all that much. The problem still exists.

Sophia places a hand over mine and taps my knuckles.

"Please don't worry. I can see I've troubled you. Wait in here for Aleksander to come back, then have something to eat and go to sleep, Okay?"

"Yes. Thank you."

"I'll see you at the dinner tomorrow." She gives me that

heartwarming smile again. The reminder of dinner tomorrow and knowing the whole story just makes me feel like vomiting.

She might be nice, but what is everyone else going to be like? I have a strong feeling they won't be like her. Maybe that's another reason why she's been coming here. She probably feels sorry for me.

"I'll see you then," I say, and she dips her head for a curt goodbye.

Five minutes after she leaves, Aleksander walks into the sunroom with a scowl on his face. He's clearly annoyed he has to do anything for me, and looks more put out than usual when he tells me to come into the kitchen.

We don't talk as he makes up a plate of cookies and hot chocolate with milk and cream he prepares on the stove.

Before he hands it to me, I notice him put some spices in there, like cinnamon, nutmeg, and something red.

The red bits float on the top and puff out the way marshmallows would, but I don't think they're marshmallows.

"Thank you for making this for me," I tell him.

"I suggest you head to bed when you're done," he replies. "If I were you, I would not be worrying myself over Mr. Dmitriyev. It's not uncommon for him to be away for the whole night. Especially if he has *new* company."

New company.

The way he said that, in that obvious way, can only mean he thinks Mikhail is with a woman.

If that's true, I'm so foolish to worry about him. And even more stupid to make myself look so obvious that a man who can't stand me was summoned to get me hot chocolate and cookies.

"I wasn't worried about him," I lie. "Why worry about him when I have myself to worry about?"

He says something in Russian he knows I won't understand, then marches away and leaves me.

I look down at the cookies and decide to throw them and the hot chocolate away. I don't want anything from that man.

I feel like such an idiot. What the hell must he think of me?

I've been so engrossed in getting from one day to the next that I haven't paid as much attention to the staff as I should have. The fact that still none of the maids speak to me suggests they've already formed their opinions on me. The fact that Aleksander is rude as fuck is also not good.

It means they see no need to respect me, and the only person who would have given them permission to behave like that is Mikhail.

Which takes me right back to the question I asked him the other night about what would happen after the wedding.

You only treat people the way I'm being treated if they're temporary.

I make my way upstairs, shower, and change for bed. I climb beneath the sheets and try to summon sleep.

It doesn't come. More hours pass, and instead of sleeping, I think of everything, and my mind keeps going back to the question of what I'm going to do.

Speaking to José would have eased my mind to some extent. I've dared not mention his name for fear of what Mikhail would do.

And where is Mikhail?

Is he really out with some woman?

Do I care?

I roll onto my back when something pulls on my insides, and I realize I do care, and I'm conflicted and confused because I shouldn't.

I knew I was just a plaything. Something like taking my virginity would mean nothing to him. I've become the statistic I knew I would, and he's probably either chasing another virgin or with one of his women.

I'm so very foolish, because this here is a sneak peak of what it's going to be like to be married to him.

As soon as the thought races through my mind, the sound of something smashing downstairs has me bolting upright.

It sounded like glass breaking. Like either something fell on the ground and smashed or someone threw it.

Or what if it was someone breaking the glass of the window to break in?

There are guards everywhere on the grounds. I don't think anyone could just break into this house. Who would be so foolish?

Then again, didn't Raul try to kill the whole Dmitriyev family? If someone helped him and that someone is still at large, why wouldn't they do something as simple as break into Mikhail's house?

The sound of heavy boots coming up the stairs makes my nerves scatter until I realize I recognize the sound pattern of the footfall.

When you're like me, when every minute of every day is a test of survival, you take note of things like that. Sounds, smells, and that eerie feeling that makes the hairs on the back of your neck stand are all signs to pay attention to.

The footsteps move straight past the room, and the sound fades after a few seconds.

He's back, and he's not coming in here.

Something has obviously happened.

I slip off the bed and open the door. The automatic hallway light is already on and shows droplets of blood on the marble floors.

I suck in a breath when I realize the blood leads down the whole hallway.

What the hell happened?

My prior thoughts fade and my concerns return telling me to follow the blood trail.

So I do.

Chapter Twenty-Four

Natalia

I find myself on the third floor.

The floor where Mikhail's office is located, and one of the places of the house that are restricted to me.

Although I'm fully aware I'm breaking a rule by coming up here, my curiosity has overpowered me. I'm not sure who wouldn't be curious after seeing the trail of blood taint the immaculate floor.

I have that feeling again, like I'm walking around in a horror film and every step is taking me closer and closer into the unknown.

I turn the corner and notice the dim lights on in the hall ahead. This whole area doesn't look like it's for work purposes, and I haven't seen an office yet.

Since the blood trail leads to the hall, I continue following it.

I walk right into the grand hall, and my breath is stolen away when my gaze lands on the most beautiful paintings and sculptures of ballerinas.

Large and small paintings cover the walls. The entire wall to my left is dedicated to the largest painting of a ballerina in what I'm guessing must be *Swan Lake*, and she is the black swan.

The sculptures are set out gracefully across the floor. There must be well over a hundred of them. Some made of crystal, others of stone. All beautiful. I can't help but move closer to take a better look.

When I do, I realize straightaway that the ballerinas are the same person. The same woman. It's the same woman in the paintings, too.

There's something the artist captured about her face that is evident in everything.

It's the emotion. It's sadness, but there's a twinkle in her eyes. The emotion is more pronounced in the paintings because they're a clearer depiction of what she looks like.

I move closer to the *Swan Lake* painting and take note of her honey-colored eyes. The sight grips me, and I think of where I've seen those eyes before.

Mikhail.

Is this woman his mother?

Is that who she is?

Apart from the eyes, I can't quite detect any resemblance, but that doesn't mean she's not related to him. Sons tend to look more like their fathers, and daughters their mothers. Apart from my jet-black hair, I looked exactly like my mother, but I have my father's eyes.

Those footsteps sound on the floor again. They echo from further down the hall along with the creek of doors opening.

I watch the mammoth-sized doors ahead open out on either side to a balcony, which looks similar to the one in the bedroom, but from here I can see a larger terrace outside. I wouldn't think I was on the third floor just from what I can see.

194

I knew the house was huge, but it seems like it's so much bigger than I thought.

Because I haven't been in this section before, I have no idea where the terrace leads to. I don't think it's where I've been walking with the dog.

When I walk past one of the crystal ballerinas, I spot Mikhail ahead, and I also realize it's lightly snowing outside again.

The cold air wafts in, making me shiver, but so does he.

He'll know that I'm here in a few seconds, or perhaps he already does.

I take measured, careful steps, my bare feet frozen against the floor and my skin numb from where the cold caresses it.

All I'm wearing is a nightdress made of silk with little straps securing it to my shoulders.

He's dressed for the weather in a black biker jacket and black slacks. The same clothes he had on last night. Blood drips from his hand, lots of it. He's wounded, and as he moves around, the blood continues to drip.

This section of the hall has paintings covered up with dust sheets.

I watch him take the sheet off one of them sitting on an easel. It's the closest painting to the opened doors. The sheet floats to the floor, and he stands in front of the painting. Because of the angle it's placed in I can't see what the painting is of yet.

But I can see him clearer now, and know he's hurt.

There are bruises and blood on his face and all over his neck. It's on his jacket too. I'm not sure if all that blood is his. In fact, I'm inclined to think it might not be from the way it's splashed all over his face.

So, if it's not his, it means he's killed someone.

He's killed more people.

With that in mind, why am I still moving toward him?

I continue and look at him as he smears his bloody hand all over the painting. It's such an odd thing to do.

Really, Natalia, you think odd is the best word to describe that?

There's a good reason why I've been describing the things I've seen this man do as comparable to a nightmare or a horror. It's because that's where monsters and fucked-up psychos live.

What I just saw him do is what I'd expect a psycho to do.

When I get closer and realize the painting is an unfinished one of a beautiful girl with soft brown hair and bright blue eyes, I'm inclined to agree with my assumption whole-heartedly.

That's when I stop in my tracks and observe.

Who is she?

She's someone else, not the ballerina, but the girl is wearing a tutu and has a bright smile on her face.

I think the same artist did the painting.

I'm not sure.

One last smear of blood on his thick fingers goes over her face, removing her smile.

He says something in Russian, as if he's talking to the girl in the painting, then shakes his head.

"I got them, killed them all, but nothing will bring you back. Not you or Mother," he says in English this time, and I realize the girl in the painting must be his sister. "There's nothing I can do, Talia."

There's a slur to his words like he's been drinking, and when he moves to the door, I notice a bottle of wine in the corner.

He picks it up and takes a long swig, finishing the contents. When he's done, he throws the bottle into the painting. It bounces off the surface and falls on the floor, smashing.

I realize now that's what I heard downstairs. It was another bottle.

My legs tremble, and I feel that urge to run, run far away. Yet I'm rooted to the floor like vines are holding my feet down.

I take in a slow breath. That's when he turns and looks at me.

"What are you doing in here, Malyshka?" His voice, harsh and cold, cuts into me. "You were told not to come up here."

"I'm sorry. I saw blood on the floor and... You've been gone since last night."

"Go back to bed, princess. You don't want to be around me right now."

"What happened?" I don't know if I'm making the mistake of my life by asking questions I shouldn't be asking, but I'm compelled to nonetheless.

"Nothing that concerns you. Now go. Get out." He points to the door. More blood drips from his hand.

"You're hurt."

"I'm always hurt, princess. This is just another day with new pain." A menacing smile inches across his face. The menace doesn't reach his eyes, though, like it usually does.

There's too much pain lurking in the depths for anything to reach them. I know I should listen and get the fuck out, but that pain reaches out to me.

Maybe it's because I recognize it. I've felt it and seen it in myself.

I chance walking up to him and stop a breath away. He stares down at me with those cold eyes, assessing me, and I gaze up at him.

"What room is this?" I ask, trying another angle.

"A shrine."

That's exactly what it feels like.

"It's a shrine for them," he adds.

Them.

His mother and sister.

"Mikhail, let me dress your wound. You're bleeding."

He chuckles off-key. "What the hell does a cartel princess know about dressing wounds?"

The answer to that is, she would most likely know nothing, but *I* do. I know because I'm not a princess. I'm the pauper.

Tentatively, I reach out to touch his hand, as if I'm touching a predator who could devour me any second now, but he steps away from me.

"Don't touch me. I have their blood on my hands."

"Whose blood?"

"The men I killed."

My heart freezes in my chest. I was right. He's killed again.

"Who did you kill, Mikhail?"

"The men who bought my sister and thought it was a good idea to torture her so badly she had to beg for death."

My God.

My soul trembles. Only hours ago, I talked to Sophia about Mikhail's sister.

Hours ago I could only assume what must have happened. Now I know.

I can only imagine how she must have suffered.

"Look at her," he says, staring at the painting again. The blood has completely defaced her image. "She was sixteen when I did that painting of her."

He did the painting?

My eyes widen.

I don't know what shocks me more. Glancing around the room, I look at the other paintings and wonder if he did them, too. They seem older, though.

Gritting his teeth, he steps around me then walks away and through another door to our left.

I follow him and see it goes back into the hallway. He continues down it and opens the door at the end.

This leads into an office. This is where I'm not supposed to be.

He takes off his jacket, and I gasp when I notice the deep

knife wound running down his shoulder. It's sliced through his shirt, and the whole sleeve is practically gone.

He opens another door at the back that leads into a little bedroom area. This office is equipped to work and sleep in. There's a bathroom in there, too. That's where he goes next as he continues taking off his clothes.

This is the first time I've seen him naked and not taken note of how good his body looks.

What I look at now is his wounds. There's another gnash on his back.

He steps into the shower and turns on a heavy blast of water to wash over his head and wounds.

Blood flows down the drain as I stand there and watch him clean himself off. I watch until he decides to turn off the water minutes later and turns to face me, resting against the granite wall of the shower.

"Why are you still here?" he mumbles.

"I told you I wanted to dress your wound." Which has already started bleeding again.

He grabs a towel and wraps it around his bottom half before stepping out of the shower.

He walks toward me, then reaches over my head to the cabinet and takes out a first-aid box.

He doesn't give it to me, though. He ignores me and walks back into the office, where he opens the box and starts trying to dress the wound himself.

I ignore him and look into the box myself. It holds more than the normal stuff you'd find in a first-aid box. There's a bit of everything, and I find just what I need to close the wound until he can get himself to a hospital.

He sits down and starts fumbling with a bandage pack, but there's a tremor in his hand either from the wound or the alcohol. It's stopping him from getting a good enough grip to open it.

I take it from him. He glares at me, but as soon as I open it and get down to business cleaning his wound, he allows me to take care of him.

All he does is watch, and while I know what he must be thinking, the part of me that wants to be me keeps going.

I find something I can use as a makeshift suture, then bandage both wounds.

When I touch his face to look at the cut on his cheek, he catches my wrist.

"Leave that one," he orders, but he doesn't let me go. I shudder. I know he sees my fear. There's a spark of something sinister in his eyes that heightens my senses. "Are you afraid of me, princess?"

"What do you want me to say to you?"

"We're getting married in a few weeks. Maybe we should start with the truth."

He holds my gaze, and a different type of fear coils through me, reminding me I'm a lie. He's going to marry me and find out he married the wrong woman.

We will never start with the truth.

"One more time, are you afraid of me, princess?"

"Yes," I breathe.

"I don't think you're as afraid of me as you should be, or you wouldn't nurse the guy who killed your father, no matter how cruel he was to you. You'd still view me as the monster. The question is, why aren't you?"

I press my lips together and think of my answer.

I view him as the monster, but when I think of how he slayed Raul, I view him as my savior.

I can't tell him that. Ever. And I'm only safe in those moments in my headspace when I think of how he defeated Raul. That's it. I can never voice those thoughts to anyone.

"Do you want me to think of you as a monster, Mikhail?" I ask. "Is that what you want me to think of you?"

He looks me over before answering, and his face softens somewhat.

"No, I don't."

He releases my hand and continues to stare at me.

"Where did you learn to do this?" He glances at his shoulder.

"It was something I was taught in case of trouble." It's the wisest answer I can think of, and it seems to work.

He stands and holds out his hand to me. "Baby, come and lie next to me."

I take his hand, and he leads me out to the little bed. He gets on it first, and I climb in next to him.

He turns the lights off and slips an arm around me.

The moonlight is the only light we have so we can see each other.

He lowers his head to kiss me briefly, and I kiss him back.

"Go to sleep, princess."

I close my eyes but don't sleep for a while. Neither does he.

But I drift off eventually with thoughts of tonight weighing on my mind.

* * *

I'm woken the next morning by the light shake of my shoulders.

When I open my eyes and find Aleksander looming over me, I sit up straightaway and pull the sheets closer, even though I'm wearing clothes.

Mikhail isn't here. It's just Aleksander and me in the room.

He straightens and gives me that look of disgust I'm now accustomed to. Probably because I found my way into the place he told me not to visit.

"You have a visitor, Miss Alvarez," he informs me.

I give him a narrowed look. "Me? Is it Sophia or the seamstress?"

"José Diaz."

201

Oh my God in heaven! José. I get to see him.

I jump off the bed, not caring what I'm wearing.

"Mr. Dmitriyev has allowed you fifteen minutes with him. He's out on the terrace waiting for you," he adds.

"Thank you."

I rush out of the room and head down the hallway I came up last night so I can grab my coat from the room.

When I do, I run outside to the terrace. I have to hold back tears when I see José standing by the balcony waiting for me.

I try to hold them back but fail, and I become that little girl I was years ago when I first met him as I rush into his arms.

He holds me, and for the first time, I truly appreciate the fatherly warmth he shows me.

"Mija," he mutters, holding me closer.

Aware of the presence of guards, he pulls away and glances nervously over my shoulder.

I look, too, and that's when I notice Mikhail standing in the hallway inside the house.

He gives us a nod and walks away. This is because of what I did last night.

It has to be. Whatever the reason, it's what I need right now.

"We don't have much time," José reminds me. "Let's sit over here."

We sit side by side on the little bench, and I feel like eons have passed since we last saw each other.

Where we sit is private enough to talk, but we still have to be careful.

"Are you safe, my dear?" he asks.

I nod. "Yes."

"He hasn't hurt you?"

"No. I'm not hurt. But I'm so scared. I've been scared every day that he's going to find out my secret."

"I know. I wanted to come before now, but this is the first he's allowed me." He nods. "The house in Mexico was burned down. I managed to destroy everything inside there before the guards got to it that would give the secret away."

"Oh my God, you did?"

"Yes. I got rid of all of Adriana's pictures and the ones Raul had of him and his family. Everything."

"Thank you so much."

He takes my hands into his.

"You're more than welcome, mi amor, but you know that's not going to be enough. It won't. You can't stay here and live this life. I did my best, but it's still risky. I was only able to get rid of what I could in the house. We don't know what could come from the outside. We don't know what Mikhail could find."

I nod. "I know. What am I going to do, José?"

"There's nothing you can do, so don't even try. My powers are limited, but I'm still trying to get you out of this mess. I'm still looking for an escape route. All I can say is, be ready to leave when I find one. Things are happening that might work in our favor."

My heart races. "Like what?"

"People are still trying to kill Mikhail and his family. When that happens, we leave."

When. He said *when*, as if he was sure.

"You think that will happen, José?"

"I don't know details, and I probably won't. Whatever is happening is big, with people who are above anybody we've ever dealt with. My only concern is you. The only way I can see out of this is Mikhail's death. Until then, I'll play nice and look for another way out. Either way, you have to get out because someone will find out the truth and kill you. You hear me, Natalia?"

"I hear you."

I'm listening, and now that I'm even more aware of the situation, my heart aches.

203

Someone still wants Mikhail dead. If his death means my freedom, I should want him dead, too.

But... I don't.

I don't want to die, either.

"Be ready to leave the moment I give you the word."

"Yes."

Chapter Twenty-Five

Mikhail

I'm in my office waiting for Eric to arrive. He should be here in a few minutes for a quick visit. When he leaves, I'll try to catch up on the work I wanted to do yesterday.

I'm standing by the window.

From here, I can see Adriana and José sitting on the terrace.

When I came up here, I found myself moving over to the window to watch them. I'm not even sure what I'm looking for anymore.

I know there's nothing romantic going on between them and everything is as they both say.

What I'm looking at tells me that Adriana really does view José as a father figure.

There's just something that keeps playing on my mind.

If I'm being honest, I'll admit I'm still jealous, just not the way she would think.

I'm jealous of the closeness she has with him. I don't want her to be that way with anyone who isn't me.

Herein lies the problem.

I shouldn't be thinking like that about a woman I took as a pawn in my game.

A pawn she will become in three weeks from now when I give her my name.

Every time I'm with her, though, she reaches a place inside me I never thought could be reached. She went there last night.

I specifically didn't want her in that room. The hall where memories of my loved ones are now stored because I didn't want the presence of anyone connected to Raul to taint it. But her presence didn't do that. She calmed my pain and my rage.

I don't know what the fuck I planned to do, but chances were in the state I was in, I would have probably destroyed everything in that room.

And then I would have hated myself for it after.

My father did all the paintings and sculptures of my mother. They're all of her. He was obsessed with her, and that was how he showed it.

All the ones the princess would have seen. The one she saw me desecrate was mine. As well as all the others under the sheets.

My father gave me the paintings and sculptures when I bought this house because he knew I'd be the only person to appreciate them. I did and still do.

He gave them to me because like him, at one point in my life, I used to paint.

My father stopped painting when his arthritis, which he hides very well, got the better of him. But I stopped because of Ivan.

I stopped just before college, and my reasons were foolish when I think of it.

Ivan thought I was less of a man because of my art. His taunts played on my mind, which eventually made me stop.

I've never wanted my brother to have anything to hold over on me, no matter how big or small. So, I was willing to get rid of something that balanced me for a greater cause. I knew one day, I'd have to go up against him, like I am now, and being the best Bratva leader was the only thing that mattered to me.

Sometimes, my heart goes back to that place, probably seeking peace. It did last night. Right back to the painting of my sister I never finished.

I went for it because there was no fucking point in finishing it.

A tap on the door has my head turning.

It's Eric, and he looks concerned.

It's understandable after the way I lost my shit the other night.

"Have you cooled off?" he asks.

"No." I've only calmed down a little, but I'm still ready to kill.

After meeting with Tony, Eric got the names of the men who'd bought my sister, names I didn't have before. Our team was able to find an address in Chicago, and a few witnesses.

The key witness was a woman who worked in the house who'd fed Talia and gave her water. It was her who told us Talia had to beg for death, and she also confirmed Felipe was there and took part in the torture and rape. She said there were others, but she didn't have names.

At that house we found parts of Talia. Literal parts. Her head and an arm and a leg.

That was what I buried the other week. Pieces of my sister.

I lean against the wall, while Eric sits and regards me.

"I'm going to have to tell my father something, Eric," I state. It was in agreement to keep things under wraps until I knew how big the problem was. "He has to know what's going on."

"I know. I thought that the moment Tony started talking. Can I just advise you to only talk to your father for the moment?" Eric offers. "I think the fewer people who know, the better. Especially if this is coming from inside."

"Yeah. I'll be seeing him tonight. I'm going to talk to him then." My father doesn't like business being discussed at these socials, but this is an exception of great importance.

We're going to have to tighten security and put certain things in place. The wedding is going to be an event we're all going to attend, but then, so will our allies from different brotherhoods and syndicates. Nothing might happen there, or it might.

"I don't have a clue who this person is."

"I know."

"The best I can come up with is that one of the brigadiers might want to overthrow us. That's the only way any of them can climb ranks. As for the company, the same rings true. Everything is kept in the family."

"I'll keep looking through Raul's files. I plan to spend the day working on it."

"I owe you."

"No worries, friend. Like I said, if there's something to find, I'll find it."

And so far, he has.

He just hasn't hit the mother load yet.

But I have a feeling he will.

Chapter Twenty Six

Mikhail

Adriana looks beautiful.

The other day, I thought about how many beautiful women I'd been with and how she was right up there with the best of them. I take that back now, because I'd push to call her the most beautiful woman I've ever seen.

I can imagine the women who are going to be at the dinner tonight will be envious.

The most beautiful thing about the princess is that she doesn't know how beautiful she is. That makes her even more desirable.

I don't know how that works, but it does.

Minutes ago, I walked into the bedroom and had to stop by the doorway to look at her as she stared at herself in the full-length mirror.

She still hasn't seen me yet.

She's wearing a black sleeveless cocktail dress that enhances her perfect frame.

I selected that dress for her for tonight's event and had it delivered earlier.

She looks stunning in it, like it was made for her.

Her hair is down in loose graceful waves around her shoulders, and her face is lightly made up.

She's the kind of woman who carries natural beauty and doesn't need too much of anything. When she does add anything at all, whether it's clothes or makeup, it's more than striking.

The most elegant I've seen her look was when she was fitting her wedding dress. Before that, it was in Mexico right before I killed Felipe.

She could have all the beautiful dresses in the world, and I'm sure each would look like it was made to fit her, but my favorite thing is her naked body.

I allow my gaze to run over her body and take in every inch. It must be the heat of my watchful glare that makes her turn around. Her cheeks flush when she sees the way I'm looking at her.

I never hide my intentions. Never have and never will. It's not my style, and I won't start now.

I purposely stayed in my office all day because I wasn't ready to talk to anybody.

Or specifically her. She saw a side of me last night I didn't want anybody to see. I asked for it, though, because I drew attention to myself.

The way I am now just for looking at her.

She knows I want her, which makes her less afraid of me. I meant what I said last night, though, when she asked if I wanted her to think of me as a monster.

I don't, and that's in violation to what I set out to do.

"Thank you for the dress," she says first.

"Looks nice on you."

"Thanks. And thank you for allowing me to see José."

"No worries."

"How's your shoulder?" She brings her hands together.

It still hurts like a bitch, but I've had worse done to me. Whatever she did helped.

"It's good. Thanks for patching me up, princess."

"You should still go to the hospital."

I've had enough of hospitals. "I don't need to. I'll be fine. Are you ready?"

Nerves fill her face. "I think so. Who's going to be there? I... just want to know."

I should have told her before now. "My father, Sophia, my brother, an aunt from my mother's side, and two cousins. That's it."

She looks more nervous than before, but we have no time for nerves.

I have important business to discuss with my father.

I hold out my hand to her, beckoning her to come to me. "Malyshka."

She steps forward and walks toward me, taking my hand.

The maids all look when we walk down the stairs, everyone gazing at her in adoration, even the ones who don't like her.

I know of the tension that exists in the house, and I'm partly to blame for it because I didn't want the staff talking to her. That was mainly because I didn't want them treating her unfavorably.

Aleksander is loyal to me, but he has a big mouth I don't like sometimes.

When we get in my car, I realize this is the first time she will have gone anywhere with me and our first outing as a couple.

A quick look in the mirror shows me how good we look together and how she fits me.

We don't talk on the journey to my family home, but I know she has questions. She'll have questions about last night I won't want to answer, and she's curious about the room.

I knew when she'd entered the room long before I saw her,

and I knew the room would fascinate her. It's supposed to be fascinating.

When we arrive at the house, she looks so nervous her skin has gone pale, and there's a tremor in her hands as she brings them together. I can imagine she must feel like the lamb going to the slaughterhouse.

Even when we get out of the car and she straightens her shoulders like she's finding strength, I can tell she's still nervous.

So, I take her hand.

I know I shock her, but I hold her hand like she's mine because she is.

When we walk into the house, everyone is in the living room, where we normally meet for canopies first.

We're the last to arrive, and we get the attention I expected we would as my family stop what they're doing to look at us.

"Hello, everyone," I say. "This is Adriana Alvarez, my fiancée."

Even she looks at me when I give the announcement.

Sophia smiles sweetly. I avoid looking at Ivan because I clocked him the moment we stepped through the door and saw he was looking at her, just like I knew he would. I'd bet the motherfucker was counting down the hours until we arrived.

Father is the first to get up and make his way over to us. I'm not sure what to expect from him, but when a small smile cracks his wrinkled face, I feel more at ease.

I think out of everyone, Adriana was most worried about him.

"Good to meet you, my dear. I'm Sergei Dmitriyev, Mikhail's father and Pakhan of the Baranov. Welcome to my home," my father says, holding his hand out to shake Adriana's.

She takes it and returns his smile. "Thank you for inviting me."

Father cuts me a glance, and I know from that he's all right with her. He was always going to be all right with my plan, but being okay with her is a different matter altogether.

"I can see for myself the rumors are true," Ivan cuts in, walking up to us, too. "Adriana Alvarez is definitely a beauty."

I don't want him to touch her. I hardly want him to look at her. But I'd be completely overreacting if I said anything to him now or stopped him as he reaches out his hand to shake hers.

"I am Ivan Dmitriyev, Mikhail's brother."

"Pleased to meet you."

She shakes his hand, and I notice how he grips hers when she tries to let go.

The asshole lifts her hand to his lips and kisses her knuckles.

"And you," he replies, releasing her.

Adriana glances at me, probably sensing my disdain for my brother's display of affection for what's mine.

"Okay, now that we're all here, let's go to the dining room," Father announces.

I'm sure he noticed my temper rising, too.

Moments later, we're all seated around the dinner table, Adriana sitting next to me and opposite Ivan, who continues to fucking stare at her.

The only opposition I feel comes from both my cousins Marsha and Louise, my aunt Denise's daughters, and I know the animosity isn't down to their grief over my mother and sister. It's jealousy.

Sophia, as always, lessens any tension and guides us into talking about things a normal family would discuss.

I need normal tonight for many reasons, and she provides it with her talk of flowers.

When the evening approaches that natural pause, my father motions to me, signaling he's ready to talk. Before we arrived, I told him I needed to talk to him, so he was aware I'd be discussing business tonight.

I lean close to Adriana, and she looks at me.

"I have to step out for a few minutes. I won't be long," I tell her.

"Where are you going?" she whispers.

"I just have to talk to my father. When I get back, we're going home."

"Okay."

"Don't worry. I'll take good care of her," Sophia cuts in.

"Thanks, Sophia."

I leave, following my father out of the room, but when I look back, Adriana is staring after me, and fucking Ivan is looking at me, too.

Father and I head to his office on the ground floor, where we sit together.

He has that weak look again, like he's had enough.

I'm sure he has.

"Well done, son. She's a nice girl," he states. "I'm sure we've enraged many in Raul's alliance just for having her."

"I'm sure we have."

"Are your plans still the same?" He raises his thick brows.

When I posed my idea to him about killing Raul and marrying his daughter to get control over the cartel, the plan was to either kill Adriana as soon as I didn't need her or dispose of her by some other means. Of course, killing her would be the ultimate ending of revenge. In just one week, my mind has changed.

I can't kill her, but I can't see myself keeping her, either.

I still don't know what I'll be doing when I cross that bridge of marriage yet.

"I'm playing it by ear," I decide to say.

"I leave it in your good hands, my son. What you've done so far is the sign of a good leader."

"Are you dropping hints, Father?" I decide to aim for light-hearted so he can take the heavy stuff easier when we start talking about it.

He chuckles. "No, I'm not dropping hints."

"But you already know who the next Pakhan will be," I state bluntly, and he nods.

"I do. I always did. I did years ago. But this part is necessary to seal the deal. My decision can change like the wind."

"And you want to meet me at the lake house because?" I quirk a brow.

"We won't talk about that tonight. That's an important meeting I want to have with you, just not now."

"Okay, I'll wait."

His expression grows serious. "You've found something more to worry about, haven't you?"

"I have. It's not good, Father."

I quickly fill him in on what's been going on but leave out the part about it being someone inside the brotherhood. I'm saving that for last because he's not going to take that well. He's spent his life as Pakhan establishing loyalty among the ranks. It's what he'll be remembered for.

By the time I finish, he looks like he's ready to breathe fire.

"So, we don't know any more about this contract?" he demands.

"I believe it's someone from inside our brotherhood," I finally say, and the blood drains from his face.

"Our brotherhood, Mikhail?" His nostrils flare.

"Yes, Father. It makes sense, and now's not the time to second-guess or pussyfoot around the shit. It would have been someone in our circle who would have known our movements or been feeding information. I don't know if it's one person or a group, but we need to watch our backs."

"God in Heaven. This just goes from bad to worse."

"I know."

"Where are we at now?"

"I want to keep this between us for the moment, and I suggest an investigation on everyone who's working for us."

"Everyone." He says this more like a statement than a question.

"Yes. We can't afford to slip up. Eric is still checking things out."

He nods. "Okay. And agreed. I will speak to Aiden Romanov personally and thank him for lending us one of his finest men."

I dip my head. "Father, you know Eric would have helped outside of our alliance of the Bratva."

"Yes. It's a shame we can't have such faith in our own men. I can't begin to tell you how this makes me feel." He bares his teeth and balls his hands into tight fists that shake more because of his ailments. "Someone we know and trusted with our lives was watching us, and they took your mother away from me."

"I know how you feel, Father."

He shakes his head. "My son, I know you loved you mother and sister with all your heart. It's commendable how you took care of them. But you don't know how I feel. Your mother was the love of my life, and you kids were the result of that love. The only way I could show my love for her was in my art. When I couldn't do that any longer, I took comfort in just being with her. When you meet the woman who feels like the other half of your soul, nothing can describe what it feels like when you lose her."

Few things grip me to the point where I feel in touch with my soul. He always seems to guide me to that place. I have no words of comfort for him, and I feel inadequate for it.

"It doesn't feel like it's enough to tell you how sorry I am."

"Because nothing is enough, my son. Nothing will ever be enough. Loving her was my strength, and now it's my weakness. Weakness is a curse in the Bratva. To be weak is to sign your death certificate, yet I chose it, and now it's crippled me. There's a hole in my heart that can never be filled again. Now that she's gone, all I look forward to is death."

The lifeless tone of his voice buries a hole into my own heart and disarms me. He's right about weakness and love. Love is the fastest way to become weak because your enemies use it against you to destroy you from the inside out.

My father looks destroyed.

Somewhere in the back of my mind, a voice warns me not to allow the same thing to happen to me. It's laughable, though, because I always thought I was incapable of such love. But perhaps the voice beckons to me now because I've encountered my match. A woman I've been obsessed with owning and staking my claim to her body since the first look I got of her.

This is a dangerous thing that could cost me, and I can't allow that to happen.

Father draws in a measured breath and tries to calm himself. I can tell he's still worked up. I expect him to be, and it must be eating him up from the inside out that he can't be the ruthless leader he used to be.

If he were his old self, there's no way he'd allow anyone else besides him to be out on the street searching for the truth and justice.

"I promise you I will fix this," I tell him, and he nods.

"I know you will. I'm grateful for the way you've literally come back from the dead and taken this on."

"Thanks, Father. Remember we still have control of the cartel. That's a big win the enemy never anticipated. They also never anticipated me. I wasn't supposed to survive."

"No, you weren't."

"So, take comfort that I have this in hand."

I need him to believe me and trust my capabilities. Especially for the goal I have in mind. Like fuck am I going to allow him to choose Ivan to be Pakhan when I have all the skills it would take to lead the brotherhood the way our forefathers did.

217

That's why I need to stay focused. It's imperative *now* more than ever that I do.

He rests a hand on my shoulder and nods.

"I do, Mikhail. I do take comfort in all you do. And I trust you to figure this out. You have my permission to do whatever you see fit and use whatever resources you need to, to accomplish this task of securing the company and the Brotherhood."

"My thanks, Father."

This week, I allowed my lust for a woman I'm supposed to be using to get the better of me. I need to gain control of my ability to think and eradicate this problem hanging over our heads. Our future and safety depend on it.

My future and safety depend on it, as does everything I've worked so hard for.

I can't allow anything to clash with that, not even Adriana.

No matter what I feel for her.

Chapter Twenty-Seven

Natalia

The women moved into the sitting room, where the maids brought out little cakes for us to eat.

I was grateful to get away from Mikhail's brother. I don't know where he is, but I didn't like the way he was looking at me. Or should I say leering. There's a big difference between simply looking at someone and gawking at someone's body.

He reminded me of Raul's guards. The way they used to leer at me and undress me with their eyes made me sick.

I couldn't exactly be disrespectful toward Ivan, but I don't think I'm wrong in what I saw.

I also didn't miss the tension between him and Mikhail. It was very obvious.

I can tell Sophia is trying to get us all talking, but the three women with us don't seem to like me very much.

They've been talking about their vacation plans for the Easter holidays, and I've been sitting here sipping on a glass of fruit punch.

Mikhail hasn't been gone that long, but it's been long enough.

The youngest woman, who might be a little older than me, keeps cutting me dirty looks and glancing at her sister, who snickers as if she's privy to some secret joke.

I forgot their names as soon as I was told them because of the horrid way they were both appraising me.

Their mother seems slightly nicer, but I think she's probably being nice because of Sophia.

Another look comes my way. I was pretending I didn't notice her looking at me, but I'm done doing that, so I look right back at her, glaring, which surprises her so much she looks away quickly.

God, I need air.

I can't deal with shit like this now.

If we're leaving soon, I don't see why I have to sit in here with them treating me like I'm a fucking leper.

I push to my feet, and Sophia glances up at me.

"Are you okay, dear?" she asks. "Forgive us for getting carried away with our traveling plans. It's been a while."

"I just need some air. Is it okay to go out on the terrace?" I reply.

"Of course, that's no problem."

"Thanks."

They all watch me as I walk out, and I'm sure as soon as the door closes, I'll be the talk amongst them.

I don't care. I can't care. Their lives are different from mine, and so are their life experiences. When you've been through what I have, women being bitches are the least of your worries.

Besides, I'm only receiving the treatment I expected to get coming here.

It's just good it's not coming from the one person I worried about the most—Mikhail's father. Although I don't know what he's talking to Mikhail about.

I can't worry about that, either.

Everything José told me is on my mind.

Nothing is sitting well with me, but I have no power.

The only power I have now is my present behavior.

I have to keep doing what I'm doing.

So, I keep pretending I'm Adriana Alvarez.

The problem is not knowing when things will happen. It's all so risky.

I could have this whole escape route in mind, but what happens if I'm discovered before that time?

That's not going to be good for me.

At least I know José was able to buy me more time by getting rid of everything I was worried about in Mexico that could identify Adriana.

Knowing he'd done so eased my mind. Only to a certain degree, though, because the threat of exposure is still very much there, and neither of us knows or will know where that threat will come from.

I just wish there were something more I could do for myself. It's not fair José has to do everything.

What would I do, though?

What can I do?

And what can I do in this confused state I always find myself in when I'm with Mikhail?

I think I'm at the point where I can accept that I feel something for him.

I know I do.

I can feel it stirring inside me, no matter how much I resist.

The feeling truly hit me last night in full force as I took a peek into his soul and saw the man who lay inside the monster. My heart has been a pattering mess since.

Throughout the day, as I've thought of him and my conversation with José, my heart has turned over and locked in confusion.

I want to push it all away, but like the flames of fire, he

entices me to him. I keep touching those flames, moving my hand deeper and deeper into them even though I know I'm going to get burned.

"Enjoying the view?" comes a voice from behind me that sends a shiver of ice down my spine.

When I turn to see Ivan watching me, my skin erupts with goose bumps. The pimples scatter across my flesh and tingling my scalp.

It's amazing. It's cold enough out here for my breath to hang in the air. I don't have my coat on, and my shoulders are bare, but I wasn't cold until this man approached me.

What is it about him that feels so off to me?

He is creepy, but there's more to him. All the warning bells are going off in my head, telling me to beware and be careful of what I say.

"I just needed some fresh air," I answer, and he takes that as an invitation to come closer.

There's a hint of a smile on his face. Not a friendly or humorous smile. It's one that has a taunting vibe tacked on to it.

He looks different than Mikhail. So different I wouldn't think they were brothers, but they both have striking similarities to their father. Ivan has light blue eyes, paler skin, and lighter brown hair. Whereas Mikhail has darker features, and his skin almost has the same olive tone as mine.

Ivan is also slimmer built with leaner muscle, while Mikhail has muscles on muscles. The brothers couldn't be more different.

"Was it too stuffy inside? The women can be a little overbearing in their chatter." His smile widens.

"They were okay. They were talking about traveling. Since I haven't travelled much, it was interesting to hear."

He observes my face and narrows his eyes for a fraction before looking me up and down.

It's weird to be so analytical right in front of someone's face.

"Is something wrong?" I ask when he continues to assess me.

"I don't think so. It's just that you look familiar, but that wouldn't make sense."

My mouth goes dry, and I find it hard to swallow past the lump in my throat.

How awful it would be to come this far only for this man to recognize me. But how would he recognize me?

Raul kept me away from his business associates, and if I saw any of them, they never saw me.

I never saw Ivan at any point. Never.

With that reasoning, I shake my head and gather my strength, but I still search my mind and try to figure out why he'd think I look familiar.

"I definitely don't think you've met me before," I tell him. I don't know where I find the courage to speak with such confidence, but I do. "My... father kept me away from his associates."

"Of course," he agrees, dipping his head. "Kept you on a leash, so to speak. I guess there was just something in you I recognized, but I must be mistaken."

The instant he says that, something hits me.

An idea strikes, and I think of where the threat I was worried about might come from.

My mother.

There's a chance he could have met my mother. Both my parents had dealings with Raul's associates. I'm not sure in what ways she would have known him, but it seems like it's possible they met.

The first thing anyone who meets me who's met her says is how much I look like her.

My only differences are my hair and eyes. Those are my main Mexican features, but when you look at me, you can find the underlying Caucasian features she inherited from her Irish roots.

Jesus, what do I do if he links me to her?

He straightens and seems to shrug off the idea, but I can already tell he's moved on to something else in his mind.

"How is Mikhail treating you?" He steps a little closer and rests his hands on the stone rail.

"Fine. He treats me fine."

That smile returns with a wicked glint lurking in his eyes. "Enjoy it while it lasts." He slants closer to me, and a rake of shivers courses down my body. "I'm sure that will change after the wedding."

I rivet my gaze to his, realizing I'm back at that place again with that question hanging over my head. What's going to happen to me after the wedding?

He seems to have the answer I seek.

"In what ways will things change?" I ask in a small voice.

"Let's not kid ourselves here. Do you seriously believe my all-powerful, conquering villain of a brother is going to tie himself down to the daughter of the man who killed his mother and our sister?"

I note the way he says *his mother* and *our sister*. I realize then they must not have the same mother. That's why they look so different.

I think Ivan must have wanted me to know that, or he wouldn't have said it. Or maybe he wasn't aware he did. I feel like he doesn't waste words, though, like everything he says is designed to hit where it's supposed to hurt most.

It's working.

"My brother is not the kind of man who will tie himself to one woman, and he certainly won't do that with you."

"What will he do with me?" My heart squeezes, and I try to fight back the burn of tears in the backs of my eyes.

"I'm sure once you stop being his favorite fuck toy, he'll sell you for a pretty penny."

Sell me?

Everything inside me freezes in the cold air enveloping us.

Mikhail is going to sell me?

I'm going to be sold. The same terrible fate I feared before. The same terrible fate I thought I'd escaped.

I wish I could believe this man was just taunting me, but why would he do that? Why would he be so crude to rattle my brain if it wasn't true?

"He'll sell me?" I can scarcely get the words out.

Ivan reaches out to touch my cheek and lean even closer. The flicker of desire in his eyes confirms there's no mistake in my prior thoughts about his interest in me.

"Sell you or give you to me. I'll happily take you, Adriana Alvarez." He moves to my ear, and his breath whispers over my skin. "Maybe by then you'll need a hard fuck from someone who can fuck you properly."

Fear grips me in its icy claws, and I find it hard to move away from his callous words.

It's the sound of someone clearing their throat behind us that makes Ivan move away from me.

When I see Mikhail standing by the doorframe, my awareness returns, and my first instinct is to run to him.

How could I feel like that, though, if he'd sell me or give me to his brother when he's done with me?

I'm not safe with anyone or anywhere. That is the only true thing and the only fact I can trust. No matter what he seems to feel for me.

"Keeping my wife-to-be company, brother?" Mikhail asks with a sarcastic edge. He sounds like he's trying his best to hold it together.

"You know me," Ivan replies.

Mikhail grits his teeth and starts speaking Russian. I have no idea what he's saying, but the sharpness and firm timbre in which he speaks suggest it can't be anything good.

Ivan answers back in the same tone, but a mocking smirk lights up his face.

Mikhail finally sneers and holds out his hand to me.

"Malyshka, let's go," he states, with his eyes blazing.

I take his hand again and allow him to lead me away from Ivan.

I feel Ivan's cold stare on me with every step I take. Even when Mikhail and I get in the car and drive away, I feel it haunting me like a bad dream.

I glance at Mikhail when we get on the open road and wonder how he could call me his in one breath and give me away in another.

Maybe that's just the type of monster he is.

I need to know what he's planning.

If it's what Ivan said, I'm screwed. There will be *no* escape route for me.

Chapter Twenty Eight

Natalia

We drive back home in the same silence we left in hours ago.

It settles over us, and I'm so lost in my thoughts I'm too afraid to breathe.

I can tell he's the same and that heated argument, or whatever the hell it was he had with his brother, has put him in a bad mood.

Mikhail has spent most of the journey clenching the steering wheel like he wants to wring someone's neck.

When we get back to the house, he maintains his silence and walks with me upstairs to the bedroom. All the while I try to think of a way to talk to him and ask the questions weighing heavily on my heart.

It's late, so I expect we'll fall into bed, but he doesn't look like he's going to. He looks like he's gearing up to go out again.

He watches me as I take off my heels and walks over to me to help me undo the zipper on the back of my dress.

He continues to stand behind, and we both look at our reflection in the long mirror. It scares me how good we look together. Staring at the reflection of ourselves is like looking at someone's idea of a joke that ended up working.

Like throwing spaghetti on a wall and watching it actually stick like glue.

His warm fingers flutter over the bare skin of my back, snapping my mind back into focus.

"I don't want you talking to my brother if you can help it," he mutters.

I turn around to face him.

"Why?" After what Ivan said to me, I sound foolish to my own ears for asking that question, but I want to know why *he* doesn't want me to talk to his brother.

"Because I say so."

"You think just because you say so, it's reason enough for me to be rude to your family."

He grits his teeth. "Just fucking listen to me. I don't want you talking to him or be alone with him. He's not a good person."

"And you are?" I know I'm poking the beast in the worst way. I can't help myself. Everything is making me crazy, and I hate that there's nothing I can do to save myself from this mess.

"Malyshka, do not let me punish you. You won't like it. It won't be anything close to what you liked previously."

He steps away and heads toward the door, confirming my thoughts of him going out.

"Where are you going?"

"To work."

"It's late."

He opens the door, and I want to scream and shout. I want to beg him to stay and tell me what he's going to do with me.

I don't want to be sold or given away to someone like Ivan.

Desperation gets the better of me, and I pick up the paperweight on the table and throw it into the wall.

It smashes, and he stops in his tracks then turns back to me.

"What the fuck is wrong with you?" he growls, his eyes blazing

"Are you going to sell me?" I choke out. Just saying the words to him fills me with terror. "Is that what you're going to do to me after the wedding? Sell me? Or give me away?"

An uncontrollable tear slides down my cheek, and another follows. I hate crying, and worst of all, crying in front of him.

All I need now is for him to be the ruthless bastard he is and tell me yes.

But I'm the devil, too, because here I am, planning to escape the moment his back is turned or the instant someone puts a bullet in him to take him down.

But the thing about that is, I couldn't do it. I couldn't just run away and leave him to die so I can save myself. But he could sell me without batting an eye.

He walks back to me and stops a breath away to level me with a stare.

"Who told you that?" he asks.

"It doesn't matter. You never did answer me that night when I asked you, what you wanted with me. You told me to go back to sleep. Why can't you just give me an answer to a simple question? All I want to know is if you plan to sell me once I stop being a fuck toy."

"Fuck toy?" he mutters pensively, and then his face hardens in understanding. "What did my brother say to you, Adriana?"

He knows.

"He said you would sell me or give me to him."

His eyes darken with rage, and I swear the vein throbbing on the side of his head is going to pop.

He crowds me against the wall, and when my back hits the smooth wallpapered surface, the air leaves my lungs.

"Is that what you're going to do, Mikhail?" I whisper, and he crushes his mouth to mine for a raw, unapologetic kiss.

He ravishes my lips, kissing me like he wants to possess me. He's always intense. *Always.*

This time, however, feels like he's desperate to take that last piece of me I try to hold on to for myself. His hungry lips consume me, and I take what he gives me knowing I've gone over that line of reason and crossed over into madness.

This is insanity. It crawls into my mind and weaves an invisible web of temptation I have no hope of escaping.

Only he could do this to me.

Only he could break me down like this with just a kiss that makes me relinquish my heart, body, mind, and soul.

He cups my jaw, and his lips wander over my cheeks, my eyes, my chin, my nose. Then brushes over my lips at the same time he lifts my dress up to my hips and pushes his fingers into my pussy.

He moves his nose over mine, inhaling me as he undoes his belt buckle and shoves down his pants.

Lifting my leg to hook it around his waist, he positions his cock at my entrance and rubs along my sex.

He lifts my jaw next and lowers his head so my eyes are in line with his. A wicked smile dances on his lips.

"No. My answer is no. Malyshka. I'm not going to sell you or give you to anybody, because you're *mine.*"

I'm already wet for him, so when he thrusts into my pussy, my body welcomes him.

I can't answer, but I don't need to.

My body does the talking for me when I slip my arms around his neck and I pull him back to my lips to kiss him.

I do that.

Me.

And he welcomes me like he's mine, too.

A jolt of wild sexual energy lances through me like fire, and pleasure steals the remaining breath from my lungs.

His pumps speed up, plundering my body, going deeper and deeper inside me as he fucks me hard and sure.

Every touch, every kiss, every careless whisper of sweet nothings in Russian sends me closer to climax. Then it comes. I come, and mindless ecstasy cripples through my body and our hearts pound together, beating as one. Our bodies quiver, sharing the release, and we both surrender to the force that's been driving us together.

Even when I feel him come, he doesn't stop kissing me or touching me.

We continue just like this, and I know everything will be different when we stop. Nothing will ever be the same again.

Chapter Twenty-Nine

Mikhail

"Ride me, baby," I tell her, squeezing her hips as she straddles my cock and moves over me. She looks like a fantasy come to life when her hair bounces as she does, and her gorgeous tits move up and down in front of my face. "Harder, fuck me the way you want to."

She does exactly what I tell her to do like the good girl she is, and the sizzling sensation that pours over my soul eradicates any thought and responsibility from my brain.

I have that mind-fucked feeling a drug would produce where I can't think of anything that's not her, and in the moments I do, I remember my threats to Ivan to watch himself. She wouldn't have known what I was saying because I spoke in Russian. I didn't want her knowing of the bad relationship I have with my brother just yet.

I'm sure she guessed, though. It wasn't hard. And when I see him next, I'll make sure he gets the message loud and clear to leave my woman alone.

I just need one more time before I leave.

One more time.

Seconds pass by, then minutes, then hours, and I can't make myself stop.

It's worse than the other night when we were like this.

We fuck until we fall into sleep, and all plans of what I had to do get pushed to the back of the shelf.

When the sun comes up and we open our eyes, I'm inside her again. I take breaks to get us food and water, and then I find myself back inside her.

I've lost my mind and given in to recklessness, taking comfort in the fact that my phone hasn't rung, which generally means I'm not needed.

By no means does it mean I don't have any work. There's so much to do, but I can't stop touching her.

The sun comes up again, and we're the same.

I have her on her hands and knees, fucking her from behind in her sweet pussy and in her asshole.

The day ends the same way, and I close my eyes, feeling the changes and the gears shifting in my mind.

On day three, I wake before her, and when I touch her, she's so exhausted she doesn't move, which is what breaks the spell.

That's what brings me back to reality and my responsibilities, and I make myself get off the bed.

Before I leave, I look at her and notice that she feels like she belongs to me. When I leave, I feel her everywhere, I smell the scent of her sweetness and taste her in the air.

I can't control myself no matter how hard I try to bleed her from my mind. I can't do it.

I feel some ounce of myself coming back, however, as I march down the hallway to Ivan's office at Dmitriyev Ltd.

It's early. He won't be in yet, but I can wait.

He's not going to get away with what he said to Adriana. I won't allow it. Being away the last three days has given him the respite he didn't deserve. Now he will feel my wrath.

Before I get to his office, I hear him inside, and he's not

alone. I was hoping for the element of surprise, but this is better.

I push the door open without knocking and find him fucking his new secretary over his desk.

Fucking typical Ivan. No wonder the motherfucker is early.

His secretary, who is completely naked, screams when she sees me and reaches for her clothes.

"Get the fuck out," I tell her, and she quickens her pace in putting her clothes back on.

"Haven't you fucking heard of knocking!" Ivan barks.

"No."

His secretary scurries past me, and I slam the door shut behind me.

He starts saying some shit about privacy, but I march over to him and throw a punch in his face, sending him to the ground.

I split his nose and blood sprays over his white shirt.

He jumps up ready to fight me, but I grab him by the throat and slam him into the wall.

He grips my neck and squeezes tight, like he thinks he can kill me. I have news for him because I've tasted death and been to Hell. It's going to take more to send me back there.

"Motherfucker," he hisses.

"Yes, I fucking am," I growl back in his face. "How fucking dare you tell my girl I'm going to fucking sell her?"

I knee him in his stomach, and he doubles over, releasing whatever grip he had on me.

"How fucking dare you, Ivan? Stay the fuck away from her."

He starts laughing, and the sound throws me.

"What the fuck are you laughing at, prick?" I shout.

He laughs even harder, and I shove him away from me.

He stumbles back into the wall.

"I'm laughing at you, *brother*. Look at you."

"What the hell is funny about me?"

"You can't even see it, can you? You have the same flaw as our father, stupid over a pretty face. It only took less than two weeks for you to lose your mind over easy pussy, and that's why you will never be a good leader."

"Shut the fuck up." I move to throw another punch, but he blocks me and catches my arm.

"Struck a nerve, have I? Look how long ago I saw you and said what I said to your girl. It took you three days to come and find me. She was upset when you left. I'm sure she would have told you right off the bat what your big brother said to her, and yet it took you three days to get here and kick my ass." He pauses and laughs. "Newsflash, Mikhail, you stink of sex and love. You reek of it. Love is overflowing from your eyes. You're in love with her, aren't you?"

"Shut the fuck up."

"How can you love the spawn of the man responsible for your mother and sister's death? How can you think that's okay? How, Mikhail? Look what they did to Talia, and yet you've come in here to beat me down. Me, your brother, your family. You've come to kick my ass over pussy. Shame on you."

I wrench my arm free from him and glare at him.

I want to tell him to shut up again. I want to tell him he's wrong about me.

I want to say I don't love her and list all the reasons why I can't be what he's accusing me of, but my lips won't move.

I step back and bare my teeth.

"Stay away from me and mine, brother. I mean it."

He answers with a chuckle, and I leave before we can really get into it and fight like we've been known to in the past.

We were both holding back there, and if I fight like I want to this time, I'll probably end up killing him.

I stumble into the atrium and find a corner by the water cooler where I can take a moment to myself.

I can't be in love with Adriana.

Love was never in the cards, and I know better than to fall for her.

I can't be in love because I know it will be my weakness, and I can't be weak right now, or ever. Now is the time for strength.

What Ivan said regarding our father and my mother pricks at my mind. I can't argue with him. Not when Father bared his soul to me nights before.

If anyone ever needed an example of what love should look like, all they needed to do was look at my parents. My father told me himself he was waiting for death.

I just had to fill in the blanks. Before my mother was killed, he looked forward to spending the rest of his days with her, however little time he had left.

Now he wants death so he can be with her.

Losing her destroyed him.

I can't lose myself like that.

I've moved past the fact that Adriana is Raul's daughter. That doesn't bother me anymore. If I were hung up on that, I wouldn't be contemplating anything right now.

This is about me. I can't be me if I succumb to something I know will cripple me eventually. Doing so goes against me as a person.

The only thing to do to stop that from happening is to go back to the original plan of business. Marry the girl and take the cartel.

That's all it needs to be. That's all it *should* be. And the only way to free her from my mind is to avoid her and put that wall back up I had in place when we first met.

That is what I need to do.

I go through the day with that in mind, working until late in the night to catch up on my workload from the last three days.

Just before I pack up to leave, I get a message from Eric asking if he can meet me at home.

I realize he must have something for me to look at, but it's the fact that he wants to meet me at home that piques my attention.

I head home as quickly as I can and find him in my office waiting for me.

He's holding a manilla envelope.

"You better sit down for this," he states the moment the door closes.

I release a tired sigh and sit opposite him on the leather sofa.

"What did you find?"

"It's not good, but I'll keep my opinions to myself and allow you to form your own." He hands me the envelope. "That was in one of the emails. It was heavily encrypted. When I opened it, I saw the reason why. It's the contract. Raul's copy of the assassination contract."

My scalp tightens with this information.

I open the envelope and pull out the three-pages long document.

I don't need to read the whole thing.

The top paragraph tells me everything and changes the game entirely.

This contract is to secure the deaths of the following parties:
Elena, Talia, and Mikhail Dmitriyev.
Following their deaths, shares of equal values will be
distributed to you once the ownership of Dmitriyev Ltd. and the
Baranov Bratva are transferred.

I stop reading when a stone drops in the pit of my stomach and shock slams through me.

All this time, I believed the assassination attempt was on my family as a whole unit. I thought it was about all of us.

But it wasn't.

It was just about my mother, my sister, and me.

Why?

"It was never about everybody."

"No, Mikhail. It was not."

I stare at Eric, but he looks like he's already formed his conclusions.

"My past has taught me to keep my mind open. I told you that sometimes, the answer is right under your nose. You and I have been friends for quite a few years now, and we've done a lot together in that time, so believe me when I say I've been a friend to you and I'm doing exactly that when I say this." He stops for a moment and presses his lips together. "Someone was watching you. They knew your every move. They think they have the power to do shit like transfer shares of the company equally, but only when the ownership is transferred. They also wanted you, your mother, and sister out of the picture. There's only one person I can think of who would fit that description."

There's only one person I can think of who would do this to me, too, but I can't believe he'd do all of this. Kill *me* maybe. But my mother and sister?

Why not?

He would do it if he stood to gain something and they were in his way.

We were all in his way.

"Ivan," I mutter, and Eric nods.

"Yes, old friend."

Chapter Thirty

Mikhail

I remember when I had my first fight with my brother.

I was eight and he was eighteen. We went on a camping trip, and he was supposed to be watching me while our parents went out.

He told me to play by the river and urged me to go past the signs that told everyone to keep away because it was dangerous.

Of course, I fell in the river because the reason the signs were there was the ground being unstable.

The current was so strong I couldn't swim against it, yet Ivan stood on the bank watching me go down the river, crying for help.

Someone heard me screaming. It was an old man. He jumped in and saved me.

When our parents got back, Ivan lied and told everyone I disobeyed him and ventured out against his caution.

I got in trouble, but that night, I tackled him about his lie. I punched him, and he broke my arm. Another lie was told about how that happened, and because he was older, everyone

239

believed him. No one would believe an eighteen-year-old would do such a thing to a little kid or try to drown him in the river.

I must have been around eighteen before our parents started listening to me.

It was clear starting back then that my brother wanted me dead. I just couldn't understand his deep hatred for me.

Now I see. I truly, truly do.

I stand and walk over to the window, resting my hands on the white wooden ledge.

"Mikhail." Eric says my name tentatively.

It takes me a moment to return my focus to him, and when I do, I can tell he knows I'm going to lose my shit.

"Ivan actually teamed up with Raul and fuck knows who else to get rid of my mother, my sister, and me." I speak the words more to myself than him. "All so he could take over the empire."

Seeing I'm having a hard time grasping the truth, Eric simply nods.

"I might be wrong, but that hardly ever happens when I have strong suspicions." He looks uneasy. "I know things are already tense between you and your brother. The last thing I want to do is cause more problems, but I wouldn't be a friend to you if I didn't call it like I see it, or think it is. I would do the same to anyone else. I'm basing my conclusions on how things look to me."

When I think of it, things look that way to me, too.

We thought the problem had to do with someone big and powerful. Someone more powerful than Raul. Ivan is exactly that.

We thought someone inside the Brotherhood was helping Raul. Ivan is exactly that.

We knew the person had to be watching our every move and would know our whereabouts at all times. Ivan was exactly that. Except he didn't need to watch anybody. All he had to do was ask, and we'd tell him.

It was easy to isolate everyone on the night of the attack because Father was sick. That was the opportunity to split us up.

Ivan knew Talia really wanted me at the performance because I hadn't seen her dance all season. He also knew neither my mother nor father would have both wanted to miss her performance, so he would have been best placed to go to the office and do Father's work. Also, that Sophia would have offered to take care of my father.

It would have been easy for him.

Father told me the investigation team came back with the all-clear on Raul, yet Eric found fault and hinted at the possibility that they missed things on purpose. If such was the case, it makes sense now because my father also said Ivan personally assisted them.

So, either he covered things up, or he has them eating out of the palm of his hand.

Fuck. I can't believe this.

"I really can't believe this."

"I can't either, and I have no hardcore evidence. Just suspicion that points toward him."

I could deal with this possibility if this was just about me, but my mother and sister are dead. Killed in the worst ways possible because of him.

Because he wanted to be Pakhan and take over the company.

"Something doesn't add up," he adds.

"What else?"

"I feel like there must be more to it than just the leadership and the company. That's more about you. He wouldn't have needed your mother or sister dead if that's all it was."

"No, he wouldn't. He wouldn't have needed them dead at

all. Just me. I'm the one standing in his way of the leadership for all."

"Then we need to look at the reasons why he'd want the three of you dead. Do you know what is in your father's will?"

I shake my head. "No. No one is supposed to know that. Not even my father's lawyers. Not yet. He's been secretive about it."

"He must have told someone something. The ticking clock is all based around when he chooses to pass on the leadership and ownership. Maybe he told Ivan something, or Sophia, and Ivan found out. I guess that part is irrelevant. The part we need to worry about is you being a loose end. He's still going to want you dead."

God, this is shit. All of it.

"I wonder what stopped him from killing me while I was in the hospital."

Eric thinks for a moment. "Your father had you under strict supervision, and the Voirik were called in to assist. If people are working from your brotherhood with Ivan, they might not have had access to kill you."

"God. He never told Raul I was alive, either. Both he and Felipe looked shocked I survived." They both looked like they'd seen a ghost.

"Did he offer to go with you to Mexico?"

"He didn't." And I was so hyped up on rage and grief I never questioned it. Then again, I wouldn't because he was here *investigating*.

"So, maybe he wanted you to kill Raul. Think about it. If the plan was still on and you were in a coma, then he might have just been watching and waiting for you to wake up and find out what you remembered. If you died, it would have made no difference to the plan. You being alive, though, identi-fied Felipe and, of course, Raul. So, they both had to die."

"My God. All this is happening, and the more we talk, the

242

more I suspect him. But I can't say anything to my father without proof. This is going to break him."

He gives me a sympathetic stare. "I'm still working on the files. There's still a lot to go through, but I'll get it done and hopefully find something there. I suggest we focus on watching Ivan and seeing what we can get that way."

"I'll track his every move."

"You're going to have to be careful with who you trust, Mikhail," he cautions. "You don't know who else might be working for him."

Damn it. "It could be anybody I know."

I think of Sebastian and hope like fuck my brother didn't sway him. I doubt it, but I don't know. That's the fucking problem with betrayal. Those who fit the bill to betray you are the people closest to you. It wouldn't work otherwise.

"Let's keep numbers small for now. You and me. If we need more muscle and brains, I got the hookup in L.A. I'll come here to meet with you. I don't think my presence at the office will help. We need Ivan to think you're on your own. In the meantime, I'll check everyone out, and him, too."

"I keep saying I owe you."

He smirks. "We'll talk about that when you repay me." He pushes to his feet. "Sorry for the bad news, old friend."

"It's okay."

It has to be.

* * *

As the hours tick by, I'm aware of the two new elements I now have to contend with.

Ivan's treachery and the woman in my bed upstairs who's wondering where I am.

I have to deal with both.

I can't allow my brother to take over, and I can't allow the woman to make me soft so I slip up and don't recognize the danger for what it is.

The next morning, I come up with a plan to set things in motion.

Something that seems like another joke the universe is playing on me.

I wonder if it is when José Diaz walks into my home office. Aleksander is just walking away after ushering him up here.

José must be wondering why I sent for him and why I'm not meeting him at Dmitriyev Ltd.

"Close the door and sit," I tell him.

He does and sits in the same chair Eric was in last night.

"Is everything okay, Señor?"

"Not exactly." So far, this man is the only guy in this game who doesn't have anything at stake and doesn't have anything to lose.

Nobody has promised him anything except his life in exchange for his help.

The only thing he values is that and Adriana.

"What's going on?"

"I need to change up your work a little," I reply. "I need you to split your time between the office in town and working here on the grounds of my home."

He narrows his eyes in confusion. "What do you want me to do here?"

"You'll be working here with Sebastian. I need you to watch over Adriana. But I also need you to watch everyone else."

"Everyone else, including Sebastian?" He straightens.

"Everyone including Sebastian, and everyone who works for me."

Understanding forms in his eyes. "You trust me that much to watch your men, Señor?"

"No, I don't trust you. In fact, I don't even like you. But if I told you the princess's life could be in danger and someone worse than me may take her to get control of the cartel, I know you would protect her with your life. Is that right, José?"

He nods without thinking. "I would. She's like a daughter to me."

"Then do this for me. You notice something wrong, you tell me, and more importantly, you don't speak to anybody else but me. Got it?"

"Sí."

Chapter Thirty-One

Natalia

I remember the days not so long ago when I would wish the minutes and hours away and pray I wouldn't see Mikhail.

I would spend my days with Snow, walking the grounds of his home to pass the time and gather my thoughts.

I was a mess every time I saw him. Now I'm a mess not for seeing him.

Over two weeks have passed now since we last saw each other.

We're supposed to be getting married in a few days.

I know he's been at the house, though, and this isn't a case where he's been away. Aleksander has been given me Mikhail's orders. At other times, I've felt eyes watching me.

His eyes.

But every time I turn and look for him, he's not there. He's nowhere.

I know I'm not seeing him because we went too far over the line, and it disappeared.

That's why.

If I have any sense, I'll retreat, too, and protect my heart. What the hell do I expect from a man like Mikhail Dmitriyev?

Love?

Do I truly expect love when everything is so wild and reckless when we're together? We've never actually sat down and had a conversation that didn't end with him doing something sexual to me.

The only time might have been my first day here when he told me I was as evil as Raul.

We have nothing in common, and he's supposed to be my enemy.

He's just been the sensible person out of the two of us and severed the link before it could grow any stronger.

I'm pretty sure I won't see him until our wedding day.

That sounds so weird.

We're getting married, and we'll have a loveless marriage.

I'm a fake, and he's my captor.

We exist on lies and secrets.

A mockery to any vow we'll be taking when we say, 'I do.'

If I survive, this is what life will be like because we aren't supposed to be.

This sham is an arranged marriage for business purposes, and I forgot that somewhere along the way. As I lay beneath him repeatedly, I forgot who he was supposed to be to me.

There was never a question of love in the mix. And since I'm not who he thinks I am and I was never supposed to be here, things are working out exactly how they're supposed to.

At least I know he's not going to sell me or give me to Ivan. And the only good thing to come of this time apart is seeing more of José.

He's been working here at the house, but because Sebastian is here, too, José and I hardly have the chance to speak like we did that day over a week ago.

I still take comfort in seeing him. It's something, and if he's around, I know I'm safe and there's hope in some form.

I just wish there weren't this hole in my heart or this empty feeling in my soul when I think of Mikhail.

This coming weekend will mark one month since he's been in my life. One month of chaos with this constant push and pull of my heart.

When I asked José more about what was going on, he said things were still the same and Mikhail just wanted more security here. Of course, that just made me curious about what else was going on to make Mikhail want additional security. I didn't push, however, because I knew José would have told me if there was anything more to tell.

I've spent the day outside with Snow. The weather is getting better as it transitions to spring. It hasn't snowed all week, and there's a hint of warmth in the air. When you spend as much time outside as I do, you notice things like that.

When it gets dark, I head back to the house to put Snow in her room.

There I see José waiting for me.

"Just checking on you," he says with a little smile. He crouches down to pat the dog on her head for a moment before he stands. "How are you doing?"

"I'm okay," I lie. "As okay as I can be."

"I'm sorry I have no news for you."

He says the same thing each time.

"That's okay. At least I'm safe."

He reaches out to pat my head the way he used to when I was little.

"When we're free, I'll get you an ice cream. The biggest one we can buy," he promises, and I can't help but chuckle. It's been so long since I smiled it feels foreign to me.

"Ice cream, José?"

When I was little and life was normal, my parents would meet up with José nearly every weekend. We'd go to the beach, and he'd get the biggest ice cream cone for me. It was he who took that picture I have of my parents and me on the beach. That time, he came with us to see my grandmother. Those are some great memories.

"Never too old, my little chica. You will always be my little girl, and I am your second father. So, I can promise you ice cream when I get you out of this mess. That's the first thing we'll buy when we get our first taste of freedom. I'm sure your Papito will forgive me for giving his little girl sweet things."

"Yes, I'm sure he will, and you can buy me anything you want. Let me take care of you, too."

He taps my head again. "No. I promised your father I would always take care of you. That's my job. Nothing is required of you. Only to live. You hear me?"

I nod, but I promise myself if we do get out of here, I will look after him, too.

"We just have to take each day as it comes," he adds.

Talk of leaving has me thinking about Mikhail again, and my curiosity stirs.

"Where's Mikhail, José? I haven't seen him at all. I just want to know where he is, or if he said anything to you about when I might see him again."

He looks me over without saying anything, and I think he can sense that my questions run deeper than mere curiosity.

"You have feelings for him," he states, worry now clouding his eyes.

"It's not that." I run a hand over my head and try to smile past my embarrassment at being caught out.

"You can't fool an old fool, Natalia. I can see it. You can't give your heart to a man like that, little one. You will get hurt. I assure you, you'll get hurt. Don't do it. This is a means to an end and not the path any of the people who loved you would have chosen for you. Please don't make the mistake of falling for a man who can't give you what you need."

He touches my cheek, and I nod, agreeing with him.

I agree. I just can't get my heart to listen to me.

I'm still trying to get my heart to listen on Saturday as the limousine pulls up at the church.

Sophia is sitting next to me. She is my only company, and apart from José the only person who will be here for me.

She seems excited but I'm so nervous I feel like I might throw up.

I'm on autopilot as I walk in through the back entrance of the church, where I'm supposed to go in for the bridal march.

We've arrived just in time for the nuptials.

"You look beautiful, dear." She fusses over me, straightening a wisp of my hair and removing an invisible piece of lint on my veil.

"Thanks."

"Are you ready?"

I'm not sure what to say. I'm not ready. The only thing I could be ready for is running through the door we came in and jumping into the first vehicle that will get me out of here.

I don't want to go through the doors in front of me. Those doors will lead to my groom.

I don't want to see him and face the rejection on his face.

I don't want to have these strong feelings for him I never asked for, only to feel like I'm nothing but a business deal.

I don't want to feel that thing inside me luring me to love him because that will push me to accept the lie I always was to him.

So, no, I'm not ready.

But saying no was never an option.

"Yes," I tell her, and she smiles.

"Then God speed." She opens the door, and I take a peek inside at the people waiting for me.

This part should be simple.

I have no father to walk me down the aisle and no one here for me.

Our vows are simple, too. Two paragraphs of a handful of words.

As I look inside the church and see his guests, nothing about this feels simple.

The pews to the left hold the cartel heads and some of their families. The pews to the right are filled with Mikhail's guests. The Bratva.

When the organist starts playing the traditional wedding march song, I move and look straight ahead, neither to the left nor the right, and I walk.

When I get to the middle of the church, I look at my groom, and he watches me, too.

His father is standing next to him, and he is next to the priest.

Our eyes lock and I want to look away, but I can't.

I feel his brother's eyes on me as I walk by, but I don't look in his direction. I just note his existence from my periphery.

Who I'm focused on is the man ahead of me who stole me away and stole my heart, too. A man I know I mustn't love.

I'm still so confused, because I think I do.

If I didn't fall for him, I don't think I would feel like this, and my heart wouldn't yearn for him.

That last time we were together, I gave him everything. Everything I said I wouldn't give. He never had to take it. I all but handed it to him on a platter so he could have it. Have me.

So, the only person to blame here is me.

When I reach him, my legs shake and my hands tremble so much the lilies in the bouquet shudder.

In the bright sunlight, those honey-colored eyes greet me, taking me in. When he looks at me in that way, it's hard to forget the way we were when we were last together.

Mikhail's eyes bore into me as I study his handsome face.

Is he thinking of that last time, too?

If he is, does he feel anything, or nothing?

Maybe what I thought I got from him is all in my head.

The priest is talking, but I don't hear. Mikhail breaks eye contact with me and looks at him, so I assume it must be time to start the ceremony.

I met Father Gabriel once in the last week when he came by the house to go over the vows with me. He's a tall man with lily-white hair and dark green eyes. He looks at both of us fondly with a smile. When we first met, I got the impression he was accustomed to Mikhail.

I have the same impression now.

"You may now say your vows," Father Gabriel says.

Mikhail turns to me and fixes his gaze to mine. I wonder how he'll speak his vows without meaning them.

"I, Mikhail Yevgeny Dmitriyev, take you, Adriana Maria Alvarez, for my lawful wife, to have and to hold, from this day forward, for better, for worse, for richer, for poorer, in sickness and in health, until death do us part."

Adriana Maria Alvarez.

A wave of nausea hits me at the mention of her name, and the stab of jealousy. Even in death, on my wedding day, she still mocks me. She still takes from me. I am the joke because I'm not real. This man I shouldn't have feelings for isn't speaking his vows to me. He's vowing to her. She is who he wants. Not Natalia Lily de Leon.

I glance at José, who I glimpsed to our far left. I'm not sure if he can see the sadness in my eyes from all the way over here, but he nods, and I return my focus to Mikhail.

It's my turn to say my vows. and he's looking at me with expectancy.

"I, Adriana Maria Alvarez, take you, Mikhail Yevgeny Dmitriyev, for my lawful husband, to have and to hold, from this day forward, for better, for worse, for richer, for poorer, in sickness and in health, until death do us part." I say the words and feel numb.

We look at Father Gabriel again. It's time to marry us. Time to seal the bond.

He addresses Mikhail first. "Mikhail Yevgeny Dmitriyev, do you take Adriana Maria Alvarez for your lawful wife, to have and to hold, from this day forward, for better, for worse, for richer, for poorer, in sickness and in health, until death do you part?"

"I do," Mikhail replies.

Father Gabriel then turns to me and asks me the same question.

"I do," I reply.

"What God joins together, let no one pull asunder," Father Gabriel declares. I zone out from there, getting lost in my thoughts.

He blesses our marriage, and when we exchange rings, I can't take my eyes off Mikhail's.

"I now pronounce you husband and wife," Father Gabriel declares proudly, and I realize we did it. I did it. I got married.

Weeks ago, I was destined for an auction block to be sold as a sex slave. Now I'm the wife of Mikhail Dmitriyev.

"You may now kiss the bride," Father Gabriel adds.

Mikhail leans forward and kisses me, but not even close to the kisses we've shared.

This kiss is empty and hollow, just like this feeling in my soul.

It feels as wrong as we do.

Aleksander approaches us, and I don't know why, but I find myself staring at Mikhail's father, Sergei, as if my mind somehow thinks he can fix this.

At least he doesn't look at me in that coldhearted manner his son is. His son I just married.

"Aleksander, please take my wife home. I have business to attend to," Mikhail says, and I cut my gaze back to his.

He's not even coming home with me?

Of course not. The business is the cartel. The men sitting on the entire side of my right reminds me of that and what I am.

Whatever we had is over. It's clear it's done and there's no trace of it left in either of us.

It's over, and we just said 'I do.'

"Mrs. Dmitriyev," Aleksander calls me by my new name. "Come with me."

I don't embarrass myself any further by saying anything.

I just do as I'm told, look away, and follow Aleksander's lead when he ushers me away.

I manage to hold it together but find myself looking over my shoulder before we leave. I'm looking back at Mikhail, but he's not watching me. His eyes are on his brother, who is staring at me like the predator who just set his sight on his prey.

There is no mistake in the interest I detect in Ivan's eyes, nor the fury in my husband's stony gaze. It means trouble.

More trouble than I'm already in.

Chapter Thirty-Two

Natalia

"**W**ould you like anything else?" Sophia asks as we step out of the store.

One of her bodyguards tags along behind us carrying our shopping bags while the other two guard us. A reminder of the situation at hand.

I'm starting to feel nearly as sorry for myself as she probably feels for me. She came by this morning to take me shopping. We've spent the day doing so.

I would have preferred to stay inside the house and lick my wounds in private rather than be on show for all to see how pathetic I am.

The pathetic wife who got married five days ago and hasn't set eyes on her husband since.

"No," I mutter.

"How about something to eat? You didn't have much at lunch. We could have dinner at that restaurant you liked last week."

Last week, I ate like a pig because I was anxious about the

wedding. This week, I've barely eaten a thing because I'm anxious about how the rest of my life is going to play out.

I keep thinking Mikhail is spending his nights with one of his women.

Every time the thought pops into my head, my stomach twists into knots tighter than a macramé.

It's doing it now. Since it's nigh on nightfall and I suspect I'm going to spend another night without him, it's probably best I refrain from eating anything because I might throw up.

"Is it okay if we just head back. I'm a little tired." I attempt a smile, and she places an arm around me.

"Of course, that's no problem. I have tired you out." She laughs heartily.

"No, it's me." Because I haven't been sleeping. It's funny. I've been spending my nights the way I thought I was going to spend my first few nights of captivity—alone and locked away.

The novelty of me has worn off like a new toy that's lost its appeal.

Or in my case, I might be more like an animal that's lost its use and been put out to pasture. Mikhail controls the cartel now, and he's taken what he wanted from me. He has no further use for me. I wonder if he'll go back on his word and sell me or give me to his brother.

Sophia cuts into my worries when she links her arm with mine.

"There's a bake sale at the hospital next week. I'd love for you to attend. There are some important people you'd be interested in meeting."

I perk up a little to humor her. It's nice of her to spend time with me. Without her I'd probably sit in that house day in and out with the dog, the only living thing in there that likes me. The staff still treat me like shit, and the house still has that unwelcoming vibe.

"That sounds great. I'd love to go."

"I'm sure you'll love it even more when you meet my

friend. He's the dean at New York University. I told him about your interest in becoming a doctor."

I can't even muster the strength to look fascinated, because going to college is not something I think I'll be able to do.

I can't start something I always dreamed of doing only to stop when the shit hits the fan and I either have to flee because people found out I'm not who I say I am or for other reasons.

I couldn't do that to myself.

All I can hope for is that one day, something will happen for me to accomplish my dreams by some other means. But again, I humor her with a smile as fake as I am.

"Thank you so much. That would be amazing."

"I thought you'd like that." She chuckles. "Come on, let's get you home."

We get home half an hour later. Before she leaves, she steeps a Slovenian tea made of chamomile and lavender to relax me.

The mood I'm in, though, would most likely require a whole field of chamomile and lavender to work.

I spend the night thinking and worrying. Not sleeping.

I'm back at that place again where out of sight definitely does not mean out of mind. Seeing my enemy would give me an idea of what's happening on a day-to-day basis.

This nothingness is driving me crazy. It doesn't even help that I get to talk to José, because he can't help ease my mind, either.

The next day, I leave the house at breakfast, not bothering to eat. I take food for Snow, and we spend the day in the woods. I disobey the rules and stay out until it's late, and I don't eat.

I see no point in making myself feel worse by sitting at that table with the maids either ignoring me or talking about me in a language I don't understand.

I knew my actions wouldn't go unnoticed, but I didn't expect Aleksander to be waiting by the door when I got back.

With that stern expression on his face, he reminds me of one of my old headmasters everyone feared because he was so strict.

"Mrs. Dmitriyev, your husband requests your presence at dinner. Now," he informs me.

"Mikhail is actually here?" I hate the way my heart flutters for that bastard.

"Yes, ma'am."

He started calling me ma'am after I got married. It's either that or Mrs. Dmitriyev. I hate both. I long to be called Natalia. I never realized how much I would miss hearing my name.

Aleksander takes Snow, and I head to the bathroom to wash my hands and take off my coat.

I catch a glimpse of myself in the mirror and wince. I look tired and like I've aged a hundred years. My hair is up in a messy bun, and my eyes are red like I've been crying. I hope Mikhail doesn't think I've been sitting here crying over him.

Summoning courage and the *I-don't-give-a-shit-where-you've-been-for-the last-six-days* attitude I practiced, I walk out into the dining room, where I see my husband.

Dressed in black and sitting at the head of the table, he reminds me of weeks ago when I first saw him looking like that.

It feels like a lifetime has passed since that happened, yet it's been only two days shy of five weeks. I can't believe so much has happened in such a short period of time, or that I've matured so much.

It's like I've been to war.

His eyes pierce the distance between us and take me in as I walk up to him.

I wish I could feel nothing and like the time apart has made me feel less for him. But the only true thing about not being with him is that it's annoyingly made my fucking heart grow fonder.

Mikhail has the audacity to give me a smile that might pass as pleasant, *for him.*

"Malyshka, out late again?" he says, enunciating every syllable of my pet name I never thought I'd hear again. "I'm fairly certain I told you to take someone with you if you plan to be out until dark."

"I had Snow to keep me company, thank you." I sit in my designated seat opposite him. He continues to regard me.

"My concern isn't having someone to keep you company. It's more for safety. Snow is too little to keep you safe."

Safety?

This is the first we've spoken since we said our vows, and he's talking to me about safety. I'm about to snap because I feel that out-of-control emotion again. If he is so concerned about my safety, why has he been gone for so long?

Tomorrow will mark a week since our wedding, and this is the first fucking time I've seen him. Prior to that it was more than two fucking weeks.

"Where have you been?" I don't care if he thinks my tone is defiant or some shit like that. I think I'm in my right to ask.

"Working." He gives me a tightlipped smile.

"How come you're here?"

"I heard you weren't eating. So, I thought I'd check in."

I narrow my eyes at him. Before I can think of what more I can say, the maids enter carrying the food.

Dinner was supposed to be served an hour ago. It seems like they were told he'd be home for dinner tonight because they prepare the usual spread they make when he's around. They do near enough the same for me, but when he's here, it's more elaborate and they treat him like the lord of the manor.

Irena, the maid who used to at least smile at me, walks out with a bottle of expensive wine.

She stopped smiling at me the week of the wedding. I guess my suspicions were right about her interest in Mikhail. I figured she was probably hoping to be the next Mrs. Dmitriyev in the family.

She's smiling now as she approaches Mikhail, and I watch

him return the smile with a real one. He's never smiled at me like that—so easy and normal.

All the smiles he's given me were either scowls or mocking smirks or taunting in some way.

They start speaking in Russian like old friends who haven't seen each other in years. I watch them feeling my blood heat, and when she giggles and he laughs, I decide I've had enough.

The only thing left is for her to sit in his lap and straddle him. I've known him for close to five weeks, yet I've never heard him laugh.

They continue talking, but I interrupt the conversation when I tap on the hard wood of the table.

They both look at me then.

"Excuse me," I say. "What are you guys talking about?"

Irena looks surprised, as does Mikhail.

"Adriana—"

"No, scratch that," I cut him off before he can have the pleasure of punishing me or embarrassing me in front of her. "You." I point to Irena. "You understand me. I've heard you speaking English before, so I know you understand me."

"I do," she replies.

Wow. Five weeks in this house, yet those are the first words she's spoken to me.

I straighten. "When you come to this table and I'm sitting here, I want to know what the hell you're talking to *my husband* about." I don't care who I'm supposed to be pretending to be or that I face death if my secrets are revealed. I've had enough of people treating me like shit. I'm not going to sit here and take it. "You don't walk in and have some secret conversation with my husband I can't understand. Do you hear me?"

"Yes, Mrs. Dmitriyev. I apologize." She dips her head and leaves.

Of course, Mikhail is staring at me with his eyes blazing when I look back at him, but I still don't care. No matter what happens to me, I'm glad I did that. It's not like Irena didn't deserve the warning.

"What the hell is the matter with you?" he asks, squaring his jaw.

"Are you kidding me? You think *I'm* the problem? The maids don't talk to me *ever,* and Aleksander is rude as fuck. Why is that? Did you tell them to treat me like shit?"

"No, they just know they're not here to socialize."

"Well, you sounded like you were socializing just fine with that girl, so I don't believe that."

"You believe what I tell you to believe."

"She got a real smile from you," I snap back. Outside my head, the words sound stupid.

"What?"

His stupid phone buzzes with a message, cutting into our conversation. When he pulls it from his back pocket, looks at it, and stands, I realize straightaway he's going out again.

"We'll finish this conversation another time."

"When are you coming back?"

He pauses for a moment, considering the answer, then shakes his head.

"I don't know. I have to work."

With that, he leaves, and I fall into my usual habit of watching him walk away.

I'm so pathetic. And listen to me; I just sounded like a crazy brat.

Or maybe I just sound like I'm in love with my husband and am trying not to be.

Chapter Thirty-Three

Mikhail

I tear down the road like a madman on my motorcycle.

I'm going way past the speed limit and taking the corners too sharp, but I need to feel something other than mind-fucked.

I miss her.

I miss Adriana and everything about her.

I miss being buried deep inside her, touching her, being around her.

But I keep telling myself what I'm doing is for the best.

I keep telling myself staying away from her is for the best.

This way, I can focus on my work and what needs to be done.

This way, I can stop myself from falling for her and our marriage can be exactly what it was supposed to be. Business.

However, at no point has it been better for me because all I'm doing is driving myself crazy.

Like now.

Weeks ago, I never thought the princess had it in her to

talk back to me with such defiance, much less speak to my staff the way she put Irena in her place.

She was right to.

I wasn't lying when I told her I didn't want an environment where the staff could socialize, but she was right to point out that I was doing exactly that.

Irena is a maid who was a friend to my sister. I gave her a job five years ago when she needed it after Talia split her work between Europe and the States.

Talia didn't need a maid anymore, so I helped out when she asked. I tend to forget Irena works for me because of the length of time I've known her. I'm probably more easy-going with her, which sends the wrong message to everyone else. Including her. I'm certain she would have thought my interest ran deeper than professional on several occasions, and the looks of interest have not escaped me.

Unlike Ivan, who would fuck every nubile woman willing to ride his cock, I don't. Contrary to what my wife believes, I have no interest in Irena.

I just wasn't thinking I'd piss off my already pissed-off wife when Irena came up to talk to me.

The whole time she spoke to me, I struggled to concentrate because all I wanted to do was reach for the woman next to me I gave my name to and reacquaint myself with her body.

I have a wife.

Me.

A wife who smart-mouthed me in a way that would have warranted a spanking a few weeks back. There's only one problem with punishment like that. It no longer works on those who have submitted, and worse, it doesn't work if it turns into fun.

Then it becomes the prelude to fucking. I was on the verge of taking Adriana right there on the table and had to hold back.

The message from Eric snapped me back into focus.

We've been watching Ivan's movements like hawks.

Nothing has come up so far. My brother is a sneaky fucker. It's hard to pin down what he's up to.

Eric wants me to meet him because he found some figures and business transactions in the system that don't look right.

He wants me to verify them because they look off.

It's easier if I help with these finds because Ivan had to do my job when I was in the hospital.

It doesn't take me long to get to get the hotel Eric is staying at.

One look at the transactions he's found tells me something's off. There's a host of transactions going to an offshore account in Russia listed under the name of a recipient I don't know. The only assumption there is Ivan's stealing from the company or paying somebody for something. I'm inclined to believe the latter because a billionaire has no reason to steal from his own family business.

I spend a few hours going over the transactions and adding what I can to my compilation I want to take to my father.

He'll be choosing the new leader in two weeks, so the clock is ticking. If I don't find solid evidence against my brother to link him to my mother and sister's murders, I want to find what I can to back up my suspicion.

I get home just before midnight, and instead of heading to the room I've been using attached to my office, I decide to check on the princess.

She's sleeping, but she fell asleep on the floor by the window. Her head is resting on the wall, and she's curled up against it at an awkward angle. I'd leave her to sleep, but I'd feel guilty for leaving her like that. So, I find myself picking her up off the floor and laying her on our bed.

Our bed.

It's the first time I've thought of the bed as ours.

I expect her to stir, but she doesn't. She barely even moves when I set her down on the stack of pillows. The dark circles under her eyes suggest she hasn't slept properly in days.

That was the first thing I thought when I saw her earlier, right after I marveled at how beautiful she is.

The lack of sleep, bad temper, and confliction are because of me.

I've been going through the same thing. I torture myself further by lying next to her, and I think of what I should have done differently on the day I married her.

I should have taken her away on an actual honeymoon. Maybe flown her somewhere exotic. Or since she's probably used to exotic from living in Mexico, I could have taken her to Russia, or somewhere else, like the Seychelles or Bora Bora.

I can imagine her walking across the white sandy beach in Bora Bora.

I think she would have liked to go there, even if she is used to exotic.

I should have done anything more than the nothing I did.

I run my gaze over her body and think of her as a work of art again. She's the kind of woman you paint to preserve the memories of feelings and emotions.

The way my father used to paint my mother.

Christ.

Listen to me.

I lie there for a while, just for a little longer, to satisfy my need to be near her before I leave.

* * *

The next day, my father is the first person on my agenda to meet before I head out to Dmitriyev Ltd.

He wanted to talk to me first thing in the morning at nine sharp, at the lake house.

Situated on the bank of Lamoka Lake and built of wood, the house looks more like a cottage than the other neighboring homes and has always reminded me of something from a fairytale.

It wasn't somewhere I went often because my parents wanted to keep it for themselves and away from everyone else.

No one would guess that a multi-billionaire owned it for its quaintness and simplicity, but my father opted for such to remind himself of the people he'd come from. Back in Russia in the old, old days of my great-great-grandfather, it would have been a cottage like this they would have lived in back in Saratov.

Saratov is one of the poorest cities in Russia, and they would have had to travel for days to get to western Siberia to work in the mines we now own.

My father's guards' car is parked out front on the drive. They aren't inside it, a sign he probably spent the night here.

The front door of the house is open, waiting for me to walk in.

I park my bike beside the car and make my way into the house.

I find my father sitting on a wooden chair on the porch at the back gazing at the shimmering lake.

He doesn't look away from the scenic view when I step out, but a smile dips the corners of his mouth.

"Good morning, my son."

"Morning."

"Everything okay at home?"

"It is."

"And your wife?" He looks at me now, but I don't know what to say.

He's been different since the wedding. I think he might take pity on Adriana. I sense it.

"She's fine."

"That's all good, son." He returns his focus to the lake and smiles again. "What do you see when you look out at the lake?" he asks.

I know what he wants me to say, but I haven't had that

artistic vision in a long time, and I don't want it now because I don't want it to make me look like I've gone soft.

"Water." I smirk.

"Smartass. Of course, there's fucking water in the lake." He laughs, then the seriousness returns to his face. "You and I don't see things like that, though, do we?"

"No, Father."

"Then tell me what you really see. Humor an old dying man."

Old dying man.

I don't want him to be dying. It's okay for him to get old, but I don't want him to go to the other side ever. But that is to come. We don't have long left.

When that time comes, I'll never have days like this again. There will just be me until Sophia goes, too. She's not that much younger than my father.

I decide to humor him and look out to the lake again. Of course, I never just saw water in the first place. So, I choose to tell him what I see.

"In the shimmer of the sunlight touching the surface, I see a fire-breathing dragon rising from the chasm of hell. It has great black wings and long, sharp teeth and eyes as red and blazing hot like the infernal fire raging from its mouth."

He nods and smiles again. "That's better. Now sit."

I sit in the chair in front of him, and his eyes meet mine.

"You shouldn't have allowed your brother to stop you from doing something you loved. Painting was as much a part of you as it was for me."

The mention of my brother has me seething, and I wish I could tell my father what I fear about Ivan.

"It seemed like a necessary thing to do at the time," I say.

"That's nonsense, boy. Complete nonsense. I hope you'll find your muse again someday, because no matter what I decide for the company and leadership of the brotherhood, you're going to need little things like that."

"It's just art, Father."

"You want to know the secret to being a great Pakhan?" he asks, and I nod. "You need balance. Little things like art help you escape reality. We are the Baranov. There is always going to be a threat to us. That is the life we have chosen to live in the Bratva. Little things like *art* help keep you sharp." He pauses for a beat. "You can't always take, divide, and conquer. You have to know when to do certain things and when not to. That's what makes you sensitive to different situations. That's how you outsmart others when they come to take you down and how you come out on top." He balls his hands into fists.

"What if the thing that balances you makes you weak?"

He shakes his head. "It can never make you weak. Something else is to blame for that."

"Like what?"

"Fear. In the Bratva, we spend so much time trying to not look weak, we're all afraid of someone discovering our weaknesses. We fear looking soft when we love, or we indulge in what we love. I have been Pakhan for over twenty years, and the things that balanced me never weakened me. I built an empire based on it and took what I already had and turned it into something legendary."

He's right. No other Pakhan has done what he has for both the company and the Brotherhood.

He gazes back out to the lake. I wonder what he sees when he looks out there. He's looking like he can see something, so I ask.

"What can you see, Father?"

He returns his gaze to me. "Her. Your mother. I always see her in everything. Now more than ever that she's gone. She balanced me, too. I've been avoiding coming out here since her death."

"How come you wanted to meet here then?"

"Because of the things I want to discuss with you. I have

things to tell you I feel you should know. Things to do with your brother and his past."

My interest piques. "What sort of things?"

"Secrets and lies, *my* secrets and lies he's never forgiven me for."

Chapter Thirty-Four

Mikhail

"What happened in the past, Father?" I give him a narrowed look.

He intensifies his stare and looks uneasy. "There's a reason why Ivan has always been so abrasive and coldhearted toward you. It's my fault."

"How in the hell is that your fault?"

"Because of the bad relationship I had with Tatiana, and how I met your mother."

Tatiana was Ivan's mother. Her name is one rarely uttered by my father for the bad memories it unearths.

"It was my meeting with your mother that destroyed my relationship with his," he adds.

As the confession falls from his lips, a stone drops in my stomach.

"I thought you met Mother after Tatiana died."

"No. It was before. I knew her many years before. She was our maid."

My mouth falls open. "What? What are you saying to me? I thought you met her at a business meeting?"

"No. She worked for Tatiana and me while she was training to be a dancer. I met her when she was sixteen. I don't know what you'll think of me after I tell you the truth, but I feel I owe it to you."

"What happened, Father?" I think I know where this story is going, and I don't like what my gut tells me. It would definitely explain a lot about my horrendous relationship with my brother.

"My marriage to Tatiana was a business arrangement because of the diamond company. That's how it became a subsidy of Dmitriyev Ltd. It came from her family. So, to merge the wealth, my father forced me to marry her. I... never loved her, though." He stops again. "All she wanted was for me to love her. I tried. It shouldn't have been so hard. I'd known her my whole life. She and Sophia were best friends, and our families were so close it was a given we'd get married. When we had Ivan, I tried even more to fall in love with her, but I just didn't. Then I met your mother, and I loved her from the first time I looked at her."

"You... cheated on Tatiana, didn't you?" I fill in.

"Yes. Yes, I did. There is no excuse, and nothing will make it right. Ivan was nine when he caught us together. He told Tatiana, and it drove her insane. I found out your mother was pregnant with you, so I asked Tatiana for a divorce. She wouldn't give it to me. Instead, she killed herself. She slit her wrists in the bathtub. It was Ivan who found her."

"My... God."

That's why my brother hates me.

This is why.

My mouth goes dry as everything starts to make sense.

I'm part of the reason his parents broke up, and he views me as part of the reason his mother killed herself. I was told she had a heart attack.

He would have blamed my mother, too, and hated my sister.

But, this is in the past, and wouldn't explain why he would want them dead now.

It would, however, be a part of the reason.

My father is right. There are so many secrets and lies.

I rest my elbows on my knees and slouch forward as his words continue to sink into my head.

"Your mother and I got married a few months before you were born."

"Who else knows the truth?"

"Just Ivan and Sophia. I'm sorry, Mikhail. I couldn't take these secrets to the grave with me. I guess I might have seemed to favor him over you in some respects, but that wasn't the case."

"I have never thought that."

"I guess you wouldn't have been at the age where it might have mattered for you to think it. But you are now. When I decided to retire, I realized I couldn't simply follow tradition. More than that, I didn't want to. You work hard, Mikhail. Ivan does, too, but he took comfort in the fact that the oldest son usually gets to be the Pakhan. There's a difference between what the two of you have done."

Something pinches my heart. "Is this your way of telling me you've chosen him to be Pakhan?" If it is, I'd have a hard time laying down my own truth for him about Ivan. Especially when I have no evidence.

"It's not, son, but I wanted you to be the first to know how I changed everything else, including my will. I changed everything for everybody."

"Everything?" This might answer the big question.

"Everything. Unlike when the inheritance passed to me twenty years ago, I felt there was enough wealth to share equally. That means the controlling interest in the company wouldn't just lie with the Pakhan."

"What did you do?"

"I gave Sophia the diamond company and split the ownership of Dmitriyev Ltd. four ways. I split it between you, Ivan, your mother, and sister. So, it will be the first time the company would have equal ownership with a horizontal line of inheritance. Meaning if something happened to one party, their shares would then be divided equally amongst the remaining beneficiaries."

And that's reason enough to want my mother and sister dead.

And reason enough to want me dead, too. This is it. The answer.

It has to be.

With us out of the way, Ivan would have inherited all of it without any problems.

As it stands now, it's down to him and me.

Shit.

I also don't think he'd be that worried about the diamond company as he would Dmitriyev Ltd. Dmitriyev Ltd. makes billions a year. That fucking contract was just about it, nothing else, so Sophia should be safe.

Who knew this was going to happen? Father would have only told someone he trusted.

"Did you tell anyone you were going to do that to Dmitriyev Ltd.?"

"Your mother. No one else, not even the estate lawyers. They'll see my wishes after the leadership changes. I also didn't tell Sophia because I didn't want her arguing about the diamond company. She's very humble and wouldn't want to keep something like that to herself, but she deserves something she can call her own."

So Mother must have told someone about the plans for Dmitriyev Ltd.

"As for the leadership, one of you will be the next Pakhan. The Pakhan gets everything else."

Which is nearly the same value as the company.

"I guess we'll know next week."

"You will. If I don't pick you, please forgive me. If I do pick you, forgive me also for the repercussions you may face from your brother. I've tried my best to fix the past, but I can't, and I hope you won't hold it against me too much."

"I... don't," I tell him, because I see no point in doing so when we only have months left together.

I don't condone what he did, and it doesn't matter that he loved my mother, but I can't change the past any more than he can.

"Then that's more than I deserve from you. That's all I have for you, son. In a week and a half, you'll know who will be the next Pakhan."

"Do you still know who you're going to choose?" I'm curious.

"Yes, but I'm still waiting. My heart and mind need to tell me the same thing. I'm going to come here the night before the big day so I can feel your mother's presence. She'll guide me in accepting my answer. I've invited Sophia to come here on the morning. She will know first. My sister deserves to be the first to know something this important to me. You both love her, and I suspect she'll play a big role to whoever I choose."

"She most definitely will." I nod, agreeing.

Rising to my feet, I dip my head with the respect I always show him.

He nods too with the same respect but stops me before I walk through the door.

"One more thing. Maybe another bit of wisdom from an old fool."

"What?"

"You don't have to be afraid to love your wife. There is no need for it, and no one would fault you for it. I don't."

My lips part to tell him that's not a problem, but when I look at his face, I know he can see straight through me. There's little point bullshitting a person who can do that, so I nod and leave.

* * *

It takes me a few hours to digest all I was told this morning. After I get back from my first meeting, I find José outside my office waiting to speak to me.

He should have a report for me on things at the house and cartel business.

"What would you like me to start with first?" he asks.

"Cartel business." I lean back against my chair and try to focus. I need the easy stuff first.

"Everything is done. All Raul's assets have now been transferred over to you. The lawyers completed the last transaction yesterday. Everything is now in your name, and things can basically run on autopilot in some respects," he explains. "I may need to go to Mexico in a week or so to continue discussions on a project that was in progress before Raul died. Of course, with your permission."

"Yes, that's fine. You can go." Controlling the cartel is my biggest accomplishment and something I'll be remembered for, but I'm glad that part is over. It's easier on my mind to focus on one thing at a time. Right now, that's not the most important thing. It never was. It was more of a side quest.

"What about your report?" I ask.

He looks uneasy. "Sebastian and your men at the house seem to be clean. I don't think you have to worry about them, but I'm still keeping my eyes open. I did notice something weird at the docks yesterday to do with your brother though."

I straighten immediately. We have a shipping company located at the docks. I sent José on an errand for me. "What did you learn?"

"Ivan met with a guy who used to work with Raul when he needed to import goods. I don't know the guy's name. Raul worked in secrets to keep a tight handle on things. He's a guy like Tony, a middleman. I think he might just be his replacement. What I didn't know is why he was meeting with your brother." He eyes me with suspicion.

José is no fool. I'm sure he's already put two and two together.

"Let me worry about that." I'm not going to talk to him about Ivan. "What time did you see them?"

"Late last night, about eleven. They were in the alleyway at the back."

Dammit. There are no cameras in the fucking alleyway, which is probably why Ivan met the fucker there.

"Thanks. Keep doing what you're doing and if you see my brother with that guy again, call me straightaway."

"Sure will. You be careful, Señor. Blood is thicker than water for a reason. Blood can drown you quicker."

Don't I know it.

Chapter Thirty-Five

Natalia

The gentle breeze caresses my skin, and I can smell the oncoming rain.

Angry storm clouds cover the heavens, but the sky refuses to crack open and allow the rain to fall.

I'm not going to stay out too long today. Not until dark.

I went out by myself for a walk out by the lake so from where I am I can still glimpse the terrace of the house from where I'm sitting.

I just needed fresh air.

Things were more tense in the house after last night, but this morning, Irena said good morning to me. So did the other maid. Aleksander was just as abrasive but not as rude.

I figured Mikhail must have spoken to them.

I was almost sure he was in the room with me last night, lying next to me on the bed. I thought I'd fallen asleep on the floor, though. I was so tired I couldn't remember.

The scent of him hung in the air when I awoke. I must have imagined his presence, because today was another day of nothingness.

Today marks one whole week since we got married. I don't even know why I'm bothering to take note of the time. It's not like it makes a difference to anyone. It won't make any difference to me.

It's just because I'm the one with time on her hands, watching the days go by. Each day that passes leaves me wondering what the next will be like.

I've been caged in this house, and although I've been allowed to wander around and go shopping with Sophia or one of the guards, I still feel like I'm locked up.

Or like I'm on a deserted island with no real hope of escape. All there is, is what's around me.

Not to mention the fact that I'm in New York. A place that's new to me. People are different, and I have a new language in my ear I can't even make heads or tails of. Sometimes, people can pick up certain words and try to piece together the meaning of a conversation. I can't do that when it comes to Russian.

All I know is *Malyshka*.

No matter what tone Mikhail uses to say it to me, the endearment has always sounded like a word of affection expressed by my lover.

God, I am pathetic.

Is it because he's the first man I've been with, why I can't shake him from my mind? Is it that? Or maybe the word *husband* has more meaning to me than it should.

I don't think it's either of those things. I think it's him.

The problem is him and what he broke down inside me to make me feel for him.

I can tell myself I resisted, but the thing I was trying to stop myself from feeling was already there. All he did was unleash it. Now that he's abandoned me, I'm trying to rein it back in.

The shuffle of footsteps makes me turn my head.

I nearly jump out of my skin when I see Ivan walking

toward me. I was so engrossed in my thoughts I didn't hear him.

This is the second time this has happened to me. Once again, he's crept up on me, catching me off-guard.

I stand and face him, wondering why he's here and if Mikhail might be home, too.

All these weeks I've been at this house, he hasn't come by once. What brings him here today?

"Relax, princess, I just came to say hello to my new *sister-in-law*." He smiles.

What do I say?

I don't have the fire I possessed last night, and that warning voice in my head tells me not to mess with this man.

Or underestimate him.

I remember how he looked at me at the wedding, and I can't forget what he said to me back at his father's house. Both occasions told me I needed to be very careful of him.

"Hello," I say.

"How is married life treating you?"

I'm sure he can tell married life is not treating me very well.

I'm also sure there's more to his question than what he's really asking.

Something more along the lines of when my expiry date might come up and my husband decides to sell me or give me away.

"I'm fine, thank you."

"Enjoying the fresh air?"

"Yes."

He steps closer and I wish he wouldn't.

The air in my lungs freezes, and my spine tingles with uneasiness. I wish he would leave me alone. It's clear, though, he has an agenda, and I am it.

"You know what? I remembered why you look familiar to me."

God, not this again.

Not *this* again. What is he going to say to me this time?

I keep my gaze trained on him. "Why?"

"There was a woman who worked for Raul. Very, very beautiful. You reminded me of her." His smile widens, and I feel myself shrinking away. "You have the same look of fear in your eyes."

Something hits me when he says that—a memory of something I shouldn't have heard.

It was my mother telling my father she'd been attacked by one of Raul's business associates.

Raped.

She said he'd raped her. My father wanted to do something, but she begged him not to. She knew what would happen if he did anything. It meant death.

My parents kept it from me.

My *mother* kept it from me, and I know it happened at least two more times while my father was away working. He didn't know about those times. I heard her crying in the bathroom and saw the bruises on her legs.

My mother would have been so hurt if she knew I knew, so I pretended I was none the wiser.

When Raul tried it with her, she'd had enough. That's why it was so bad and probably why it was the last time for anybody.

A deep cold seeps into me, working its way into my soul. Why is my gut instinct telling me this devil in front of me did something to my mother?

"That's an odd thing to say," I tell him.

"Maybe it's how everyone who was around Raul looked, right? Scared and afraid."

I don't know what this devil suspects or how he'd pieced the truth together, but it's clear he knows something is up with me.

According to what José said, unless Ivan has proof, he wouldn't be able to figure out I'm not Adriana.

But he knows something is not right with me.

I just can't establish what he might know, or suspect. All he seems to have so far is the strong resemblance to my mother, which will give me away because that's a striking element that could pick me apart.

"That's enough," Mikhail's rough voice cuts in, just like it did that night and I'm grateful to hear him.

Ivan and I turn to see him marching over to us. His hair looks windswept, and he's slightly out of breath, like he's been running.

"Why are you talking to my wife?" he demands, glaring at Ivan.

"Chill out, brother, I dropped off some stuff Father wanted you to have."

"Yes, Sophia told me. My phone was off when Father called, so I didn't get the message. That doesn't answer my question of why you're speaking to my wife."

Ivan chuckles. "Unbelievable. Since when is it a crime to speak to someone?" He squares his shoulders when Mikhail walks closer, doing the same.

"What do you want, *brother*?"

I can tell now there's bad blood between them and it doesn't matter that they're brothers. I've seen Mikhail when he's angry. Back in Mexico, he looked like he was ready to bring forth the end of the world.

But this is different. There's a different look in his eyes that's just as murderous but fueled by wrath and madness.

"I was simply getting reacquainted," Ivan explains nonchalantly. "The wedding was so rushed. You never even had a reception or anything for me to congratulate you. You could have at least made it look more normal and not like the business transaction it was. If only for the other guests who didn't know the truth of why you married this poor girl."

I already felt bad enough. The reminder of what I am makes me feel worse.

Just then, drizzles of rain trickle down from the sky. The heavens are ready to crack open and pour. A metaphor for the way I feel inside.

"You can leave now," Mikhail tells him.

Ivan smirks and then walks away.

Mikhail's fists ball at his sides. We both gaze on at Ivan until he's on the terrace and back inside the house.

Mikhail turns back to me, and as our eyes lock, I note how drained he looks. He also smells like he's been drinking. Not as badly as that night I went into the hall with the paintings, but enough for me to smell the whiskey on him.

Raul drank whiskey. So did Felipe. They always smelled like it.

"What did he say to you?" Mikhail demands, moving closer to me.

I take him in. I'm so focused on his eyes that I almost miss the dash of color on the collar of his shirt.

Because he's always in black, the smear of red lipstick pops. It's the only color I've seen on him. Another woman's lipstick.

The hole in my heart grows wider, deeper, faster, and I shake my head at him.

I imagine him with someone else, touching her the way he would touch me, possessing her body the way he would mine and it makes me sick.

Bastard.

The message he got last night could have been from her. He was out all night, or away from me a good amount of time. Fuck, what am I saying?

I have my times all mixed up.

It's almost dark again. He could have been with her all day.

He reaches out to touch my face, but I back away, out of his grasp.

"Where were you?" I ask, hating the quiver in my voice.

"Working."

"Liar," I choke out, feeling like the pot calling the kettle black. I have no right to call anyone a liar. None whatsoever. But I don't care right now. I feel so foolish. While I've been here worrying myself over him, he's out fucking around.

"Why do you think I'm fucking lying?"

"There's lipstick on your collar, Mikhail." I point to it, but he doesn't take his eyes off me. "Were you with one of your women?"

Why am I asking a question I already know the answer to? If you don't want to get hurt, don't do things that will hurt you.

I'm digging my own grave. When his face hardens and he doesn't answer me, I do the only thing I can understand his silence to mean and accept the answer must be yes.

It shouldn't hurt me. I shouldn't care. I should remember this arrangement we have is a means to an end for us both, yet the tears running down my cheeks say otherwise.

They speak of my heart, and I can't fight that.

They also speak of my rage, and suddenly, my hand flies up and connects hard with his cheek.

"Bastardo," I cry. "I hate you. Te odio diablo," I shout, telling him I hate him in Spanish and calling him the devil.

The sky cracks open as I rush away from him.

But I don't get very far.

I thought I might this time because I didn't expect him to come after me.

That's my mistake. Not only did I strike him, but I defied him. That means punishment. The sadistic bastard will use the opportunity to punish me.

He secures a hand around my waist and yanks me against him.

"Let go of me," I yelp, kicking against him.

"Fucking stop it."

"Leave me alone. I hate you."

The falling rain quickly turns the ground slippery, and my kicks and thrashing send us both to the ground.

He reaches for me and moves himself on top of me, pinning my hands above my head to stop me from moving.

"I didn't cheat on you," he growls.

"I don't believe you."

"I didn't."

"It doesn't matter. I'm a business transaction, remember?" My tears pour and fuse with the raindrops on my face. "So, it's not real. We're not real. I'm not really your wife, so you can fuck anyone you want."

"I didn't cheat on you, Adriana," he grates out in a firmer voice. Hearing that name makes me snap. I keep forgetting I'm supposed to be her. He hasn't called me that name since we took our vows, and now that he's said it, I want to scream at him and tell him I'm not Adriana Alvarez.

"I was at a bar, drinking. I switched my phone off because I needed some time to myself. That's why no one could reach me," he continues. "A waitress I know propositioned me. That's how the lipstick got on my collar. I said no and left. I was on my way back to work when I heard Ivan was on his way here. Now I'm here. That's the truth."

I glare at him and think about what he's saying to me.

He never tells me anything and explains himself to no one. Everything he's told me so far has been by chance and slowly drip-fed to me.

So, I know when he's talking like this to pay attention.

The rain falls on us, soaking us both, but I can't take my eyes off him as he stares at me like he's looking into my soul.

"I can't cheat on you, princess," he says, and it's like the guard over his eyes falls away. "I can't get you out of my head."

I know the truth when I see it. I know the truth when I feel it.

I can see it in his eyes and hear it laced in the tone of his voice.

"Then what happened to you? That day you left before the wedding, everything changed."

"I crossed the line I didn't know I could cross. Now that I have, I don't want to go back."

"Then don't," I whisper, and something twinkles in his eyes.

A shimmer flickers between us. An entity of understanding within a crackle of energy.

He lowers his lips to mine, and I move to him, too, kissing him the way we used to kiss. Not like that kiss we shared when we said 'I do.'

This is the kiss to rival all, revealing more truths, and I allow myself to love him.

He picks me up, scooping me into his arms, and rises with me, but his lips don't leave mine.

He walks back into the house with me just like that. I feel the maids' eyes on us. Neither of us cares who sees us, though.

We reach the bedroom, where our clothes come off layer by layer and he makes love to me.

We actually make love. I feel the difference in his touch.

Passion grips us, claiming us, claiming me, and I know I crossed that line, too, and I don't want to go back.

There's only one problem—one of us is still a liar.

Me.

I love him, but I'm not the woman he thinks I am.

When he finds out who I am, I'm not sure love can save me, and neither will his obsession.

Chapter Thirty-Six

Mikhail

The silver moon beams down on the princess as I open the grand oak doors in the hall I christened the shrine.

That was what this room felt like when I got out of the hospital.

Everything in here was supposed to be a reminder of good memories my father had of my mother. To me, they felt like memories of what used to be and what will never be again.

Tonight, I look at my wife and focus on her.

Moonlight is what I want her in. Nothing but moonlight touching her skin.

There's something enchanting about watching her in the silver glow I want to capture. It is the only thing I'll allow to touch her that isn't me.

When night fell and the moon came out, I decided I was going to paint her.

I want to paint her in moonlight and show her what she looks like when I look at her. I want her to see herself the way I do when she balances me. I thought it was something else, like she tamed the beast inside me. It's not that, though.

It's the other thing my father spoke of.

Balance.

We spent all night and day in that bed, and I found myself thinking that maybe this will work. Maybe I wouldn't get screwed by love, and maybe I didn't have to retreat.

As I look at her now, I realize the fucked-up thing was me thinking I can give myself permission to love her. I never had a choice.

The last few weeks told me that truth.

She was the one thing I stole that backfired on me.

I stole her life, and she stole my heart. But there is more about the two of us neither is saying.

We're far from okay. *I'm* far from okay and actively choosing to forget the sword of fate hanging over my head, gearing up to sever me from this world.

Nothing about Adriana and me will feel okay until the right things are done.

I'm the villain in our story.

I'm not supposed to do the right thing for anyone else except me. I'm supposed to do what benefits me.

I'm supposed to be willing to do what I must to be the ruthless Bratva Pakhan I'm working hard to become.

But I wasn't supposed to fall in love either.

Neither was she.

Even now as I look at her, there's love in her eyes, and I know she can see it in mine.

But in her, I can see love as clearly as the trouble also lurking within them, telling me something worries her. Something more than me.

Again, I think of what her secrets might be.

Right now, I'm being selfish and taking her with me as I escape reality.

She looks around the room at the ballerina sculptures and the paintings with fascination.

She doesn't know what I want to do to her yet.

I'm sure it will surprise her. The idea still surprises me.

"They're all so beautiful," she states.

I watch her floating around the closest sculpture of my mother, and all I can think of is how beautiful my wife is.

My wife.

"My father created them all," I tell her, and her eyes widen.

"Your father? Really?"

"Yes."

"They're amazing, Mikhail."

"Yeah, that's what he used to do to balance him." I borrow his words.

She looks at the largest painting at the end of the room then back to me.

"The ballerina is your mother, isn't she?" she asks tentatively.

"Yes. This was my father's way of preserving what he felt for her. Art captures emotions and visions. Each piece is a memory."

"That's beautiful. What about those?" She points to the paintings I did that are covered with dust cloths.

I walk over and remove the cloth.

She gasps when she sees the first one. It's of the snowy landscape in Siberia. I painted it when I was sixteen.

"These are mine," I tell her. She walks closer to the painting.

The rest aren't displayed. I didn't have the respect I do for my father's.

"You did this?"

"Yeah. My last painting was the unfinished one of my sister you saw weeks ago."

"Why didn't you finish it?"

"Ivan. He tainted my love for art."

"Ivan?"

"I'm sure you can tell we're not exactly fond of each other."

"Yes, it's very clear."

"He's my half-brother, and he's always made it his duty to point out we're only half related. He's also always done some shit to screw with my mind. We grew up believing he would be the next Pakhan. I didn't want to get cast out when that happened, so I got stronger and got rid of everything that made me appear weak. The unfinished painting was part of that decision. It wasn't until recently that I learned I had a shot at being leader." That's all I'll say regarding Ivan for now. I also don't want to talk about him anymore. "I want to paint tonight, Malyshka."

She smiles, and it's an even better sight.

"What do you want to paint?"

"You."

Her delicate lips part. "Me? You want to paint me?"

"I want to paint you naked in the moonlight. You naked lying on that chaise." I point to the chaise by the window. She looks at it.

"Me... you want to do that of me?"

I nod. "Yes, Mrs. Dmitriyev. So, take your clothes off for me."

A sensual flame brightens her eyes as she slides the straps of her dress down her shoulders. The dress floats down to her feet.

I watch her take off her bra and panties, too, and step out of her pumps.

All she is wearing now are my rings. The wedding ring and the engagement ring.

"Is this what you want?"

"You know it is. Now lie down on the chaise."

She does what I ask. As she lowers herself to the velvet

chaise and the moonlight beaming through the doors and windows touches her, she looks exactly the way I imagined.

Everything about her is beautiful. Her olive skin, her gorgeous eyes, that long flowing hair, and her perfect body.

I don't miss the fact that I must have found that muse again my father spoke of.

I just never thought she would come to me this way.

I walk over to the unused batch of canvases I got eons ago and my paint, hoping they haven't dried out. They should be okay in the little boxes I stored them in.

The princess watches me as I set up to my easel.

She offers me a smile when I sit and start sketching her.

"That's the most you've told me about yourself," she states.

"Want to know more?" I push away a lock of hair from my eye.

"Yes."

"What do you want to know, baby girl?"

"What's your favorite color? I don't think it's black, although you always wear it."

"The sky," I reply with a smile.

"The sky?"

"The sky has different colors at different points of the day and night."

"It does," she agrees.

"Your favorite color is lilac," I tell her, and she smiles wider.

"How did you guess that?"

"I pay attention."

"What's your favorite food?" she mutters.

"I don't have one. I eat everything. What about you?"

"Ice cream."

I chuckle at that. "Then I'll buy ice cream, cover you in it and lick it off you."

She laughs, and I pause to commit the sound to memory. I continue to stare, and she notices my fascination.

"What?"

"You just gave me a real laugh." She said something along those lines the other night when I was talking to Irena.

"I did. Now stay just like that and tell me what your dreams are." A person always shows the most emotion when they're talking about their dreams.

She stills and rivets her gaze to me, clearly surprised by the question.

She looks away briefly, into the moonlight. The light catches her eyes, making them look brighter.

"I want to be a doctor," she says barely above a whisper.

"A doctor?" I check if I heard her right. She nods.

I'm surprised by that because of who she is.

"I've always wanted to be a doctor."

"I didn't know that." I wouldn't know, because I never asked and would have never guessed that a Cartel Princess would have such big dreams.

"I didn't think you'd want to know."

"I do. You still want to be a doctor?"

"Yes."

"Then that's what we'll do."

Her skin pales with shock. "Really? You'd allow me to do that?"

"Of course." I almost sound normal. I'm listening to myself, and I know I'm glossing over the important things we should be talking about, but it's like I want to do anything and everything to make her happy. Anything to make up for the way I stole her life.

"Thank you so much."

"You're welcome. Talk to me about it, Malyshka."

She does. She speaks for one hour while I paint her.

My first painting in nearly ten years. I haven't lost my gift at all.

I capture every aspect I want of her body. Everything my obsession guides me to paint and highlight the expression on her face as she talks about her dreams and the arousal I see in the tight, taut peaks of her nipples.

I capture the glint of the ring on her finger branding her as mine and the way she looks at me.

Even when I'm done, I watch her as she continues talking. This is the longest we've ever spoken.

"My God, I've just talked non-stop."

"That's okay. I'm done now."

"Can I see it?"

"Come take a look."

She reaches for her dress and wraps it around her body before she walks toward me.

When she sees what I did, she sucks in a breath and brings a hand to her heart.

"Oh my God. I can't believe that's me. That looks amazing."

"I'm glad you like it."

"I do." She leans forward and kisses me. "I forgot to ask you what your dreams are."

As I stare back at her, I ask myself the same, and I know the answer.

Reaching for the edge of the dress, I tug it from her body.

"Right now, I just want you. Can I have you?"

"Yes."

I stand and pick her up, but I don't carry her back to our room like she thought I was going to do.

I carry her out onto the terrace and set her against the wall where the moon shines on the surface and over her.

This is how I want to take her.

"Out here?" She looks around nervously.

"It's just us. No one can see. Now give yourself to me."

I claim her lips and then push her against the wall and claim her body, fucking her hard the way I like to fuck.

Madness consumes us quickly, and we share one of those wild nights we got lost in weeks ago.

I take her everywhere in the house all night. By morning, she's out cold.

I have to go to work, so I can't stay in. There are also things to do with Ivan I have to check on today.

Instead of leaving her the way I have in the past, with nothing, I pull a white rose from the bouquet in the hallway and leave it on the pillow next to her, so when she wakes up, it's the first thing she'll see.

I leave it with a note simply saying, "Later."

That way, she won't have to wonder if I'll be back or whose bed I'll be sleeping in.

She'll know I'll be coming back to her.

Before I even make it down the stairs, my phone rings. I answer quickly when I see it's Eric.

"Hey," I say.

"Can you come to the hotel? I found something I need you to look at."

Fuck, I wish I could feel some accomplishment at him finding something, but every time I get a call like this, my stomach sinks.

"Of course. What did you find, Eric?"

"Just come." His voice has that cautious edge again. "It's best I show you in person."

"I'm on my way."

Eric has things set up so our phones can't be tracked or tapped into. His reluctance to give me a hint about what he found means it's something big again. Something he wants me to see in person.

Shit. What the fuck is it now?

I get to the hotel half an hour later, and the moment I read Eric's face, I know what he's going to show me is worse than the previous shit.

"What is it?" I ask.

"Come and sit."

I do, and he heads over to his desk to retrieve a document. When he returns, he sets in front of me.

"I've finally finished checking through Raul's files. This was one of the last documents I found. It was encrypted, but it wasn't amongst his emails. It was on his computer listed in a secret file. It looks like he was still working on it, preparing it to be sent out."

He hands me the sheet of paper from the document. When I look at it, the first thing I see is my wife's beautiful face.

There's a picture of her at the top of the sheet. It's a standard full-length picture of her dressed in a black tunic. There's nothing amiss about the picture itself, but I notice her eyes.

They are what looks amiss. Her eyes are brimming with that internal pain I witnessed weeks ago and she looks like she's lost the will to live.

When I scan down to the details below the picture, my eyes are glued to the details listed for her name.

At first, I think my eyes must be screwing with me, then I think this must be wrong because it says here that the name of the woman I'm looking at is Natalia Lily de Leon.

Further down, there's a listing for her for sale in the virgin auction for two million dollars.

My hands tremble, but I'm not sure what this emotion is I'm feeling or if it's possible that I'm feeling a myriad of them.

I pick out the burning sensation of anger and rage, but both are fueled by hurt. Like someone stabbed me with a knife in my heart and twisted it to make sure I could feel the sting of betrayal.

"What am I looking at, Eric? What the fuck am I really looking at?"

"Your wife isn't Adriana Alvarez. This woman is."

He hands me the rest of the document. It's medical records and the image of a woman who looks more like Raul.

Her name is Adriana Alvarez.

Everything I thought about the woman in my home that never made sense does now.

The scars on her back, the absence of the engagement ring, her behavior, her personality, her pain.

Her.

She never begged for Raul's life, but she was worried about José's.

I stole the wrong woman.

I *married* the wrong woman.

And the woman I stole lied to me.

Chapter Thirty-Seven

Natalia

The first thing I see when I open my eyes is a beautiful white rose.

I lift my head and study it. The little note on plain white paper says, "Later."

I pick up the rose to inhale the scent.

It brings a smile to my face, and I think of the last few nights I spent with Mikhail.

I smile wider when I think of the idea of going to college and pursuing my dreams.

Could I really have it all?

Could this really work out for me?

Could I have the man and the dreams and finally live a life where I'm free?

I allow myself some reprieve to dream and savor the feeling of being in love.

That smile on my face is there for about five minutes, maybe less, before it recedes as I once again think of the lie I am.

I pull my head out of the clouds and climb back down to reality.

How can I have the man and the dream and live my life in freedom when I have this big lie hanging over me?

How can I do that?

The plan was to escape at the first opportunity, but I can't do that now, and it should be my number one goal.

I already knew I couldn't live the lie, so escaping was the only option. It was always the *only* option.

Of course, the path would have to open for me to have the choice. Right now, I have nothing.

When I first came here, I was worried about death. I was worried Mikhail would find out I wasn't who he thought me to be and kill me, and José, too.

I'm still worried about that.

But now I'm worried about love lost.

I never factored this in. I never even thought about it because there was no way I thought I'd fall for him.

Now, I don't know what the hell I'm supposed to do.

Should I tell him?

I shake my head at myself and the craziness of the thought. Telling him would be a terrible idea.

And it's too late. The time to tell him was long ago, and I'd be in the same danger now as I was then.

I'm stuck in a lie that's going to become more entrenched with every day that passes. And I can't go back to where things went wrong. Things went wrong for me long before I met Mikhail.

I can see in his eyes that he must feel something for me. I'm not sure he loves me, and I doubt he'd still love me if he knew the truth. I think the cartel would be more important to him than anything else.

That was my purpose.

My only purpose.

I always knew he could do whatever he wanted with me after we got married.

I glance at the clock on the wall and realize I've missed breakfast entirely and it's lunchtime.

The last few days wiped me out, but it's not like I have anything to do here.

I get dressed quickly. When I sit in front of the dresser to do my hair, a knock sounds at the door.

Thinking it's Aleksander coming to haul me downstairs for food, I stand and gear up to tell him I'll be down in a minute.

But when I open the door, it's not Aleksander standing there.

It's Sebastian.

I don't really talk to him. Mostly because he's scary. Not as scary as Mikhail, but scary enough for me to be wary. He's also never said much to me or showed any desire to speak to me other than relay some order from Mikhail.

He looks me in the eye with his dark green ones and straightens.

"Mrs. Dmitriyev, I need you to come with me. Your husband wishes to see you."

"He's here?" *At this time?* Mikhail hasn't been home at this time in weeks. At least not when he's left for work for the day.

"Yes, come with me, please."

"Of course." I walk out of the room and follow him as he marches ahead of me.

This is odd.

Sebastian has never come up to the room to get me before. Both he and José have been on the grounds of the house for weeks now, and they've barely come inside, much less upstairs.

When we get downstairs and I don't see the staff or smell the food that's normally ready at this hour, my nerves spike.

Where is everyone?

I look around for them as I follow Sebastian, but no one's here.

Suddenly, I wish I could see Aleksander's scowling face or the rude maids, because something isn't right.

And... I think I might know what it is.

I believe something's not right even more when Sebastian reaches the door leading down to the basement and opens it.

This is the second place I was told not to enter when I first got here. It looks like I have permission now.

But why?

"After you." He waves a hand motioning for me to walk through the door.

I walk in, but truthfully, I want to run away.

He's behind me now, and any hope to run is gone. He must have preempted I'd want to flee.

The stairs are made of stone and are wider than the steps in the house.

It feels more like a dungeon than a basement. I'm used to dungeons, so I would know.

Another one of Mikhail's guards stands at the bottom of the stairs. His name is Levka. He's another from his senior security team. A sure sign something is definitely wrong.

Why would I need two of his best guards to usher me to him if it wasn't?

He knows.

Mikhail knows the truth.

I can feel it in my bones.

I can feel it all over me, so I don't bother to ask questions about what's happening. I just move like I'm walking to the gallows. I know there's no hope left. This time, no one will save me.

I'm taken to a metal door, and the guard in front of us opens it.

"Go inside," Sebastian orders.

I do, and that's where I see Mikhail standing at the far

corner of the room which looks more like a prison cell—so yeah, I'm in a dungeon.

His back is turned to me, so I can't read his face. He has one hand behind his back, and the other is holding something.

When the door closes behind me, he turns, and I see his face.

That's when I know I'm right.

He knows.

He knows the truth.

The truth about me.

God. I'm sure of it.

His face resembles the way he looked when he first came to get me from the dungeon in Mexico. Back then, however, there was a mocking edge to him, like the conquering villain.

That edge isn't there now. There's something sinister lurking in his expression, and the eyes he's looking at me with now make me find it hard to believe this is the same man from the last few nights.

It can't be the same man who painted me and told me I was his dream.

It can't be the same man who called me his and told me I belonged to him.

It can't be the same man who stood before me and became my husband.

But it is.

This is what he looks like when he's been lied to.

I need to say something. Anything.

I need to say something... even if it sounds foolish. It will be worse if he speaks first. I'll look much worse than I already do.

"What's happening?" I mutter. My words are barely audible. "Why are we down here, Mikhail?"

"This is where I bring people to interrogate them. No one can hear them scream or suffer down here. Down here, they don't see the light of day. Often, they never see it again."

"Is that what you want to do to me?"

"We'll see, *wife*."

I fight back tears and will myself to be strong.

"It turns out a lot was happening right under my nose and the joke was on me the whole fucking time." His eyes blaze with fury, and his nostrils flare. "I have a penchant for telling when someone is lying, but the trick is, it only works if I ask a specific question. Now, I asked you everything under the sun that I could, except the one thing that could have screwed with me. I never asked you your name."

The air expels from my body, and the blood freezes in my veins.

"I'm sorry," I say.

"What was that?" He rushes up to me and grabs my arm, then he holds up the piece of paper so I can see it.

The paper shows a picture of me with all the details of everything he was never supposed to know. My name and my listing for sale in the virgin auction.

He knows the truth. The confirmation makes the gravity of the situation strike me a hundredfold.

This is the moment I feared.

"You're sorry!" He rips the blouse I'm wearing off me and tears off my skirt. "You're fucking sorry?"

"Stop it!"

"Fuck you. Fuck you for doing this to me."

"I'm so sorry, Mikhail. I'm so sorry. I thought you were going to kill me."

"You were right to think so." He tears off my bra and panties next and shoves me against the wall that hold chains running through a loop.

"Please, forgive me. Please... I'm so sorry."

"No."

I scream when he catches my face and holds me down while he grabs my wrists and binds my hands to the chains above my head.

I'm crying so hard I can barely see. He steps back and looks at me with vengeance in his eyes, and I know I'm dead.

"I'm the one who's sorry," he says. "You truly had me fooled. Had I only asked you your name, I would have known straightaway that you were lying about who you were, Natalia de Leon."

The tears still flow from my eyes like a river, and my soul weeps, but hearing my name spoken from his lips awakens something inside me.

How I longed to know what it would sound like to hear him say my name and not hers. Not Adriana's, but mine.

Now it doesn't matter because I was right.

Nothing was enough to save me. He doesn't want me.

He wanted her.

He fell for her. Not me.

I stand here loving him so hard, but he was obsessed with the illusion of the Cartel Princess. Not the pauper.

"I am going to kill you, but José gets to go first."

"No, please! Don't kill him!" I scream.

"He's just as much of a liar as you are, Malyshka. Neither of you knew who you were messing with when you concocted this little game of yours. You're about to find out."

The sobs pour from my naked body. I feel like I'm about to turn inside out from the gamut of emotions that assails me, but he's done talking.

Done with me for now.

His heavy boots carry him away, and as the metal door slams shut, locking me in the dungeon, all I hear is myself screaming and crying.

He's going to kill José.

Then me next.

My mind is fractured, but my heart hurts even more as it breaks and splinters into a million pieces.

Chapter Thirty-Eight

Mikhail

As I march up the stone steps leading from the basement, I know I've gone completely crazy and lost my mind.

I say nothing as I walk past my guards and head out to the driveway to get back on my motorcycle.

No one but Eric and I know anything.

I told the house staff to stay away from the house for the day, and Sebastian and Levka to meet me there.

I left Eric at the hotel close to two hours ago. I was so enraged I rode around for an hour before I contacted Sebastian and got him to carry out my orders for the staff and himself.

I tear down the driveway and through the gates of my home like I've come straight from hell and head down to the docks, to the shipping company.

That's where José is, and my guards there have instructions for that

motherfucker.

That motherfucking liar.

He fucking lied to me, and now I know of his affinity for the girl—*Natalia*—I know why he did what he did.

Natalia.

Natalia de Leon.

That's her name. Not Adriana Alvarez. She isn't Raul's daughter.

I don't know whose daughter she is or what she was to Raul, but she was most likely a maid or one of his servants.

I don't know why she was wearing the wedding dress when I first got her, and I swore she was kissing Felipe when I crashed into that hall back at Raul's estate in Mexico.

Fuck, fuck, fuck.

Every fucking thing is a mess, and the real Adriana could be alive somewhere in Mexico or fucking hell.

That means I have no cartel.

If people find out, I'm fucking screwed. It could cause a war from the men who signed their allegiance to me in blood.

If that happens, blood is all there will be, and I will have to kill men who would be assets to me.

I gave her the choice to marry me or die, knowing I could take the cartel the hard way, but that would have never been a benefit to anybody. If you want something the way it is, you try to preserve what makes it good.

But listen to me. As if my rage is really about the fucking cartel.

It's not.

I admitted it the other day. Taking the fucking cartel was just a side quest. Something to teach those who crossed the Bratva a lesson they would never forget. It was something to warn enemies away from thinking they could come and kill me and mine without consequence. I wanted to take the thing they revered and crush the man who led it.

Taking the cartel was never something I needed, though. Not for anything. So, my wrath isn't about that.

It's about her and the lie she represents to me.

My wrath is for myself because I dropped my guard and loved her.

Hearing her real name in my head makes sense in different ways, and I think I knew the answer all along. I think I knew she couldn't have been the woman I'd heard such horrendous stories about.

I think I knew.

I pull up to the parking lot at the shipping company and head straight to the back where I gave orders for José to be taken.

When I get to the warehouse and see him sitting on the chair with two of my men standing on either side with guns, I rush him and land a fist straight in his face.

Both he and the chair go flying backwards.

My men here don't know what's going on, either, so when they exchange curious glances and probably wonder what the fuck is going on with me now, it's understandable.

"Leave us," I bellow, and the two leave José and me in the room.

José rights himself but doesn't get to do much before I land another fist in his face and grab him by his throat to shove him against the wall.

"You fucking liar. You lied to me this whole time and made me believe the woman I married was Raul's daughter." I cut to the chase and spare us both the bullshit of explaining by shoving the sheet of paper in his face.

His eyes go wide when he realizes what I'm holding, but there's a defiance about him that irritates me even more.

I want him to beg for his life and explain himself, but he doesn't.

"Fucking talk!" I shout in his face. "Say something to explain your fucking self. I spared your life."

"You want me to say sorry?" he counters and smiles. "You won't fucking hear that word from me. I'm not saying sorry to you or anybody for what I did. You act like I owe you something, but I will never owe you for nothing. You fucking spared my life so you could use me."

It's like a light switches on in my head and I realize the truth in his words—all his words.

"Why did you lie about her?"

"Because, amigo, you're the devil, Mikhail Dmitriyev. You are the fucking devil, el diablo, and we were all in a game of survival. She's not from our world. She doesn't belong in it, and I wanted her to have a way out. I wasn't going to stand by and allow you to kill her. That's what you would have done if you knew the truth."

"Where is the real Adriana?"

"Dead. She was one of the first to get killed. She was on her way out when you came in. She left Natalia to do her fucking wedding dress fitting so she could go fucking around. That's why Natalia was in her dress. Natalia was her maid. She suffered that fate after Raul ordered Felipe to kill her father. Before that, she had to watch Raul rape and slice her mother's throat right in front of her." His eyes cloud, and so does my heart as his words sink in.

"Natalia was to serve his daughter until Adriana married Felipe, then he was going to sell her," he continues. At that moment I remember how she freaked out when she thought I was going to sell her. "That's what her life was supposed to be. Death. Then you came along like a fucking wild card, and I saw a choice. Either she died at your hands or someone else's. Being with you was the lesser evil. It gave me more time to think about how I was going to get her out."

"You were going to take her away?" I seethe.

"Of course, I was. I still planned to do so even when I saw you were in love with her."

His words sting me deep in my core, like acid being poured straight into my throat.

"I'm..." I want to tell him that I'm not in love.

I want to deny it, but the fucking words don't come.

"Can't say it, can you? Can't tell me you're not in love with her?"

"Shut the fuck up."

"You told me to talk, so I'm going to sing like a fucking canary. You're in love with her, so her name shouldn't make a difference to the way you feel about her. All the people who matter think she is Raul's daughter, and the assets have all been transferred to you. You have control over the fucking cartel. So, knowing who she is shouldn't make a difference to you. All you would need to do is love and protect her. You just won't accept what's so obvious to everyone else."

I throw him on the ground and continue to stare at him, seething, my blood boiling.

I don't want to accept that he's right, but the shitty thing about this is still the sting of betrayal, and the joke is still on me.

I fell for her, but I still don't know how she feels about me.

"I'll kill you if you talk," I threaten.

"If I cared about death, Mikhail Dmitriyev, I would have allowed you to kill me in Mexico. Men like me have their spot reserved in hell. That's a surety, so I don't care about my life. I care about hers, but you already know that."

"Why? Why do you care about her so much?"

A tear runs down his cheek. "It's my fault she's in this mess, and my fault Raul killed her parents in such a violent way. If not for me, she would never have known Raul. My drug addiction got her father mixed up with him. She was a little girl when she first became his slave. Ten years old. Only ten. In my eyes, she's still a little girl. I had to stand by and watch that girl's life change and turn into hell. So, you don't need to threaten me. You have my silence for anything to do with her. I just worry about who will save her from you."

"Let me worry about that."

As I walk away, I'm sure he'll worry about what I'll do.

I don't even know what the fuck I'm doing yet, and I don't want to hear the rest of the truth.

I can't go to her yet to find out. I don't want to hear how she lied to me to save her neck. I don't want to hear those parts that are obvious. I don't want to hear how she pretended to love me so I wouldn't kill her.

I don't want to hear any of it, so I drive to the lake house, where I stay until the sun goes down and allow the onslaught of my thoughts to get the best of me.

Chapter Thirty-Nine

Mikhail

It's not until late that I decide to head home, and I only do so because I think of how I left my wife naked, alone, and scared in the basement, which will be dark now.

Leaving her like that for the rest of the night would make me more of a devil than I already am.

She must be terrified. She was terrified when I left, and still, she begged for José's life. She didn't beg for her life. She screamed for his, pleaded for his. All she asked for in regard to herself was forgiveness.

My mind is numb by the time I reach home. With no staff around, the place feels barren of life.

When I walk down to the basement and open the door, all I hear are her quiet sobs.

I switch on the light, but she doesn't move. Her head is still bowed and she's still crying.

I feel like a bastard for leaving her like this. The sight is testament to the devil I am.

I hurt her just as much as Raul did. I added to her misery when all along we had an enemy in common.

Raul was our enemy. He killed my mother and sister, and he killed her parents.

I remember her nightmare, when she begged for her mother's life. I recall thinking I never knew she'd witnessed her mother's death. I was right. The real Adriana didn't, but Natalia did.

I remember asking about the whip marks on her back and wondering why Raul would treat his daughter like that. I was right again. He didn't treat the real Adriana that way; it was Natalia.

When Raul screamed and bawled out his eyes before I killed him, it wasn't because I had his daughter. It was because he realized my mistake and knew I'd already killed his Adriana.

He knew the woman I had was the wrong one but couldn't tell me because I'd sliced out his tongue.

The woman before me never deserved any of that. I don't need to know her for any length of time to know that.

She doesn't belong in our world...

José's words come back to assault my mind with a vengeance.

If she doesn't belong in our world, she doesn't belong with me.

That's one truth I know like I know my own fucking name.

It doesn't hurt me any less to know it, though.

A few steps into the room, and the obsession I've felt when I'm with her hits me.

By the time I'm a few inches away, madness takes me again. Madness takes me when I think she played me and made me believe she loved me.

It's only then she raises her head and looks at me.

Her face is red and swollen from crying. Her lips move, but no words come out.

It's clear she thinks I killed José.

I see that pain in her eyes again. That agonized look from

weeks ago. Except now I understand her, and the pain mirrors my own because of the losses she's had in her life.

"I didn't kill him," I tell her, and obsession brings back the jealousy I felt weeks ago.

"You didn't?" she chokes out.

"No."

"What are you going to do?"

"I don't know."

"I'm sorry."

Every time she says that, it irks me.

I rest one hand on the wall over her head and lift her chin with the other.

"Which parts are you sorry for, Natalia?" I try out her name with less angst. It feels right. "Sorry for the lie. Sorry that it didn't work out? Sorry I found out you played me?"

"I didn't play you. Please don't believe that. Everything I did with you was real. I never lied to you about my feelings for you."

She's never told me what those feelings are, but I've seen them, or at least what I thought I saw.

"Maybe I just saw what you wanted me to see. I certainly believed what you wanted me to believe."

"No."

"You lied about who you were to save your neck. How am I supposed to believe anything you say?"

She stares at me, and tears fall over the edges of her eyes.

"Ask me. Ask me how I feel about you. You said you could tell if I was lying. So, ask me," she pleads.

I tighten my grip on her throat and press my forehead to hers. I consider what she's asking me to do. This will be the first time in my life that I would have done this.

"Ask me, Mikhail, or kill me now," she mumbles. "Death will hurt my heart less than this. I don't know what else to do."

I lift my head from hers, and when I look into her eyes, I

detect the answer there in the depths. I don't need to ask the question.

What I see is what I always saw.

Her hazel eyes gleam with a sheen of purpose that steadies everything inside me and anchors my own feelings.

Nobody has ever looked at me like this.

I remember my father talking about how he felt about my mother. He described her as the other half of his soul.

That's how this woman feels to me. Maybe it's the same reason I refused to even consider something was off with her.

Her eyes brim with tenderness and passion, of unspoken promises and love. There is no mistake in what I read in them.

Or what I feel.

Instead of asking her anything, I move to her lips, and she reaches for me, too. The chains around her wrists clink. I think to take them off, but I don't want to break this moment for anything.

Hungrily, I kiss her lips, demanding she give me more, and she does.

She doesn't hold back, and all she gives me leaves my mouth burning with fire.

I catch her tiny waist and run my fingers down to her pussy, feeling how wet she is, how ready for me to fuck her.

The moisture of her sweet nectar in her delicious pussy sliding over my fingers hardens my cock, and there's only one thing I can think of doing right now.

It's the only thing I always think of when I'm with her.

I shove my pants down my waist and take out my aching cock.

I push her up against the wall, and as I slam into her welcoming heat, I don't hold back. A pleasure-filled moan tears from her lips, but I keep kissing her, and I keep fucking her.

I keep possessing her.

She wraps her legs around my waist as I drive into her body harder and faster. I release her only to shove my pants down further so I can angle her against the wall to fuck her properly, but she grinds her hips against mine and presses herself closer to me.

"Don't stop touching me," she begs, pushing away from the chains. "Please."

"I don't plan to," I vow. The words carry more strength than the vows I spoke on our wedding day.

I press her to me and allow the downpour of the raging pleasure to enslave me. Waves of ecstasy throb through my body and my dick as I fuck her.

When she comes, arching her back and screaming my name, clenching my cock with her slick walls, my balls tighten, and I lose control.

The rawness of our shared climax sends me over the edge, and I hold on to her, kissing her still, taking her with me.

It takes a while for us to calm down from that height of pleasure, and even when I do, I don't want to let her go.

Nevertheless, it's me who moves first, because I'm the one who should speak first.

I cup her face and gaze down at her.

"I love you, Natalia," I tell her.

A beautiful but weak smile graces her face. "I love you, too, Mikhail."

"I know."

I release her chains and scoop her up to carry her up the stairs.

As I walk, more truth hits me.

I've never told any woman, apart from my mother and sister, I loved them.

This one is the first, and as I look at her, I know she'll be the last.

She doesn't belong in our world.

José's words hit me again.

He's right. That means if I do love her, I can't keep her in my world.

Chapter Forty

Natalia

I lie cocooned in Mikhail's arms.

Neither of us has slept.

Since the dungeon, we've been wrapped in each other, making love, and he's hardly stopped touching me.

Now he's lying next to me. Holding me close to his heart.

I have so much to say to him, but I'm afraid to break the silence and shatter the moment. I don't know what's going to happen next, but I know he's thinking about it.

I told him I loved him, and now that I know how he feels about me—me, Natalia—I want to savor the feeling, if only for a few more hours. But it's clear neither of us can sleep because there's still plenty to worry about.

Me being me changes everything for both of us.

I was so scared in that dungeon. I truly thought Mikhail was going to kill José. I spent the time flitting between worrying about José and thinking about what my lie did.

I never expected the shift in Mikhail's mood when he came back.

I don't know what happened when he met José. I know he

talked to him, though, and something was said to change the tide of what could have been, because Mikhail was different when he returned.

He's been even more different as the hours have gone by. His touch feels remorseful, and he keeps kissing the bruises the chains left on my wrists.

Warm fingers trace along my back, and Mikhail presses his lips to my forehead.

I meet his gaze and his lips for a brief kiss.

"Go to sleep, princess," he whispers. In the moonlight, I can see the wealth of worry in his eyes.

"I can't sleep."

"You need to. Don't worry about anything. Go to sleep."

He covers my hands with his, and I notice his wedding ring. His fingers lock with mine, and I think of how he feels like mine again. That's what lulls me to sleep.

It feels like a few seconds have passed, but when I open my eyes again, it's morning and he's not beside me.

I sit up, thinking first that he's gone to work, but then I catch sight of the open sliding doors.

I reach for my robe and pull it on, then walk out onto the balcony, where I find Mikhail sitting on the little bench.

He's shirtless and smoking a Cuban cigar. His hair is ruffled and seems a little longer like that.

A lock falls over his eye when he looks at me. He tucks it behind his ear and reaches his hand out to me.

I walk toward him, and he puts the cigar out.

I smile when he pulls me into his lap and kisses the bridge of my nose.

"Good sleep?" he asks.

"Yes. Are you going out today?"

"I have to. There are a few things I need to take care of, but we have to talk first."

Talk.

My heart squeezes, and I look away. He, however, guides my face back to meet his.

"Natalia, you know we have to talk, don't you?"

I nod. "Yes."

He lifts my left hand and kisses the bruise on my wrist. That remorseful look enters his eyes again, and he kisses my skin once more.

"The first thing I need to say is I'm sorry for the way I treated you yesterday."

I'm shocked by the apology. He apologizes to no one.

"I understand why you did it."

"That doesn't make it right. You're my wife. I... just lost my shit, and I shouldn't have. I don't want you to be afraid of me. I'm not a monster. I'm not. I don't want you to think I am."

"I don't."

"Thank you. I've... been doing a lot of thinking."

"Because I'm not the princess anymore," I fill in.

"Yes and no."

"How did you find out?"

"I don't want you to worry about that."

"Did you speak to José?"

"I did, and he told me what Raul did to you and your family."

I was right.

"Are you disappointed that you got the maid?"

"I don't think you could ever do anything to disappoint me, Malyshka." He shakes his head. "I think it's time I tell you what's going on and what needs to happen after it's resolved."

"What's going on?"

"I've been investigating Raul's activities with a friend of mine, and so far, it looks like he and Ivan joined to plan to kill my mother, my sister, and me."

I suck in a sharp breath.

"Ivan?"

"Yeah. I don't have evidence yet, but the evidence I found

so far points toward him. I don't know who else is working with him, but that's what's happening."

"But he's your brother."

"Baby, that means nothing. He wants to be Pakhan, take over the brotherhood and the business. After that incident, I was in a coma for a few months, and I'm sure he thought I was going to die. With me out of the way, he gets it all. My father will reveal who will be the new leader in a few days' time. I don't know what I'll find out in the meantime or after, but I will search heaven and earth trying to find it and eliminate him before he can get to me and mine again."

I feel prompted to tell him what Ivan said to me. "I think he knew my mother," I tell him, and Mikhail tenses.

"What?"

"When we first met at your father's house, he told me I looked familiar. I knew that was impossible because Raul kept me away from his associates and I never saw any of them. Then last week, Ivan said I reminded him of a woman who worked for Raul. I look exactly like my mother, Mikhail."

"Do you think he knows the truth about you?"

"I don't know. But he said I have the same look of fear in my eyes. My mother was attacked a few times before Raul killed her... I don't know if that's how Ivan knew her."

His skin pales. "Jesus, if you see him, call me. I'll instruct the staff to inform me if he comes here. Do not speak to him or anyone. You hear me?"

"Yes."

"What will happen if he finds out the truth about me?"

"Nothing. He's no fool. He knows people think you're Raul's daughter. He would be an idiot to make them think otherwise because I'm sure he wants the cartel, too. To ally himself the way he did with Raul, he would have had some agreement with him I don't know about yet. So, owning the cartel is going to be an asset."

"But he could only get the cartel if you..." My voice trails off.

"If he killed me? Yes." He looks out to the expanse before us and returns his gaze to me. "I don't want you to worry about that. Ever. Or worry about someone capturing you to do what I did to you. José said you don't belong in our world. You don't. I've had to accept that you don't belong with me, either."

My lips part, and a heavy weight pulls on my heart.

"What do you mean?"

"I'm going to do my best to keep you safe, and when I figure out what's happening with my brother, I'm... I'm going to set you free."

"But, Mikhail—"

"It's the right thing to do." He holds my gaze, and I can't look away. "I'll make sure you'll be able to do everything you ever wanted to do, like med school. And José will be right alongside you. That's what's going to happen."

I don't know what to say to him. When I was first captured, this would have been a miracle I could only wish for. Now that it's happened, I can't wrap my head around it.

I don't want him to set me free.

"You said I was yours," I mumble.

"You are. You are mine, so if I love you the way I say I do, it's for me to take care of you. It's my responsibility as your husband to make sure you have the life you deserve, even if it's not with me. I'm not a good person, Natalia." He cups my face. "Staying with me will always mean possible captivity and danger. You should be free of the cartel, and the Bratva, too. You know I'm right."

He kisses my lips and sets me down on the bench.

I'm so numb I can't move.

One more kiss is placed on my forehead before he leaves, and as I watch him walk away, he looks back at me then continues through the door.

* * *

"Hi," José says when he walks up to me.

"Hi."

I didn't think I was going to see him today, but it makes sense after that conversation I had with Mikhail this morning that he'd come by.

He joins me on the little bench by the lakeside, and I look over the bruises on his face.

"Are you okay?" I ask.

"Yeah, I'm an old, tough fool. These are just scratches." He chuckles. "How are you feeling?"

"I'm okay."

He sighs and leans forward onto his elbows. "We've had one hell of a ride, you and I, haven't we?"

"We have."

"Mikhail spoke to me earlier. After I finish my work at the shipping company tonight, he wants me here full time as your bodyguard. Until we leave."

"He said that?"

"He did. He said he spoke to you about leaving. I had a feeling you wouldn't be feeling all that thrilled about leaving him, whenever that might be, so I thought I'd come by and check how you were."

"I'm not okay with it. I should be thrilled. But I'm not." I blink a few times and shake my head. "How did I get here, José? I'm supposed to be happy. It worked out in the end for both of us. Look how far we've come and what's happened to us. How could I not want freedom?"

"It's not that you don't want freedom, mija. That's not the problem at all. The problem is love lost. The sacrifice and what freedom costs." He nods with conviction. "Mi amor, Mikhail is right, though. You'll be safer away from here for several reasons. I don't know the full details about what's going on with his brother or what Mikhail plans to do to him, but if he fails, then neither of us wants you anywhere near here or the Bratva. You specifically can't be. His brother has his eye on you, mi amor. That's not good."

It's not.

And that's a problem I'll have no matter what my name is.

Chapter Forty-One

Mikhail

Eric looks at me cautiously as I enter his hotel room.

He has one more night here before he heads back to L.A., then he'll be back again next week.

He asked me to stop by after work. Just to talk.

Fuck knows I need to talk, but I'm also tired.

It's been a long fucking day, and I can't wait to see the back of it. I just have one more stop after this. I need to check in with José at the docks before I head home.

"Feeling better, old friend?" he asks, motioning for me to sit.

I lower myself to the chair and shake my head. "I don't know."

We spoke briefly on the phone, and I filled him in on what happened and what I decided to do regarding Natalia.

As right as it feels, it's weird thinking of her new name. It helps that I thought of her as the princess or my Malyshka.

"Well, for what it's worth, I spent some time going through whatever records I could find on Adriana Alvarez and erasing them from existence."

I straighten. "You can do that?"

"I *did* do that." He chuckles. "Raul went through great lengths to conceal his daughter's identity, so it wasn't that hard to find the little information that existed on her. I just erased it. That way, no one can accidentally stumble upon it."

"Jesus, Eric. Thank you."

"No worries. I thought you would appreciate it no matter what you decide to do."

I dip my head. "I do appreciate it. Sounds like you think I might change my mind."

"I think you're in a weird situation right now. Things could change and you might want different things. You might want to keep her."

Keeping her sounds like a dream my heart wants, but I can't think about that now.

"I can't see past this trouble and nightmare. We started off the wrong way. Everything about our first meeting was wrong. She watched me kill and threatened her life." How the fuck can I want what's best for her and keep her in the same breath? "I was so fueled with rage that I would have probably killed her had I known who she was."

"Mikhail, I think any of us would have behaved the way you did given the circumstances. I don't know anyone who would have been able to think straight if they'd gone through what you did."

"I don't know. It's not in my nature to be calm or patient. I flipped out, and if given the chance, I would do it all over again because it's the same fucking pain. She deserves someone better than that. And what's fucking worse is, Ivan wants her."

Worry clouds his eyes. "What makes you think that?"

"I know him. She also told me he could have known her mother. He said there was a woman in Mexico who worked for Raul who she looked like." That played on my mind, too. The moment she told me he'd said the fear in her eyes was the same as the woman's he knew, I was certain he'd done something to her mother.

"Fuck. Well, that's a long shot, but something we need to be aware of. I don't think he'd do anything about exposing her identity if he ever found anything out. It would be foolish to do that and put the ownership of the cartel in disarray."

"I thought so, too. But the important part is him knowing. Eric, if anything happens to me—"

"Fuck you," he cuts me off, and his face contorts into a scowl. "Don't tell me that bullshit. We're working hard so nothing *does* happen to you."

"I know, but I have to be real. Something did happen to me once before. It was close, Eric. Right now, we're not any closer than where we were days ago. We can't find shit on Ivan, and whatever my father decides regarding the leadership will still put me at odds with my brother. Ivan is still going to want me dead because we'll have equal shares in the company. He's plotting my death now as we speak." That's the realistic picture of what I have to face. "If anything happens to me, please promise me you won't let Ivan take my girl. Don't let him take her. He won't plan to keep her the way I want to. If she ends up with him, it will mean death for her. I can't let that happen."

That motherfucker will use her until she's of no use to him, and then he'll do exactly what I thought I had the heart to do—sell her or give her away. Except, whoever he sells her to or gives her to will be the same type of sadistic bastards who killed Talia.

My girl will suffer the same fate and beg for death.

"Okay, I will make sure she's safe." Eric sighs. "Keep your ear to the ground, Mikhail. Try to stay focused. I'm heading out tomorrow, but that doesn't mean I won't be working on things behind the scenes."

"Thanks. I owe you."

"You keep saying that."

"Because it's true."

He chuckles. "That's all I got for you."

"Cool. I'm going to speak to José about locking away Raul's files."

"Good. Talk to you tomorrow."

I give him a curt nod and leave.

The docks are fortunately not far from the hotel, so it doesn't take me long to get there.

There aren't many staff around, either. I should be about five minutes, then I'm out. This is José's last night here, too.

I felt he's the best bodyguard Natalia could have.

When I reach the door, my steps slow when I notice droplets of blood on the ground leading to the door of the warehouse he works in.

I reach for my gun when I notice more blood by the door.

Walking carefully, with my gun ready, I push the door open and freeze mid-stride when I see José on the floor covered in blood and his throat slit from ear to ear.

His lips are blue, his eyes wide open, lifeless.

He's dead.

* * *

As the hours have ticked by, one person after another has come to investigate what the fuck must have happened here.

The only thing that's been on my mind is how I was going to break the news of José's death to Natalia.

I have no idea what fucking words I'm going to use to tell her that the man who was like family to her was killed. He's dead.

Clearly, he saw or heard something he shouldn't have, and someone here is working for either Ivan or one of my enemies.

José's death also means my plans to protect my wife the way I wanted to have just gone out the fucking window.

I was supposed to be home hours ago, so she's going to be wondering where I am.

I had Levka and another guard head to the house, while Sebastian has been here with me looking through the surveillance and talking to people who would have noticed José. I just finished the last recording while he's been busy questioning the porter, the last person on the list to speak with.

The fucking cameras in the warehouse he was working in weren't on.

That doesn't just fucking happen. This is where we do our arms trafficking under wraps and other shit of the illegal variety. So, the cameras have to be working.

The security guard said everything was working this morning when he checked, so it's obvious someone switched them off.

I haven't noticed anything out of the ordinary on the recordings the other cameras picked up. I didn't think I would. Whoever is screwing with me is allowing me to see what they want me to see.

I walk into the little foreman's office Sebastian has been using to talk to the workers. He's still talking to the porter.

They both look at me when I walk in.

"Anything so far?" I demand.

The porter looks like he's going to shit himself.

"Nothing," Sebastian replies. "He says José left the premises before lunch, and no one saw him come back on site."

I narrow my eyes. To get back on site, someone would have had to see him.

Unless he went directly to the warehouse loading bay, and the fucking cameras aren't working for us to establish that.

"No one saw him. I've been here all day," the porter adds.

"That's fine. You can go," I reply. "If you think of anything else, call me."

"Yes, boss."

The porter gets up and leaves.

Sebastian shakes his head and opens his palms. "I don't know what else to do."

"You head home, too. I'll need you at the house twenty-four-seven starting tomorrow night. Switch things up with Levka."

"Sure thing."

He leaves, too.

I lean against the wall with my head pressed against it, thinking about my next move.

I saw José this morning. We talked about what I wanted him to do. Aleksander said he was at the house around lunchtime, and he wasn't there for long. I'd given him permission to talk to Natalia, so I expected him to go to the house.

That time frame checks out, but not after, and there's a huge gap when no one saw him.

I had him doing some odd jobs for me when he wasn't working on the cartel stuff. That's why he was mainly here. It's not uncommon for a person to be working inside the warehouse itself amongst the containers and deliveries without being seen for hours. What makes this particularly weird is that normally, a few would have encountered him because of the job I gave him.

This all stinks of Ivan. I'm no longer pussyfooting around the truth.

José saw Ivan talking to a guy who worked for Raul. He saw them here. Maybe something like that happened again.

I know what my gut tells me. It's screaming at me that José must have witnessed Ivan do some shit and he killed him.

When, though?

When did it happen?

My phone rings. I answer straightaway.

It's Eric. He came by when I first found José's body. He looked at him with the coroner. He seemed to have suspected something more.

"Hey," I say into the phone.

"Hi, are you still at the docks?"

"Yeah."

"The coroner just finished his first examination. I went with him because José's wound looked off to me."

"What do you mean?"

"Like he got it after he died," he replies.

I grit my teeth. "*After?*"

"Yeah. I wasn't sure, so I thought I'd check with the coroner, and I was right. The cause of death wasn't slashing his throat. It was poison. There's a needle mark on the back of his neck. It also looks like he died a few hours before his throat was slashed, and I don't think it happened at the docks."

Holy fuck. If it's a few *hours*, that matches the statements I've been getting.

"So, someone poisoned him first, then brought him back here to the docks to make it look like he was attacked?"

"Yeah. That's what it looks like."

Fuck. I feel like I'm heading deeper into a maze, and I can't find my way out.

That makes no sense.

None of that makes sense.

Ivan, what the fuck are you up to?

"The other thing is, I found José's car parked about two miles from your house behind an alley," Eric states. "My guess is that's where he was killed."

"If he was behind an alley, maybe he was watching someone."

"I think so. I have a cop associate who works in forensics looking into it for me. I asked him to keep an eye out if anything else crops up."

"Fuck, this keeps getting more complicated."

"I know. I'll check in again if I have anything else for you."

"Thanks."

He hangs up, and I release a haggard sigh.

More things keep happening, and I still don't have answers.

Now I have to break Natalia's heart.

Chapter Forty-Two

Natalia

I t's nearly sunrise.

I woke a few minutes ago, unable to go back to sleep.

I'm still lying in bed with the lights out, and all I'm doing is gazing out the window at the bright moonlight.

Mikhail didn't come home last night, and I've had no one to ask questions to because it was late when I realized he wasn't coming back.

The house is heavily guarded outside, but in times like these, I feel alone.

Alone and left to my thoughts and my worries, which is almost as bad as being in a room full of people who aren't talking to you.

The only times I experienced this type of worry was back in Mexico when I was little and growing up on the plantation. Living there was awful, just awful.

I used to worry about my father when he worked away. I worried something would happen to him. Something was always happening to the men who did the drug runs or any work, really, they did for Raul.

I also worried myself sick about Mom and me being safe while he was away.

Papa would leave, and Mom and I were left alone in that little plantation house. The men on the grounds were so vile and disgusting. They were always wolf-whistling at my mother and propositioning her for sex. Then, when I got older, they did the same to me.

Sometimes, José would come around to check on us, and his presence alone would keep us safe because they knew he was Raul's lieutenant. They didn't want to get in trouble with him, or worse, Raul.

I shuffle to sit up when the door handle turns.

When Mikhail pokes his head in, I switch the light on.

He walks in, and the moment I take note of the tentative expression on his face, I know something more has happened.

"Malyshka, you're awake," he breathes.

"I was worried."

I slip off the bed. He walks toward me and gives me a quick kiss.

He then sits me back down on the bed, and as he touches my face, a flicker of sadness dulls the light that normally shines in his eyes.

I notice he hasn't said that there's nothing to worry about.

"Something's wrong," I say. When he nods, my stomach and chest tighten. "What's happened?" I'm afraid to ask.

He takes both my hands into his and holds them.

"Baby, it's José," he replies. His tone is low and distant. Too distant for him. "Something's happened to him."

A sudden heaviness expands my core, making my heart squeeze then go numb.

"What... happened to him, Mikhail?" I choke out.

"I'm sorry, baby, he's... dead. He was killed."

My hands fly to my mouth, and I shoot up to my feet. Tears well in my eyes then spill over and run down my cheeks.

"No." I shake my head. "No. It's not true. It can't be. I saw him yesterday. He's not... dead. It's not true, Mikhail. No."

Mikhail moves closer and holds me by my shoulders.

"I'm truly sorry." His voice holds more emotion than I've ever heard.

I continue to shake my head in disbelief and then finally snap when I realize he's not correcting what he just told me.

When I think of José and the man he is to me, I break. The tears come harder, draining my strength, and I scream as my knees give and I fall to the floor.

Mikhail pulls me close to him, folding me into a soothing embrace, but I'm so broken I can't feel him.

I can't feel anything besides the sadness that tears me apart.

"José," I whisper through my tears.

Mikhail pulls me even closer. The rapid beat of his heart is the only thing that anchors me from slipping away into the sadness.

I can't even ask what happened to him because all words are frozen in my mind.

* * *

I don't know how long I cry for. I remember it being dark outside, then the sun rose. Then night fell again, and I still cried. The only difference as the time moved was me moving from the floor to the bed.

It seems all the grief I've suffered in my life has come pouring out of my soul.

First for Mom, then Papa, now José.

I don't have anyone left now who was close to my heart, and I know the clock is ticking over my head when it comes to Mikhail.

He stayed with me, holding me, but I still can't feel anything. I can't feel him even when he touches me. It's like the numbness has suffused my being and I will never feel anything again but this sadness.

It's late in the night when Mikhail tries to get me to eat some fruit Aleksander brought up earlier.

I haven't eaten anything, and I don't want to. I've just been sipping on water and orange juice here and there. I can't remember the last time I ate.

"Natalia, please eat something. I need you to eat something, baby." Mikhail holds out some grapes to me.

I shake my head and rest it back on the headboard.

"What happened to him?" I finally ask. Those are the most words I've spoken since I got the news. "What happened to José?"

I've heard Mikhail on phone calls talking about it, but he never said enough or gave enough information for me to grasp what happened.

He sets the bowl of fruit back on the nightstand and looks at me.

"I think we should talk about that another time."

"I want to talk about it now." I dab away the tears that fall with the heel of my hand.

"Malyshka, there are some things you're better off not knowing."

I stare at him long and hard, and I can't help but feel angered because he's deciding for me again.

"How can it be better if I don't know? How can you say that to me?"

"I know why I say that, and sometimes, I have to decide when certain things are best for others."

"Like how you decided it's better for me to be without you?" I throw back and he looks like I just slapped him. "Those are all my decisions."

"No, they aren't. This isn't about me and you. You're grieving, and I don't want to make the pain any worse than it is."

I look away from him, then roll onto my side, dismissing him.

"Natalia."

"Please, just leave me alone," I rasp as another bout of sadness takes me. "If you aren't going to tell me what happened to José, leave me alone."

He sighs, and my heart sinks when his footsteps connect with the floor and I hear him close the door behind him when he leaves.

Slowly, I adjust myself and search my mind for something to blame for José's death.

I know Ivan obviously had something to do with what happened, but I don't know why or how that would make sense.

What did José do to make Ivan kill him?

It's difficult to know how to piece things together when Mikhail won't tell me how José died. All he told me was José was killed. For all I know, he could have been caught in a crossfire or something just as bad.

I'm imagining all sorts of things, each worse than the last. Every thought hurts because I can't believe something happened that would lead to José getting killed, which is probably why Mikhail didn't want to tell me.

I want to blame the situation José and I got caught in, but I know I can't do that. It's not as simple as that.

We were always trapped in the situation, whether we were in Mexico or New York. His death is just one more thing and an extension of a continuing problem.

One I don't know how to get through.

Regardless of what happens, how will I get through this when I feel so broken?

I close my eyes, and the next thing I know, warm fingers graze over my cheek.

I open my eyes to see it's morning again and I'm curled up

in Mikhail's arms. I don't remember him coming back or moving into his arms.

"Do you want to go for a walk with Snow?" he asks. It will be the first time we've done that.

"Yes."

"Come, let's go. Just grab a coat."

I do just that, and minutes later, we're walking together hand in hand by the lake with Snow running ahead of us with a twig in her mouth.

We walk deeper into the woods and stop by the alcove of trees near the pond with the little ducks. There's a bench there, where Mikhail sits me down and sits next to me.

"I've made funeral arrangements for Friday," he says.

I've been in such a state that I didn't even think of the funeral.

"Thanks so much for doing that."

"It's okay. You don't have to thank me for that."

"I'm very grateful."

"I know you are, and I'm sorry for your loss. It's strange. In the end, he was the only person I trusted to take care of you. I knew he didn't have any other agenda besides making sure you were safe. Natalia, I didn't want to tell you what happened to him until you were stronger. You're right, though. I can't make those types of decisions for you. So, I'll tell you what happened." He pauses for a moment then turns slightly so he can look at me. "I found José at the warehouse with his throat slit, but he was poisoned before that happened. Meaning someone killed him and took him to the warehouse to make it look like he was attacked."

"My God." I pull in a breath and bring my hand to my heart.

"It's reasonable to assume he saw something. Things are getting out of hand, and I've been thinking about how best to keep you safe."

"I'm safe with you, aren't I?"

"No. You aren't," he answers, and the hole in my heart widens. "You were never safe with me. So, after the leadership is announced, I'm sending you away."

That's the day after the funeral.

"That's four days' time." It's too soon.

"The sooner you leave, the better it will be for you. I'm sending you to L.A."

"L.A.?"

He nods. "I have friends there who can make sure you're safe."

"That's so far away."

"That's the point, princess. Nothing like this has ever happened. I feel stuck. I have the best people working for me, yet all I have are assumptions. I can't just walk up to my brother and kill him based on assumptions. I also know the problem isn't just about him. Everything is too carefully constructed so he's a step ahead of me. No one person can do that. So, it's not safe for you to be here anymore."

"But I love—"

"No." He shakes his head and stands up. "You weren't supposed to love me, Natalia. I'm the villain here, so I don't get the happily ever after with the wife I love, or the future I want with her. No matter what anyone says, what's happening is my fault. I could have just killed Raul and Felipe. If I weren't a monster, I wouldn't have taken you or José. If I hadn't, he'd still be alive. You can't tell me that's not true."

I don't know what to say to him, because he's right, and I don't want him to be.

The truth is something I never had a choice in changing, and neither does he.

Chapter Forty-Three

Mikhail

José's funeral was early this morning.

I had to watch Natalia break all over again. Only time can heal that kind of heartbreak. There's nothing anyone can do to soothe those wounds any quicker.

Every thought and memory of the person you loved and lost will feel like salt pouring on raw, open wounds.

It's still like that for me and continues.

The rising sun heralded the ticking clock over my head. A countdown on the time I have left with my wife.

I have two days now. Tomorrow, the day of the inauguration, and most of the day she will leave me for good.

The only people I've told she's going away are my father and Sophia, but I purposely didn't tell them *where* Natalia was going, so I could keep her location secret from Ivan.

My father and Sophia think Natalia will be staying at one of our safe houses until the problem is resolved. As an extra layer of security, it's protocol that none of us know where each other's safe houses are located.

So, they have no idea where she's headed, and they don't know about my plan of Natalia to never return to me.

She'll be under the protection of the Voirik.

I've made all the arrangements. I'm just finalizing things now with Eric.

He got back to New York earlier, but this is the first chance I've had to meet him. I couldn't leave Natalia earlier in the state she was in, but she seemed to calm as the day wore on.

I couldn't afford to lose time with her since there's so little of it.

Eric opens the door to his hotel suite the moment I knock. Like he was waiting for me.

"Hey, there," he says.

"Hi," I sigh, walking in.

We enter the sitting room, where he pours me some scotch. I fucking need it.

"Thanks." The ice clinks against the glass as I swirl the amber liquid around and take a swig. The bitterness hits the back of my throat, but the gentle buzz I crave follows seconds later.

"How are things?" he asks, resting his hands on his knees.

I'm sure he can tell my mind is fucked.

"The same." I bite the inside of my lip. "Funeral was this morning. Natalia was a mess."

He offers a look of sympathy. "I can imagine."

"Things okay with you?" I never want to make it look like I'm the kind of fucker who takes his friends for granted because of what they can do for me. I'm aware Eric is here on borrowed time. He already stayed longer than his usual amount of time. I'm sure his wife must miss him.

He's a man like me, so he'll always be thinking of his girl's safety.

His face brightens at the question, and I know he's about to tell me something about his wife.

"Summer is pregnant," he says with a bright smile.

I smile, too, because that's great news. "Congratulations, man."

I reach forward and shake his hand.

"Thank you. I never thought I'd have kids. I was that guy who never factored in the future. Until her."

His words grip me because the person he's describing is me.

"You met the right woman."

"I did, and I know I'm lucky. We've been married for years and had fun together. Now we're looking forward to starting a family."

I smile wider and wonder what that must feel like. A baby, an actual extension of them and their love.

That's not in the cards for me. None of it is. I have to accept that.

"I'm really happy for you both. We can all do with some good news. It's food for the soul."

"It is." The seriousness returns to his face. "Everything is finalized on my end. Natalia will stay with Summer and me until she gets her house ready."

"You sure that's going to be okay?"

"Of course. We have plenty of space, and Summer will love the company. I've arranged for Aiden to pick Natalia up from the airport when she arrives. He'll call once he has her secured. I don't think you'll have to worry about anything more after that."

"I can't thank you enough."

"Don't mention it." He dips his head, and I down the rest of the scotch. "As for everything else, I'm watching and waiting to see what happens after tomorrow night."

I nod my agreement. Waiting and watching is all we can do for the moment. Things have gone quiet, and they're like that for a reason.

Once we know my father's next move, I'll know mine.

"If Ivan gets the position, I'll be in immediate danger. If I get it, at least I'll have a head start."

"I pray for the latter."

Me too.

* * *

I get home an hour later, just before midnight.

I was hoping Natalia was asleep and didn't wait up for me, but the slice of light streaming from under the bedroom door is a tell she's awake.

I push the door open slowly. She's sitting behind the dressing table running her fingers through her damp hair. There's a towel wrapped around her body.

Nothing but the towel.

Before I left earlier, she was lying down on the bed, and I'd told her to relax in the bath. Looks like she took my advice.

I just wish the sight of her lithe, perfect body weren't hardening my dick and I didn't want her so fucking badly it aches.

She twists around on the little stool to face me, causing the towel to slink down her back, exposing more of her silky, opulent flesh.

Her hair falls over her shoulders and runs down her side, and the shimmer of moonlight pouring through the window touches her face.

I walk toward her and crouch down in front of her, taking her hand resting on her thigh.

In silence, we stare at each other for a few moments. The wheels are turning in my mind as I think about what to say, but every word is swallowed up by how I feel about her.

Asking her how she's feeling is fruitless.

I know she feels like shit. How else is she supposed to feel after losing a man who was like a father to her?

She's not going to feel any better than she did hours ago.

Talking about José pulls on my soul, too, because I know I'm responsible for her pain.

As I stare at her, I don't want her to remember she can't expect anything more than pain and despair from a monster like me.

Just for a moment, I want to forget what and who I am and savor this feeling I feel when it's just us. When nothing else matters.

Just her and me.

The beauty and the beast.

She reaches out to touch my face. That's all it takes for me to get lost in her.

I reach up to cup her cheeks and press my lips to hers to kiss her.

When she slips her arms around my neck, the towel slides from her body, and the huge round swells of her breasts heave against me. I run my fingers over them, filling my palms then feeling and kneading the succulent skin.

Her nipples harden at my touch. Harden and beg me to suck them while her body pleads to be fucked.

I decide to take care of her nipples first when I leave her lips and take the diamond-hard peaks into my mouth and suck them. She arches her body into my mouth, so I take more of her breast in and swirl my tongue around and around her nipple.

I fondle the neglected breast and make my way over to suck it, too. When I get my fill, I climb back up to her lips.

I haven't had her in so long, too long, my fucking cock is bursting to be inside her.

She kisses me harder, usurping control as she shows me how much she wants me. The tenderness of her lips and greediness of her passion make me forget I'm trying to stop my heart from beating for her.

The eagerness in her touch and the impatience in her kiss make me forget I'm supposed to resist the urge to take her.

I forget everything and allow recklessness to rule my mind when I think of having her one more time.

One more taste.

One more indulgence.

One more night with my wife.

Just once more, then I'll try to find my way back from madness.

Her greedy hands pull the buttons of my shirt open and push it down my shoulders.

I straighten and allow her to undo my belt, lacing my fingers through her hair when she caresses my cock through the fabric of my pants.

I love the feel of the silky strands flowing through my fingers like water, and the feel of her at my fingertips touching me the way she knows will please me.

I watch her and commit everything about what she's doing to memory because I never want to forget.

So, I watch the way she unzips my fly and pushes my pants down to take out my cock. I love the confidence she exudes as she does this, knowing she's doing exactly what I want her to.

I savor the way she licks over the head of my dick, licking off the pearly bead of pre-cum before she takes my length into her mouth and sucks me.

Fuck. She's fucking perfect. Fucking perfect and mine.

My dick grows in her hands and her mouth, aching for release. My balls tighten, and I nearly blow my load, but I control it. No fucking way am I going to finish now when we're just getting started.

If this is our last time , I want to take everything I can from her and seal it inside my heart and soul.

She stops sucking, knowing my body needs her to stop so I can fuck her now. I pick her up, and we move toward the wall I first pressed her up against when I took her virginity.

We're different people to the man and woman we were back then. Or rather, she was still a girl, and I made her my woman up against this wall.

I slam into her passage, wet and ready just for me, and she moans out loud. I do, too, because she feels so fucking good. She fits me perfectly, and I was made for her. As was my body to please hers.

Our burning bodies move together as one as I drive into her, fucking her relentlessly.

She writhes against me, moving her hips against mine, fucking me, too.

Heat streaks through me and explodes with savage energy. It tears me apart and leaves my mind reeling with delight and everything good.

She comes with a soul-wrenching cry, her body clenching mine deep to the core.

I'm not, however, finished with her yet. Not even close.

With her legs wrapped around me, I take her to the bed, where we fall down onto the silky sheets with me fucking her into the mattress.

Insanity intoxicates me, and like an addict, I indulge in more of her, going deeper, harder, faster.

When she comes again, I flip her onto her hands and knees so I can take her from behind.

She barely manages to catch her breath when I do and plunge back into her.

Her breasts bounce with every thrust, and I catch a glimpse of our reflection in the floor-to-ceiling windows. The room captures the sight of us, flesh slapping against flesh, raw and primal, mixing the scent of sex and love.

It all hits me at once as well as the epiphany of what this woman means to me.

She is the light to my darkness.

The sun, moon, and stars in my sky.

I can't bleed her from my mind because she's the other half of my soul.

That's the answer, and as long as I live, nothing will be truer than that.

Chapter Forty-Four

Mikhail

"Are you nervous about later?" Natalia whispers against my chest. She runs her fingers over my skin, and I press my hand to hers.

We're lying on the bed together. She's cocooned in my arms.

I want to take her all over again, but we needed a break before the last round. The sun will be up soon, and the spell will be broken.

"I mean because you want to be Pakhan," she adds. "Do you even get nervous?"

There's a smile in her voice, which means part of her is healing. When you can smile again after loss, even just a little, it means pieces of your heart are coming back together to fill the hole grief left behind.

"Yes, I get nervous, and I am nervous about later. I want to be Pakhan. Few people in the brotherhood get this chance, and when it was offered to me, I wanted to do everything I could to seize the opportunity. So, yes, I'm fucking nervous I won't get picked." It's been hard keeping what I suspect about Ivan from my father and Sophia. I knew knowing what I know would destroy him further, and I couldn't do that without proof. I'm hours away from the time of reckoning and feel like a failure.

"I'm nervous about Ivan getting something he doesn't deserve," I add. "Something that will give him more power. But I'm also nervous because I worry there'll be something I neglected to do that didn't qualify me for the job."

"You work hard, Mikhail. I'm not with you while you're at the office, but I know you."

I press her hand to my heart.

"I do work hard, baby."

"Then trust in that." She runs her hands through my hair and over my beard.

"You want me again." I catch her face and beam down at the seductive stare she gives me.

"Yes. I'm trying to get what I can. It will be breakfast soon, and I'll have to be jealous of the maids ogling my husband and speaking to him in a language I don't understand."

I brush my lips over her nose. "There was never anything to be jealous of. You and I speak our own language, one nobody else can understand."

"We do," she agrees, and we fall into a kiss again. Then each other.

Seconds after we climb down from the height of passion and pleasure, the sun pokes its head through the blanket of darkness and my heart sinks.

She looks, too, and knows the dawn of a new day means the enchantment has broken and we have to face a new reality.

We have one more sunrise I purposely won't watch with her.

So, this is our last.

I can't watch her like this again and suffer the temptation to keep her, nor the feeling of guilt that rides my soul every time I look at her.

I don't want to feel like I'm not good enough for her.

Those who know better should do better, so this is me trying.

And loving her even more than I did yesterday.

* * *

When I reach Dmitriyev Ltd., I'm surprised to see the meeting hall practically full of the men from the brotherhood.

No one is ever late for a meeting, but they're never this early, either.

We have about twenty minutes before the ceremony begins.

Everyone's presence heightens my awareness of the importance of tonight.

They're all dressed for the occasion and the venue. I've always thought this building with its spectacular array of crystal chandeliers and lavish European design is too elaborate for men like us. Most of us have been behind bars more times than the years we've lived on this earth, and most of us wouldn't have minded meeting in a hovel.

Everyone who is anyone will be here to witness this momentous night. A night few see in their lifetimes. Those who are older will remember when my father became Pakhan. Those who are younger will remember tonight for the same reason.

No matter how young or old the men are, they'll all be eager to be part of what happens tonight because it will be the first and only time in our history when a choice of Pakhan was made this way. A decision between two brothers.

I'm wearing a suit with the red emblems of the family crest stitched on the left breast pocket. It's the only splash of color I've worn in years. Ivan will be wearing the same. I haven't spotted him nor Father yet.

It will be all I can do to tamp down my wrath when I do see Ivan.

Motherfucking bastard.

I can't believe he's outsmarted me in such a way. He'll fucking get his.

I swear it. I swear it on my mother and sister's graves.

I swear it on mine. If it kills me to bring him down to justice, that's what I'll do, and we'll die together.

I walk into the foyer and see Sophia coming through the door on the other side. That means Father should be here, too.

She also knows the answer to this night.

She smiles sweetly at me. I don't know how to take it. Is she smiling at me because I was chosen, or is that a smile of sympathy?

I move toward her, and she approaches me with outstretched arms.

I feel her warmth before she reaches and hugs me the way a mother would.

"Look at you." She beams with pride.

"I scrub up well, don't I?" I smirk.

"Oh, Mikhail, I think we can all agree that you more than scrub up well. I'm proud of you. This is a momentous night no matter what happens. Be proud of the work you've done at the company and for the Bratva." She nods.

I try to detect any underlying tones hinting at the answer, but I can't pick up anything. That's what makes Sophia good at her job. She'll probably be the only woman in our history who will sit through our meetings and be part of the leadership.

In her lifetime, she would have witnessed two inaugurations. This will be her third.

"Thank you, Auntie."

She reaches into her pocket and hands me a little khvorost, a Russian sweet crisp pastry shaped like angel wings. She used to make them for us at Christmas when we were kids, but sometimes she'd surprise us with them.

She hasn't made any in years.

I smile as I take it and look at the little angel in my hands.

"You don't think I'm too old for this? I'm nearly twenty-nine, Auntie."

She reaches out and touches my cheek. "But you are still my little angel. Sometimes, it's the little things we remember from our past that count."

I nod. "You are right."

"How are things at home?" she asks tentatively as the worry returns to her face.

"Hard."

"You love Adriana," she notes. It's been weird hearing that name now, and stranger knowing I'll always have to keep that secret. But I don't have to lie about my love.

"I do."

"Then let's hope this gets resolved soon so you can be together again." She taps my shoulder. I don't make her any wiser about my plans.

"Yes."

"These are dangerous times, so I agree with you sending her away. It's the right thing to do. What happened to her guard will deeply affect her, and until we figure out what's going on, we can't risk anybody's safety."

"My thoughts exactly."

The door opens to our left, and I turn to see Ivan. He stops mid-stride when he notices me and puts that smug-as-fuck expression on his face.

"It's time to get seated," he informs us.

"Thank you, dear," Sophia replies.

I don't answer. I just follow Sophia when she walks ahead of me.

We enter the hall, which is now full with the members who make up the New York quarter of the Bratva.

Ivan and I walk down to the front of the room, where our father is seated at the head like the judge, jury, and executioner.

He looks worse tonight. Paler. And his eyes are duller than usual, like the light of the living has already left him.

There are two stands before his chair. I stand on the right and Ivan to the left. Sophia sits in the seat across the room but in front of the Brigadiers. The room goes silent, and Father stands.

It's time.

As I look at my father, I cast my mind back to how he was twenty years ago. Strong and defiant, ruthless, merciless. You'd know all that just from looking at him.

It was around that time when I knew I wanted to be like him, and I knew I didn't need to be the Pakhan to accomplish that. If I can accept that, I can accept him choosing my brother.

That doesn't change anything about what I plan to do to Ivan.

"My brothers and my dear sister," Father begins, giving Sophia a quick glance, to which she dips her head. "We gather tonight in our numbers to witness the dawn of a new era. A new era of leadership. In the Vory, we honor the code that was set by our forefathers, and we're ruthless bastards when it comes to conquering wealth and expanding what we already possess. The Pakhan is chosen to lead you to victory the way a general leads his army. Both my sons are worthy to fulfill the role of general, and they can both live up to everything you would expect from a Baranov leader. But only one can carry the title."

He pauses for a beat and glances from me to Ivan. When his gaze settles on Ivan, I automatically think he's chosen him, but then he looks at me, and his eyes soften.

"This has been an exceedingly difficult decision. Truly difficult." He focuses on my brother and me. "I want you both to know that I appreciate everything you have done for me and the Bratva."

"Thank you, Father," Ivan and I both say and dip our heads.

"You are welcome." He brings a hand to his heart and looks paler but lifts his head a little higher as he addresses the men again. "The man I have chosen to be your new leader is my son Mikhail Dmitriyev."

I hear the words fall from his lips, but they don't quite register in my mind until a few seconds pass.

I look at Ivan. I don't know what I expect, but it's not that nonchalant expression on his face, like he doesn't care. I know he does. He would have had to, to carry out everything that's happened so far.

The men stand and cheer, and my asshole brother steps toward me with his hand outstretched to shake mine.

My skin crawls when I grip his hand.

"Congratulations, brother," he states, but all I can do is stare at him.

He should look more cut up than he does. But he looks like he already knew I'd be chosen.

"Thank you, brother."

He's about to say something when Father starts coughing.

We both look at him in the same moment he doubles over and a coughing fit takes him.

I'm the first to get to him, panic fueling my movements. He sinks to the ground and clutches his heart, taking shallow breaths.

"My... heart," he stutters.

"Father," I blurt, my mind racing. My eyes find Sophia, who's rushed over to join us. "Call an ambulance. Now."

She takes out her phone, dials for an ambulance, and starts speaking straightaway.

Father grabs my shirt and pulls me down so he can speak into my ear.

"Be a leader, son," he whispers in a hurried staccato voice. "Be the man I raised you to be. I... know the truth."

His eyes rivet to mine.

"You know the truth?" I whisper back with narrowed eyes.

"About your brother."

Jesus Christ.

"You know?" I hiss.

He nods. "Somebody's helping him. I don't know who. Take them down for me." He coughs again.

"Father."

"Goodbye, son. It's getting dark now." He releases me and smiles. "I can see her now, Mikhail. Your mother. My angel. The ballerina. The other half of my soul. I'm going to be with her now."

His lips stop moving, then he does, too.

My mind is so fractured I can't think straight.

I hear sirens wailing but know they're too late.

He's dead.

My father is dead. Another parent died in my arms, and I'm helpless.

Rage fills me as his words fill my mind, twisting my insides and crushing the walls of my chest. I look around to where Ivan was standing, only to realize he's gone.

The motherfucking bastard left.

Chapter Forty-Five

Natalia

I stare at Mikhail when I walk down the stairs.

All I see is a broken man leaning against the wall with his dog by his side.

I don't know how I'm supposed to leave him like this.

I don't know how I'm supposed to leave him at all, and the death of his father has made everything worse.

I know what it's like to lose your parents, and now he's lost them both, too.

Like me, he witnessed their deaths.

Mikhail pushes away from the wall when he notices me and straightens, trying to look strong.

He's worn that mask of strength since he came home last night and has continued to wear it all day.

I don't even think he's registered he's the new Pakhan. He got what he wanted but lost so much in the same breath.

Now, we're about to lose each other.

It's just the two of us here, and Snow.

The house staff—Aleksander mainly—and Sophia said goodbye to me earlier today.

Mikhail takes my little bag from me when I reach him and catches my hand so we can walk out to the car together holding hands. Snow trots in front of us.

Escorting me to the airport are Levka and three of his other guards from the security team.

Mikhail hasn't gone into too much detail about what happed last night, but I noticed that more guards were here today looking like they were planning for something big. I think the fact that he's sending me to the airport with three of his top security guards says a lot about what he hasn't told me.

It must have to do with Ivan.

I have a bad feeling in the pit of my stomach, which worsens with every second that passes.

Maybe, though, that feeling stems from not knowing if I'm ever going to see him again. And I don't know what's going to happen to him here.

We stop by the Bugatti, and he places my bag with the rest of luggage in the trunk. He closes it, and the sound echoes in my heart. It's the sound of goodbye. Final and absolute.

Mikhail walks around to me and cups my face. When he presses his forehead to mine, I feel the weight of the burden he carries.

"I don't want to leave you like this," I tell him.

"You have to, Malyshka."

Malyshka. Will I ever hear him call me that again?

"Everything will be okay when you get to my friend," he adds.

"But you won't be," I point out. He releases me. "I'm so sorry about your father."

For a fraction of a second, he shows me a glimpse of the pain in his eyes.

"Even though I knew he was going to die, it feels like the world ended."

"I know." I know all too well; except I didn't know when

my parents would be taken from me. I never had time to prepare. Neither makes it easier. Death never is.

He touches my cheek and attempts a smile. "You will be okay, though, and I promise you, life won't be as hard as it was before. You'll have everything you need."

Except him.

"Will I ever see you again?"

His face tenses, and he looks away briefly then back to me.

"I don't think so, Natalia. It's better if we don't. I'll get the paperwork sorted out when I can." He pauses for a moment, and I think about what paperwork he must be talking about.

Divorce papers.

That's what he means. God...Divorce papers.

I don't know how long he needs to stay married to me regarding the cartel, but he looks like he does. Like he checked everything out. I'm sure he would have.

"That way, it will be easier to forget me and what I did to you," he says with a clipped nod.

I grit my teeth and will the tears away.

"Will you forget me so easily?" He makes it sound like it will be, and when I think of the women who will be all over him, I feel sick. Bile rises into my throat.

"No, baby. I can't forget you. Not ever," he promises and lowers his head to kiss me one last time. He pulls away before the call of passion takes us and covers my hand with his.

I look at his prison tattoos and remember how I thought of him as a monster. He's not that, though. All he's done is slay my demons and protect me.

"Go now."

He releases me and nods for me to get in the car.

I bend down and hug Snow, who barks for me, then I get in the car. I can't say goodbye to her. At times she was my only friend.

As I shuffle in the backseat, it feels like I'm not really here in this moment. As if I've programmed my body to be on autopilot.

Mikhail closes the door, and Levka starts up the car.

As we drive away, I turn to watch him through the window until I can't see him anymore. It's when we leave through the huge iron gates that everything feels like the end and my heart sinks further into the chasm of nothingness.

I feel so empty inside. So empty I can barely breathe and this feeling in my gut is suffocating.

The guards say nothing to me as the car picks up speed and we continue down the road.

I stare through the window, watching the scenery in the waning sun as an attempt to distract myself.

As the darkness takes over and we turn onto one of the country roads, I notice Levka looking in the rearview mirror at a car behind us that gets too close.

He speeds up. So does the car behind us.

The roar of a motorcycle engine sounds, and I turn around to see two motorcyclists on either side of the car.

"Jesus Christ, I think they're following us," says the guard in the passenger seat.

"They have been for a good five minutes, but I wasn't sure until we turned," Levka replies.

Oh my God. What is this now?

Who's following us?

Please, God, don't let anything happen.

We speed up more, and the car and bikes do the same. It's just us on the road. No other vehicles to the left or right of us. Nothing coming, nothing going.

"Mrs. Dmitriyev, get down!" Levka shouts.

As soon as he speaks, gun shots are fired. One hits the back tire. I bend down, but because the car is jerking so much, I'm flung across the seat. The other guard does his best to hold me, but another bullet comes our way. Something more powerful that gets through what should be bulletproof glass and lodges in his head.

I scream as blood splatters everywhere.

More shots sound, and even though the guard in the passenger seat is returning fire, it's not enough.

The motorcyclists are shooting with machine guns now, and they hit him, then Levka.

I scream again as the car runs off the side of the road with me and crashes into a thicket of trees.

I hit my head, but I shake off the pain and try to get out.

It's too late, though. I can't do anything.

The first biker pulls up beside the car and pulls a gun on me at the same time he yanks open the door.

He's masked. All I can see are his eyes.

Fuck. What am I going to do?

What the hell am I going to do?

"Hello, princess. You're coming with me," he says, reaching for my arm.

"Get away from me!" I kick him, but I'm helpless against a man like him.

He grabs my arm, then stabs me in the side of my neck with a needle.

Before I can even think about what he did to me, I black out.

Chapter Forty-Six

Mikhail

Sophia's hands tremble as she looks at the beautiful china cup on the table containing the remnants of her chamomile tea.

Her face is blotchy and her eyes red. She looked the same way last night when we left the morgue.

I arrived at her home twenty minutes ago. I promised I would come by after Natalia left to fill her in on the details I have on Ivan.

Ivan, who my men and I have been searching for and can't find.

We watched him on the surveillance cameras at Dmitriyev Ltd. and didn't find shit. I wish I could have pulled my gun on him last night and ended him, but with my father dying in my arms, I couldn't home in on my inner beast.

The motherfucker must have known what Father was saying to me, or he wouldn't have left. Or he heard some parts of the whispers Father imparted to me before he died.

I still can't believe he's gone. Having both my parents and

sister die in not even the space of six months has destroyed me. To add to the blow, I lost my girl, too.

I shake my mind free of the loss and focus on Sophia. She needs me, and she's now aware of Ivan's treachery.

We've been sitting in her living room since I arrived. Her sipping on her tea while I brought her up to speed on everything else.

She made me cup a of tea, too.

I haven't touched it yet. I'm going to need something stronger to get through the night.

Finally, she looks at me and dabs at the corners of her eyes.

"I don't know how to process this. It's too much, Mikhail." She shakes her head. "In the space of months, this family has more than cut in half. To hear that one of us is responsible for it kills me."

Her lips tremble.

"I'm sorry to bring more bad news to your door." It was the last thing I wanted to do. She needed to be aware of the danger, though.

Her guards are here, as are mine, along with the secret squad who are always with the Pakhan. They are all outside watching the place as we speak.

"You can't apologize for that. Everything is just so bizarre. All of it." She wipes away more tears. "Why didn't you come to me before?"

"I wanted evidence. I wanted hard evidence against Ivan. I guess part of me didn't want to believe it even though it was believable. Ivan is that wicked."

"When I saw your father yesterday morning, he looked like he knew something and was holding back. I didn't know he was on the verge of death. Maybe knowing his son was responsible for his wife and daughter's deaths broke his heart."

The coroner said the heart attack was brought on by an aneurysm. Because his body was already so weak, it wiped him out. He never stood a chance.

"Maybe," I agree.

"He was happy about you, Mikhail. He told me his decision was always you; that's why he decided on doing things the way he did. But he wanted it to be fair to Ivan, too. He knew the two of you would work hard and push for the position. He wanted each of you to have a fair chance, but his heart kept coming back to you."

All that time, I never had anything to worry about.

"Thank you for telling me."

"It's okay, you should know."

"I wish I could have done more. My men were trying to track Ivan, and we were so careful, but we couldn't find anything. Now we don't know which corner of hell he's hiding in. It's fucking draining me."

She reaches across the coffee table and taps my hand.

"I know. Me too. It's draining me, too. Have some tea, dear. I'll grab us something to eat."

She stands and walks out of the room.

I reach for my cup and down the contents of the tea that's now cold then set the cup back down on the table.

My phone rings in that moment. I reach for it eager for news.

It's Eric.

"Hey, have you heard anything yet?" I ask.

"No, nothing on Ivan. But something's happened, Mikhail. Natalia never reached the airport."

The moment I hear that, I bolt up.

"What do you mean? I saw her leave."

"She never boarded the plane, and I've been calling Levka and the other guards, but no one is answering their phones."

"Jesus Christ. Fuck! Maybe he got to her. How the fuck would he have known when she was leaving?"

"That's not the only thing, Mikhail." I hear him sigh, and my pulse skitters with anticipation. "My friend at the coroner's office contacted me when he realized parts of your father's initial postmortem report had been removed. When he checked it out, he found the original log made when your father was brought in, and he noticed the same poison that killed José was listed on there."

"What the fuck?"

"Yeah, exactly. It wasn't the same lethal amount that was found in José's blood, and there were no needle marks, but the dosage was enough to kill him within twelve hours. It would have caused the heart attack. He said the report suggest the poison was in his system from early that morning. I asked him to look into it deeper. I think we're onto something."

My mind wobbles, then freezes. Something he said clicks in my core, and the truth dawns on me.

Early that morning.

That's what he said.

There... was only one person my father saw early in the morning yesterday, and he would have spent the day with them.

The same person who was the only one outside my guards who knew when Natalia would be leaving for the airport and who she was going with. Once I declared who she was going with, they would also have known what car they would have taken. Levka always drives the Bugatti.

It wouldn't have been that hard to track them.

"Mikhail, are you still there?" Eric asks but sounds suddenly far away, and the room looks dim.

I hear footsteps and turn to Sophia walking up to me.

She picks up the cup and smiles wide.

"Good, you finished it," she states and then laughs.

There's something wrong with the way she looks, though.

There's something wrong with everything, and my hand feels numb. Fucking numb. The phone falls from my hand and hits the floor. That sounds far away, too, but loud at the same time.

The room spins as I reach for the sofa.

"If you'd eaten the sweet I gave you last night, you could have died peacefully with your father," she tells me in that good-natured tone I've been used to my whole life. "This way is better, I suppose. This way carries more of a punch and you get answers to the puzzle that mystified you so much."

"Sophia, what did you give me? What are you saying to me?"

I don't understand what she's saying to me, but I understand what truth is screaming at me along with the voices in my soul.

That person who was with my father all day yesterday and would have been with him in the morning was her.

That person who knew what time my wife was leaving for the airport.

It's her.

It's fucking her.

My aunt.

She's the person working with Ivan. But why?

And... what did I just drink? My vision speckles, but I fight to stay awake. I need to. I have to get out of here and find my wife.

"It's a concoction of poison from Russia they used in the war. I made this blend a little less vicious, if you will. So, you can die slowly. Just like your father."

"You poisoned my father? You did all of this?"

"I did, my love. It was me."

"What about Ivan?"

"Of course, he was right alongside me, and the only reason you couldn't find anything on him was because you were tracking the wrong person." She gives me that laugh again.

She sits back down and sets the cup back on the table.

"Why? Would you do this?" Of all the people, I never expected this from her. Not her, the last person I trusted.

Chapter Forty-Seven

Mikhail

"You poor, blind fool. You're just like your fucking father. You think because you have power, you can hurt people and get away with it. You think because you say something, we should live by your rules like mindless automatons." Sophia's face contorts with rage as she shakes her head. "Ivan's mother was my best friend. We grew up together. She was like a sister to me, and your father cheated on her with your whore of a mother. Your whoring mother worked into their home, saw they had a child, and thought she'd destroy their family by spreading her legs for your father. My *best friend* killed herself, and her little boy found her dead in the bathtub. All because of your father."

My God. This is about the past. The sins and the secrets of the past. I don't know what the fuck I'm supposed to say because it *was* wrong. Nothing about it *can* be right.

All I can speak for is the present, and it looks like there was never any time in my life when she didn't wear a mask. This is her true face.

"You waited all this time, Sophia?" I balk.

"It's called waiting for the right opportunity, my dear nephew. When you are weak, that's all you can do. Wait and watch and plan. Your father trusted me with everything. He thought I would support his disgusting idea to marry the woman responsible for my best friend's death. Like I could ever be okay with that. Then you came along and trusted me, too. Trusted me more than he did."

"I did trust you."

"Which is what made me the best spy. I knew the day would come when Sergei would have to make a choice between his two sons. It was logical. I just never thought he would go as far as changing the leadership selection rules." Again, she shakes her head. This time with disgust.

"You thought we should all suffer because of the past and the change!" My voice comes out heavy and weak at the same time.

"It's like spitting on Tatiana's grave and her son's legacy. That's all he had to look forward to as some form of redemption for what happened to his mother. We both knew your father was going to choose you. That's why he changed the rules. He would only do something like that to sidestep what he wasn't man enough to do."

Shit, she's starting to look blurry. My head slumps to the side, and my body leans with it, crashing into the wooden arm of the chair.

The fucking poison is taking effect and weakening me.

I can't move.

My hands and legs feel heavier now. But I'm going to keep fighting to stay awake.

I have to get out of here.

Natalia needs me.

"Then, to add insult to injury, my dear brother decided to split the company four ways so Ivan wouldn't get the ruling shares and I'd get no part of the company my forefathers built from the ground up. It was your mother who told me your father's plans, breaking his confidence because she thought we'd become such good friends." She hisses. "Like your father, she thought I'd be happy to get the diamond company. She didn't know she was opening Pandora's Box. Sergei thought the diamond company would be a sufficient inheritance for me. That bastard." She laughs, a crude horrible sound, or she just sounds that way because my heart is thumping in my ears. "Dmitriyev Ltd. was not meant to be split between Sergei's whore of a wife, his bastard son, his little bitch of a daughter, and the only son he should have had. It was too much. Someone had to make him pay."

I can't believe what I'm hearing.

I'd be more inclined to believe the poison was screwing with my hearing and my sight over thinking what I'm hearing my Aunt Sophia say is the truth. But it is, and I never saw this coming.

"And that person had to be you?"

"Indeed. I took matters into my own hands. I knew Ivan would agree with me. I knew all his secrets and his flaws. I knew who would join forces with me to achieve the goal. Raul was at the top of the list because he didn't like the control your father had over his cartel. He was always in some disagreement with him, so he was easily swayed when we approached him with an offer he couldn't refuse— shares in Dmitriyev Ltd. once the ownership passed, and freedom from our control. He was the only person strong enough to take you down. The others were just the masterminds."

"Others?" I rasp.

"Investors who would take the company to new heights in the grand vision I have for the future of Dmitriyev Ltd."

It makes sense now why people like Barabbas Ponteix got involved.

"What my parents did was wrong, but what you did is wrong, too. How could you think it was okay to kill them?"

When I think of Talia, my soul trembles. "My sister, what was her crime?"

"Her mere existence, my dear nephew. Her existence was her crime, and her fucking love for ballet reminded me of how your mother enticed my brother. It was me who set up her sale to make sure she died in the worst way possible."

More laughter sounds, showing how truly evil she is. She made Talia suffer the way she did.

"How could you do that!"

"Her suffering and death were an extension of what I wanted to do to your mother."

"You sold my sister to sex slavers who killed her. How dare you think she deserved such a fate!"

"Well, Mikhail. I couldn't exactly sell your mother. The sale for a woman over thirty in the flesh trade is practically non-existent. I wanted that bullet in your mother's head for the same reason I wanted to poison my brother."

"What the fuck reason was that?"

"They both had to be taught a lesson. With Sergei, though, I gave him a chance. He was dying anyway, and I'd accomplished the mission of taking away what he loved most. I decided I wouldn't kill him, and I'd allow him to die the way he wanted if he chose Ivan to be Pakhan. I felt what he decided to do with the company was one thing, but the Bratva is who we are. That was his last chance. He blew it when he chose you."

I blow out a ragged breath as my lungs constrict. I'm finding it harder to breathe, harder to focus. And she can tell.

"Everyone got what they deserved, Mikhail," she says, like she's always had the right to decide everyone's fate. "Unfortunately, you survived that night, and I couldn't kill you while you were in the hospital because my fucking brother guarded you with the best of the best. It's fine, though. Your survival took Raul out of the game once you were able to identify him, and his death tied up the risk he represented of blowing the whole operation. The goal was still achieved, and now we own the cartel."

Natalia.

They're going to use her. Just like I thought. Jesus. Everything I thought was right. Everything

Now Sophia is going to take my wife.

"Leave my wife out of this."

"If I were you, I'd worry about myself."

"You two-faced bitch."

"Yes, I am. Don't you know it's the quiet, sweet ones you have to look out for? They're the silent killers. The ones with all the good ideas. How else would a little old lady take down the new Pakhan of the Baranov?" She grins, wide and proud. "How else would a little old lady kill the last Pakhan? How else would a little old lady kill the lieutenant of one of the deadliest cartel leaders known to man? I was the one who stabbed José Diaz in the neck when I caught that fool taking pictures of Ivan while he met with Barabbas Ponteix. Me. I did it all."

"Not going to give me any credit, my love?" says a voice from outside the room that makes this moment so much worse.

Aleksander steps in, and I feel my mouth drop and the knife in my heart twist.

"You bastard," I grate.

"Sorry, Mr. Dmitriyev. Everyone has to look out for themselves and those they love," he answers, and to my surprise, he leans forward and plants a kiss on Sophia's lips.

"Of course, you helped, Aleksander. You kept me well informed of my nephew's daily activities and came up with the idea to slit José's throat."

"The two of you can rot in hell!" I shout.

"Maybe we will, maybe we won't. Maybe we'll see you there, dear nephew. You might have as much as six hours to live."

"Six ... hours?" I stutter.

"Six hours to be trapped in your mind and feel helpless. You will die in that helpless state, unable to save your pretty wife. It's the worst kind of death for a man like you. The paralysis is taking you now. Then your mind will go. When your organs start shutting down, that's it. Game over."

Game over.

She fades from my sight, and my soul screams as the helplessness takes me.

I think I hear gunfire somewhere in the back of beyond. It sounds like it's coming from outside.

I feel myself fall, but it's like my brain disconnects from my body.

As I hit the ground, my last thought is of the beautiful woman I stole because she wore a wedding dress that didn't belong to her.

But she belonged to me.

I promised her life would be better.

Now it's not going to be, and there's nothing I can do.

I will love you always, Natalia. I'm so sorry.

Chapter Forty-Eight

Natalia

My head feels numb.

And the haze of memory pushing against the walls of my mind sends off the warning that tells me I'm in trouble again.

As the thought strikes me, my awareness returns, but I'm still dazed. I can't remember what happened to me, and I hope like hell I won't wake up in Raul's dungeon again.

I shuffle, and my nerves spike when a heavy hand rests on my belly and smooths over my skin.

When fingers flutter up to my breasts and roll back and forth over my left nipple, I open my eyes, and every muscle in my body goes weak when I see Ivan staring down at me. He's sitting next to me and is the person touching me.

I jump back and crawl away, crashing into a headboard. I'm on a bed.

Where am I, though?

Where the hell am I?

I remember what happened as the question of where I am comes to my mind.

"Thought that might wake you, Sleeping Beauty," he says, running his gaze over my body. "Although I've wanted to play with those since I first met you."

"You bastard. Where have you taken me?" I look around. It's bright daylight. The sun is beaming brightly through the window, but it looks different.

I can't glimpse anything more than the sky, but the sun shines differently to how it did in New York.

He notices me looking through the window and nods.

"You can feel the difference, can't you? I always do, too, just after the plane lands."

"Plane? Where am I?"

"Mi amor, do you not recognize your homeland?"

"Mexico," I choke out.

My God, I'm back in hell, a new hell with this devil.

With a wide, toothy grin, Ivan stands.

"Yes, you're back here, and now you belong to me."

"No." I shake my head.

"Yes."

If he thinks I belong to him, he must have done something to Mikhail.

"What did you do to Mikhail?"

"I took care of him. My worthless piece-of-shit brother should be fucking dead by now."

Pain assaults my ears and rages through my body. I'm so choked up I can't even breathe.

Mikhail is dead? No.

Tears pour from my eyes, coming straight from my soul.

"You killed him!"

"Not me personally, although I wish I could have done it." He nods with regret in his eyes. "My aunt deserves all the credit."

I can't believe what he's saying to me. "*Sophia?*" He must be lying. That can't be true.

"The one and only. She killed him. She has a penchant for

poisons. She likes the way they kill. Slow and deadly. Like lies."

"Why would she kill him? Why in the hell would she do that?" I don't understand. "Sophia took care of us."

"Sophia was what she wanted you to believe. I needed someone to keep an eye on Mikhail. She was the best fit because he trusted her. That's what you call the perfect spy. My aunt created the same blend of poison for Mikhail that took our father's life, as well as your pesky little bodyguard's. José got a full dose, though, but it was a necessity. We needed to keep him quiet. A jab to the back of the neck took him down within seconds. Problem solved."

Oh my God.

What the hell kind of nightmare am I in?

"This isn't happening." I trusted her, too. I did. She made the harder days seem easier

"But it is. When you came along, I sent her to check you out because I couldn't help myself. I saw my brother's interest in you before he even met you. When I met you, I understood it, and I knew he was in love with you." His smile brightens. "I knew I could use you against him in some way because you were his weakness. I was able to get so much done on the days he spent obsessing over his shiny new toy. He couldn't see that you were just easy pussy."

"You bastard."

"Oh, please, is that the best comeback you have for me? Do you think I'm unaware I'm a bastard? I know I am, and I'll admit, I couldn't stand knowing my fucking brother got the cartel and the beautiful princess I'd heard so much about and never saw for myself. Now I have you."

"You will never have me."

He chuckles, cruel and low, dangerous. "That's what your mother said, too."

My mouth falls open, and I push back against the headboard.

"My mother?" I whisper the question, although I already know what he's going to tell me. My heart told me the answer weeks ago.

"Your mother, Lilly de Leon."

God in heaven, Ivan knows the truth. He knows who my mother was.

He knows the truth.

"That is your mother, and you are not Raul's daughter. You aren't Adriana Alvarez."

What's he going to do to me?

I have no idea what the hell I'm going to do. I have no one. When I thought I was alone before, I wasn't.

This is loneliness. This is captivity. This is hell.

"You looked familiar when we first met, and that's what gave me the inkling that something was off with you, but I didn't know what at the time," he continues. "Then it hit me why you looked familiar. I remembered her because I was fucking her for years. She was a gift from Raul every time I visited. I wanted the blonde woman with the bright blue eyes and the beauty like a goddess."

My stomach lurches. He did rape my mother. Repeatedly. Years of it.

"Your face looks exactly like hers." He returns to the bed. "I pieced the truth together, but I still thought Raul was your father until I checked her out. Not a damn thing exists of Adriana Alvarez, but look up Lilly de Leon, and details for her, her husband, and her daughter will come up. You obviously became the princess to save your neck, and my brother was none the wiser. I don't care if he ever found out the truth. You're fucking mine now, and I'll do whatever I want with you."

"What are you going to do to me?"

He catches my face. "Well, Natalia de Leon, there's a lot I want to do to you," he replies, enunciating every syllable of my real name. "We have a busy few days ahead of us. First of all, you and I are going to keep that little secret of yours. You're going to keep being Adriana Alvarez. I have business to attend to, so I'm going to be away today and tomorrow, the day after we have a meeting with the men in the cartel. I need them to know you belong to me now so they can sign their allegiance to me. When that's done, I'll fuck you all six ways to Sunday and then some. Then we'll get married. After that, I don't know. It depends on how much you can keep me interested and entertained."

He releases me and gets off the bed.

At that moment, the door to the room opens and Sophia walks in with a bright smile plastered on her wrinkly face.

Aleksander is right behind her.

I don't know how much more my mind can take.

This is doom.

Chapter Forty-Nine

Mikhail

Soft lips brush mine and ignite the fire in my heart.

My heart starts beating, and something is switching on inside me.

I'm locked away, though, trapped somewhere, and I have no awareness of anything besides the feel of soft lips and my heart.

I seem to stay like that forever, stuck in a state of... I don't know.

I feel like this could be limbo, but I'm not quite there yet.

More time passes, and then I see her eyes.

Soft hazel eyes stare down at me, and the woman I love greets me with a smile.

"Malyshka," I mutter. She nods her head.

"Stay with me," she answers.

I want to tell her all the things I said before. I want to give her all the reasons I gave before on why we couldn't be together.

But I can't bring myself to say the words.

I can't tell her she shouldn't be with me when I want her so badly I'm in physical pain. I can't tell her I'm not good for her when I want to be whatever she needs me to be.

I can't tell her any of those things because I love her and I want nothing more than to be with her.

"I love you," I say. She smiles and cries.

"I love you, too. Mikhail, you need to wake up. Please."

"Wake up..."

A beeping sound fills my ears, then memories flood my mind.

I remember how I had my girl and practically gave her away. I never fought the biggest enemy who stood between us —myself.

I was my biggest challenge, and if I had the chance, I would do everything differently and conquer my fears. I would fight to keep her.

I wouldn't choose to lie down and give up because of fear. My father warned me about fear.

The instant I think about my father, images of grief and betrayal crash into me all at once.

The loss of my mother, sister, and father, then those who betrayed me.

Sophia and Ivan.

The beeping sounds again, and I open my eyes...

Bright lights greet me, pulling me from my dream, along with a familiar face I never thought I'd see again.

Eric.

He's standing over me, and the beeping is coming from some sort of machine.

My eyes dart back and forth as I try to establish where I am. I half expect to be in the hospital, then I remember that happened already.

Then I remember everything else and try to get up.

"Hold it," Eric says, resting a heavy hand on my chest.

I lift my arm, which is attached to tubes. I'm hooked up to the machines.

"Sophia," I say, my voice coming out hoarse. "It's her. She has Natalia. She's working with Ivan."

"I know. *We* know."

"We?" My brows pinch.

"The backup plan. Aiden is here, and so is Lucca Dyshekov of the Yurkov."

"They both came?"

"Yes, they're here to help. No one else knows about your survival."

I've never been so relieved in my life. Two Pakhans are here from the two biggest brotherhoods in our alliance. Both allies of mine, and friends.

"Jesus, I need to get up."

"Mikhail, you need to rest."

"How the hell can I rest, Eric? They have my wife."

"You could have died. You nearly *did* die."

I know he's right. I felt myself shut down. I felt the end coming. "How the hell did you get to me? How am I alive?"

"You must have dropped your phone when I called and the poison started taking effect. I was still on the line, so I heard most of what Sophia said. I was able to track you, then cloak my number. I got to you just in time to get you to the hospital, where they were able to treat you with an antidote. Another few hours of the poison in your system, and you would be dead. Sophia thinks you died. So, Ivan will, too."

Shit. "How long have I been down?" Panic hits me when I think days could have passed and Ivan hurt Natalia.

"Nearly two days."

Oh God no. Not again.

God, don't tell me it happened again. I was helpless and unable to help or do shit.

"Two days?" I grate out.

"Try not to worry about that."

"Anything could have happened to Natalia."

"Mikhail, please try to stay focused."

I try and push past the fear brimming my mind.

"My guards. I heard gunfire at Sophia's house. What happened to them?" I think of Sebastian first, then the others who accompanied me.

Eric's face falls. "Sebastian made it, but he had to have surgery. He's still in the hospital. The others are dead. There were dead men on Sophia's lawn by the time I got there."

"Fuck. That fucking woman. I never guessed it could be her, Eric. I never even considered it. Did you?" I wonder.

"No, and I realized I didn't know what she was capable of or who's working for her. That's why I didn't inform anybody from your brotherhood of what happened and I had you moved here for your safety."

I look around again. "Where is here?"

"One of my safe houses. I arranged for the doctors to continue treating you here, and they brought everything you'd need. I'm working with Aiden to find the location of where Ivan took Natalia. There's a log on one of your jets for Mexico. We think he's taken her there."

That motherfucking bastard. "The cartel. I'll bet he'll do something about that now. Strike while the fucking iron is still hot."

"Yeah, I think so. Both the Voirik and the Yurkov will be ready to move in and retrieve Natalia the second I know where they are."

"Good. Thank you. Thank you for everything." What the fuck would I have done if he hadn't found me?

I would be dead by now. Now that I'm alive, I have one goal.

One mission in mind.

I have to get my wife back.

I have to get my girl back before they do fuck knows what to her. If I do, I'm not letting her go ever again.

I won't.

I sit up, testing my strength. My brain is still foggy, but I'm functional and can feel my legs.

"Mikhail, I don't think you can go anywhere."

I shake my head at him, stopping him from saying any more. "Don't you dare tell me that, Eric. You know if you were me, you wouldn't take that advice. If you heard what Sophia said to me, you know I can't not go. I have to."

This right here is where I have to accept whatever fate has in the cards for me.

Life or death. Neither matters right now.

The door opens, and Aiden Romanov walks in. I haven't seen him in a while, but he holds the same look of candor and authority he always did. He is my height and has my muscular build.

He nods at me when he notices I'm sitting up.

"We have a location," he states. "Ivan is summoning Raul's allies to sign allegiance to him."

There's only one way my brother can do that, and that's with my girl. He's going to do to her what I did.

I will kill him before I allow that to happen to her, because she's mine.

"I'm ready to go," I tell him.

"We leave in one hour."

Chapter Fifty

Natalia

Sophia sips on her tea across the room and laughs at something funny on the TV.

She's watching some old black-and-white show I don't know the name of. I'm sure the name has appeared on the screen several times, but I haven't been paying attention.

She's sitting in one of those winged armchairs with her ankles crossed over the other and her back resting against the side.

I don't know how she can be so calm, as if nothing has happened, as if she didn't kill her family.

What kind of person does that?

An absolute psychotic bitch.

I'm falling apart inside, grieving for Mikhail. The tears just pour out of my eyes at will, and I'm screaming inside. I can't believe he's dead.

I want to grab her and kill her, but I've stayed calm in her presence and everybody else who'd gone in and out of this room for the last two and a half days.

Aleksander is supposed to be outside. He's been coming back into the room repeatedly to speak with her in Russian.

Of course, I don't know what the fuck they're saying to each other. I'm still trying to decipher the words, although I'm sure it's of little use to me now.

I'm fairly certain everything that happens from here onwards is going to be the shit show I have visualized in my head.

It's a new day, and the cartel heads will be here soon. After Ivan is done with them, he'll bring me back here and fuck me. Then I'll die.

I'll die the moment he touches me. Whatever I fought long and hard to keep alive inside me will die when that happens.

If it happens.

If.

I'm still holding on to the hope I might be able to escape this.

I've been looking around the room, and when I was left alone for a few minutes, I went to the window to look outside. That's when I realized I know where I am.

This is one of Raul's estate houses in El Proyecto de Lavanda. The plantation I lived on with my family isn't far from here.

I recognized some of the surroundings and realized I'd been here a few times before with my mother. I just never went into the living quarters. It's a massive place. Just as big as Raul's house was. This room has the same high ceiling and long windows as some of the rooms at his home did. It's all elaborate. I always figured this was where his business associates stayed when they came to visit. It would make sense we're here.

Mom came here for medical supplies. This was where they were delivered.

I guess this would have been where Ivan saw her.

I can just imagine what he must have done to her. He's

about to do the same to me. It will happen if I don't get out of here.

No matter what, I have to try. Because not trying is the same as handing him a gun and telling him to shoot me.

If I don't try to live, I spit in the faces of all the people who died protecting me, who lost their lives so I could live.

So, I can't not try.

The main door is to our left. I figure I can take Sophia easily, but I worry about what will happen when I get outside. I need a weapon if I'm even going to have a chance.

Aleksander has a weapon. He's a big guy, so the problem is taking the weapon from him. The only way I can think to do that is by using her.

I don't know how that will play out yet.

I've just been watching her and assessing her to figure out what she's doing.

Ivan hasn't been back since Sophia and that bastard Aleksander walked into the room. I should have known something was up with them being together.

It was the way he did what she told him to do that should have tipped me off. I remember that night he got me cookies and he came out of his quarters to do it.

It was because of her that he did it.

What a fucking bastard.

I wonder if Mikhail knew of his treachery or who else in the house was a traitor.

It makes me sick, but I need to cast such worries aside now and think of myself.

Mikhail would want me to survive. He wouldn't want me to roll over and accept defeat, so I won't.

I'll know what to do when Aleksander returns once more.

Sophia looks at me, and her brows knit together.

"You look like shit," she states.

"So do you," I throw back.

"Little bitch." She reaches into her bag and pulls out a

syringe. Holding it up, she smiles. "Want some poison, too? I'll stab you the way I stabbed your guard."

"Fuck you. You know you can't take me down."

"I can't, but I can get the guards to hold you down. I can give you just enough poison to paralyze your limbs so you can't move while they rape you." She laughs, as if that could ever be funny. "I would be careful with my words if I were you. You're only alive because Ivan wishes it so. That doesn't mean I can't destroy you."

I can't believe I'm talking to the same person who helped me pick out my wedding dress and talked to me about my hopes for my career.

That was a façade of shit I need to forget.

This is who she is, and she just showed me something I can use against her.

The poison.

The door handle turns, and Aleksander walks in.

"The men are here. It's time to head down to the meeting room," he says to her, walking to where she's sitting.

She answers back in Russian, and the two continue talking in Russian. When he glances at me, I know she said something about me.

I don't give a fuck what she said. What I'm looking for is a window of opportunity.

He's here with the gun I have to take from him, and she has the poison.

I have to get to her to get to him, and I have to be ready to seize the moment. If I'm taken down to the meeting room, with Ivan and all his guards, the chance will slip away from me. So, I must keep my eyes open *now*.

The chance comes when she gets up out of the chair and walks toward the bathroom door.

Aleksander picks up the TV remote and switches the channel. So he's not paying attention when I leap off the bed and push myself through the air to reach her.

380

And neither is she.

Sophia doesn't look at me until it's too late. By then, I've already knocked her to the floor and grabbed her bag. She squirms to get away from me while I reach into the bag for the syringe that contains the poison.

I grab it and hold it to her neck just as Aleksander rushes toward me.

"I'll do it if you come any closer. I will do it," I cry, uncapping the needle. All I would need to do is push once for the needle to pop into the side of her neck, releasing the poison, and kill her.

Aleksander looks terrified.

"Don't be a fool. Get her," Sophia cries, and Aleksander comes at me, something I didn't expect him to do.

At the loss of hope, I do the only thing I can and decide to push the pump on the syringe expecting he'll stop.

He doesn't. Sophia screams as I push the entire contents into her neck, and when Aleksander reaches me, I slam into him. He's built like a wall, so he doesn't go down. He grabs me, securing his arms around my upper body so I can't get away.

I kick him and try to wriggle free of his hold.

He squeezes tighter, which is when I feel his gun in his left pocket. I grab it, but because of the position he's holding me in, when I cock the hammer and fire the bullet, it goes straight in his foot.

It's enough for him to release me, though, and I fire one more shot straight in his face.

Blood splatters me, staining my body, but the taste of freedom fuels me.

I'm standing here with the gun in my hand, Aleksander dead on the floor, and a look to my left confirms Sophia has to be dead, too. Her eyes are wide open, and she's not moving.

No one has come in.

Realizing this is my chance to flee, I feel adrenaline move my body and run to the door, yanking it open.

I run through into the hallway, my legs propelling me forward on the concrete floor.

I barrel ahead only to collide with a massive wall of a chest. A hand curls around my throat, lifting me off the ground.

I meet Ivan's death glare and gasp for breath when he hoists me higher into the air.

"What the fuck have you done!" he shouts in my face.

I try to raise the gun, but I can't. I can't breathe. His grip is so tight that stars speckle my vision and everything begins to blur around me.

He relieves me of the gun effortlessly while I gasp, feeling like I might pass out.

The guards enter the room, and seconds later, one of them returns, glaring at me.

"They're dead," he informs Ivan. "Aleksander and Sophia are dead."

Ivan growls and throws me against the wall. I scream when my shoulder smashes into the hard surface.

"You little bitch. You killed my aunt. You will pay for that." He hits me with the back of his hand. Blood spurts from my nose.

My face feels like it's on fire, and I heave, but he hits me again, striking my other cheek.

I scream from the pain, yelping as he hauls me up again by my throat and secures a grip around my arm.

God, it feels like he's going to tear off my arm.

"Let's fucking go and get this over with. Then I'll deal with you properly." He moves with me down the hall, hustling me forward with his guards on either side.

More come—ten more—and I realize how foolish I was to think I could escape.

I was never going to, but at least I know I tried.

This is bigger than me.

Ivan is going to kill me, too, when he's done with me. I can feel it. He'll kill me to get revenge for Sophia.

We reach a meeting hall, where I face the same men I faced nearly two months ago in this same position.

Back then I was at the mercy of a man who changed my world.

This man is not like that man, and that man is no more.

"Welcome, amigos," Ivan says, pulling me closer and pressing his face to mine. "Here she is. The princess. Raul's daughter. The reason we're here today. My brother is dead, so I will be marrying his wife and taking over. I am the new Pakhan, and you will swear your allegiance in blood to me."

A gunshot sounds, making me jump out of my skin. It came from the balcony at the other end of the room and took down the guard next to us.

All the men scramble to their feet, guns raised, but a host of men appears on the balcony.

I, however, have my eyes focused on one man.

The man I thought I'd never see again.

Mikhail Dmitriyev.

He's alive and at the head of the men with two guns pointed at Ivan.

"I am not dead, and you aren't taking my wife!" he shouts. That's when all hell breaks loose.

Bullets fly everywhere. Ivan pulls me away, but I keep looking back at Mikhail as he runs across the balcony and takes the stairs.

"He's not getting you back, princess," Ivan promises.

"Let go of me."

He pulls his gun and holds it to my head. "Come now, or I'll blow your pretty little head to pieces."

Chapter Fifty-One

Mikhail

I see Ivan hustling Natalia away with a gun held to her head, and I run.

I run with all the strength I can summon.

I don't know where it comes from, because God knows my body is still weak, but I'm sprinting. I'm moving with one goal in mind. I need to get my wife back.

Eric and the men from our combined brotherhoods follow behind me, clearing the path through Ivan's men and covering me as I rush down the hallway. So are the cartel men below who swore their allegiance to me.

I watch Ivan hurry Natalia outside, and I follow.

They're far ahead of me, which places me at a direct disadvantage.

I leap over the stairs and continue running, chasing them across the grass. He's heading for the waterfall.

He takes a set of stairs, and I can see why he went that way. There's a bridge there. Across it waits a truck.

He turns back to me and fires several shots I manage to dodge. Only just.

I'm massively off my game.

Natalia screams and stumbles, but he yanks her up and drags her. If I could just get a clear shot, I could kill him, but it's too risky with her next to him.

I shoot ahead at the path he's aiming for, but he continues.

Bastard. He knows I won't risk hitting her. That's why he's still running, practically shielding his ass with her.

"Stop, Ivan!" I call out, but it's to no fucking avail.

It's only when he notices Aiden running up toward the other side of the bridge where he was heading that he stops abruptly.

I watch confusion set in, and the motherfucker decides to head for the water instead. He's fleeing to the fucking river.

He ends up on a dusty path that leads to a dead end. He can't go any further beside what looks like a two-hundred-foot drop into jagged rock and rough waters.

They'll die if they fall in. No question about it.

Ivan stops at the end of the track, whirls around, then holds the gun to Natalia's head.

I stop when I notice the wicked smirk on his face.

He glances at the water and smiles wider. "Us and water don't agree, brother. Remember when I tried to drown you in the river?"

"So, you finally admit it," I reply, baring my teeth.

"I do. The people who matter can't hear my confession, though. They're all dead."

"They are. It didn't have to be like this." I'm talking but looking at Natalia.

She's terrified and shaking. Her eyes are wide with terror. There are bruises on her face that look like someone hit her. I can't imagine that person being anyone other than my bastard brother.

"It had to be exactly like this, because you shouldn't exist," Ivan sneers. "You should never have been born and never have been my competition. It was a disgrace. All of it. You, your whore mother, and your sister."

"Let my wife go, Ivan." I'm not interested in talking to him about the past. I had nothing to do with it.

I sympathize because he got a raw deal, but it doesn't give him the right to fuck me and everybody I love over.

"No, I'm not letting her go. If you kill me, she dies," he threatens.

"Let her go, you fucking prick. This is between you and me."

"I don't think so."

Natalia's eyes shift to the right in a suggestive way, and I catch her meaning. She's going to move to the right to give me a clear shot.

Fuck. It's risky. They're too close to the edge. Much too close. This could go wrong, but it's either that or allowing Ivan to kill her.

I decide to continue talking to him to give her the chance she needs and create my own diversion.

"Ivan, let her go!" I shout, and on realizing my words for the distraction they are, Natalia kicks Ivan hard in his shin and moves to the right.

That small window gives me a clear shot, but I only fucking manage to shoot him in his shoulder.

The impact makes him release her, and he falls over the edge, but not before pulling Natalia over with him.

She screams, and I bolt forward, thinking she's gone.

I thank God in heaven when I see her clutching a thicket of roots jutting out of the side. Ivan is just below her, holding on to more roots, and the motherfucker is tugging on her leg, trying to make her fall.

That's not going to happen.

I raise my gun, and as he looks at me, I fire one bullet into his forehead, the same way he had my mother killed.

In an instant, he falls, his cold eyes on me, hating me with his last breath.

I rush to Natalia as she slips and lean over to reach for her. I need to get her up here fast, because that root she's holding on to is going to break free any second.

"Baby, reach up to me. Take my hand," I call to her.

"I'm scared."

"Don't be scared. You have to trust me. Please trust me. Give me your hand."

She gazes up at me with her beautiful eyes, and I try to lower myself some more. I get to a point where if I lean any further, I'll go over the side.

"Come on, Natalia."

She reaches up but slips, and the hope dies in her eyes.

"Thank you for coming for me. Thank you for trying to save me. I can't do it Mikhail. I can't reach you."

"No, don't you dare give up!"

"I love you."

The branch breaks, and she screams. In that split of a second her hand flies out, I grab her, keeping my vow to myself to never let go.

I roar as I pull her up, lifting myself, too, and crawling backward with her in my arms.

She holds on to me as I press her to my heart, never letting go.

I won't.

Not ever.

The nightmare is over.

Chapter Fifty-Two

Natalia

The house feels lighter now that we're back.

Yesterday, as I drove back down the long winding driveway and set my eyes on the beautiful house that now feels like home, there was a difference about it I loved.

It felt like mine. Like somewhere I could start anew. Although I'm not really sure what's happening yet.

I'm just glad Mikhail and I aren't dead.

Since Mikhail took down Ivan, we've both seen doctors. We then left Mexico straightaway.

It's morning now, and it feels like the nightmare fog has lifted from over our heads.

Mikhail still has funeral plans for his father, which he's tending to now.

I wait patiently for him by the lake as I watch Snow chasing the ducks in the water.

When footsteps sound behind me, I turn and set eyes on the man of my dreams.

He looks like he's ready to talk to me about what's going to happen next.

I have my own speech ready for him.

He sits next to me on the bench and leans forward to kiss me briefly. "Are you okay?"

"I am. Are you?"

"Yes, I am." He shuffles to face me. "We have to talk."

"I'm not leaving you again," I cut in. "I'm not doing it. Don't you dare ask me to say goodbye to you again. The only way I'll leave is if you don't love me."

He chuckles. The sound fills my heart with hope.

"Looks like you're going to be stuck with me forever, then, Natalia."

"Really?"

"Yeah. I can't let you go. I don't want to. I can't do it. I don't know if I could spend the rest of my life without you. I still think I'm not good for you, but that makes me want to try to be what you need. All I have to offer is my love for you, so I figured that's a start."

Nobody has ever looked at me with such heartfelt adoration.

"Mikhail, that's all I need. I don't need anything else. Just you."

He kisses the top of my nose.

"Then marry me again. Be my wife again. This time as you. Natalia Lily de Leon. I want you to be my wife. Forever. Will you marry me?"

"Yes."

My heart soars into the heavens, and I lean forward and kiss my soul mate.

Epilogue

Natalia

Three months later...

We got married again yesterday and arrived at our honeymoon destination this morning.

Bora Bora looks as beautiful as any screensaver I've ever seen.

What's more beautiful is the man before me, rolling my jeans down my legs as he pushes me against the wall of our gorgeous beach house.

I giggle when he pulls off my jeans, whips off his shirt to unveil his masterpiece body, then crouches back down to kiss my feet. A line of fiery kisses is then trailed up my legs and right up to my pussy, where he pushes the fabric of my panties aside so he can thrust his tongue into my passage.

"I love the way you taste, everywhere, Malyshka," he mutters.

"I love the way you taste, too," I moan.

"You have all night to play with my body. This is my time to please you."

He lifts my leg and presses me into the wall so he can continue eating me out. I grasp his wide shoulders, dizzy with delight. Greedy for more, or anything this man has to offer me.

Every time we do this, it feels better than the last. Every time he touches me, I feel amazing.

I'm nigh on coming and nigh on going crazy from the intoxicating pleasure he gives me when he stops licking my clit and traces a line of kisses over my belly.

"I want the future with you, Natalia. I want everything. Babies and more babies."

I smile down at him. Nothing sounds better to me.

"I want that, too, Mikhail."

He stands and cups my face so he can kiss me hard. "Then let's move on to the practice stage. I'm going to make love to you for the rest of the day and all night, wife. We're not leaving this room."

He pushes his pants down and thrusts his cock into me.

"That works fine, husband. Just promise me you won't stop touching me."

"I promise. I don't plan to ever stop, Natalia."

I love hearing him call me by my name. I'll never get tired of hearing it on his lips and remembering it's me he wants when he says it.

I don't have to be anyone besides myself for him to love me.

He makes me feel like his queen.

I'll never stop touching him, either.

Not ever.

The man of my dreams. The man who will save me from my nightmares and make my dreams a reality.

The man who will be my biggest protector and guardian.

Mikhail Dmitriyev.
My husband.

* * *

Mikhail

2 years later...

I gaze ahead at Natalia.

She's playing with Lilly, our little girl who's just like her.

I thought my life changed when I married the woman of my dreams—twice. It did, but then it changed even more when I became a father to the most beautiful little girl in the world.

We named her after Natalia's mother. It seemed fitting. Then we gave her two middle names. Isabella after my mother and Talia after my sister.

So, Lilly Isabella Talia Dmitriyev is one very blessed little girl.

She's only one, but I can see those little feet walking as delicately as a ballerina.

It wouldn't surprise me if she took an interest in it, because it runs through her veins.

If she does, I'm sure I'll create a painting of her, just like all the others I have of my wife and child. My obsession now extends to both.

We're at the lake house on a break, and I'm painting them now. This is what balances me.

Now when I come here, I remember that last conversation I had with my father. As the years have gone by, it comes to mean more to me. I started painting again after Natalia and I got married and I thought of how my father loved it, and how he loved painting my mother.

I finally understood his meaning. As the Pakhan, my world is dark, and my wife and my child are my treasures that light my path and complete me.

I focus on my wife for a few seconds as I finish the brush strokes over the painting of her, and I find myself smiling, because she's one hell of a woman.

I love everything about her, but the two things that have been a constant are her strength and ambition.

She's taken these two years to be with me and Lily, and in September, she'll start her studies at New York University. I can already tell she's going to bring that fire she has in her to the medical world.

When she looks at me, I remember how I promised her life would be better.

It is.

It truly is.

I'm nearly finished with this painting now, so I put my brushes down to take a break and join my family.

The picture is only complete when I'm with them.

The universe is the artist of that masterpiece.

I walk toward them and kiss my wife and then pick up my little girl.

"Let's go for a walk," I say.

"That sounds like a good idea."

"Yeah, I get to look at you for longer."

I smile at her, and we walk by the lakeside with me holding everything that matters to me in this world in the palms of my hands.

My wife and my child—the two great loves of my life.

And it all began when I met the princess.

THE END

Thank you so much for reading Mikhail and Natalia's story. I hope you enjoyed it.
If you liked Eric, you'll definitely want to read his story in Heartless Lover, a standalone in the Dark Syndicate series.
Thank you for allowing me to share my stories with you.
Hugs and love xx

Faith Summers Collection

Series

Dark Syndicate

Ruthless Prince

Dark Captor

Wicked Liar

Merciless Hunter

Heartless Lover

Ruthless King

Dark Odyssey

Tease Me

Taunt Me

Thrill Me

Tempt Me

Take Me

Original Sins

Dark Odyssey Fantasies

Entice

Tease

Play

Tempt

Duet

Blood and Thorns Duet

Merciless Vows

Merciless Union

Novellas

The Boss' Girl

The Player

Standalones

Deceptive Vows

Acknowledgments

To my friend Dana Pittman.
Thank you for helping me bring this story to life and breathe
life into my characters.
Couldn't have done it without you.
Only you could put up with my craziness.
You know it's true. Lol. xx

And for my readers.
Always for you.
Thank you for reading my stories.
I hope you continue to enjoy my wild adventures xx

About the Author

Faith Summers is the Dark Contemporary Romance pen name of USA Today Bestselling Author, Khardine Gray.

Warning !! Expect wild romance stories of the scorching hot variety and deliciously dark romance with the kind of alpha male bad boys best reserved for your fantasies.

Be sure to join my readers list *for some exciting, mouthwatering, seductive romance xx*

https://www.subscribepage.com/faithsummersreadergroup

Join my reader group -

https://www.facebook.com/groups/462522887995800/

f

Printed in Great Britain
by Amazon

44335834R00239